HEAD ON
FIRE

PRAISE FOR HEAD ON FIRE

"I vividly recall Sifu Andy James explaining to me that the Buddha advised, 'Practice as though your head is on fire.' After these reminders, my complacency and laziness would evaporate and I'd practice with renewed energy, embracing each moment. He emphasized 'embodied learning,' by which he meant one cannot simply read books and debate eastern philosophy. Rather we should privilege actual Vipassana mindfulness meditation practice. 'Right Action' is realized internally as well as externally; it is relational and can never be compartmentalized.

"What better, then, than an autobiographical reflection on decades of practice on how the author and teacher came to embody Buddhist teachings and be a renowned practitioner of Daoist internal arts. He explains how Buddhism and Daoism 'came together' for him, not in terms of philosophical musings, but rather in terms of the practicalities of life as husband, father, friend, and teacher. Andy James's new book is a must-read."
—Jamie Magnussen, Ph.D., Associate Professor, Ontario Institute for Studies in Education, University of Toronto

"Andy James's latest book is a tour de force. A detailed account of the author's journey in following his dream. If you are under any illusion that finding your path is the hard part and once you find it, it's all clear sailing, then this book smashes that illusion. Having the courage to pursue it is when the real work begins and Andy demonstrates that courage. His personal story is captivating and the stories he includes of others are enlightening, soothing, and encouraging. I ended the book feeling, 'my head is on fire.' I can do — and must do — the work Andy is suggesting and, of which we are all capable, if we look unflinchingly into our inner Being. Anyone who picks up this book and reads it is ready for the challenge it presents."
— Donna Armstrong, author and former Crown Attorney

"I have had the distinct pleasure of being introduced to and developing my mindfulness practice with Andy James over the last decade, which has transformed my life. Andy's new book, *Head on Fire*, is a profound testament to his deep insights into the world around us and our role within it. His unique voice of inclusiveness, that there is a space for 'both-and,' helps me participate fully in each moment, opening my heart to the immense variety life has to offer. Andy calls on us to take up the challenge of self-transformation to bring about real change in the world. The time to make that change is now, as if your head was on fire! This book is a must-read for anyone seeking to ignite their inner potential and make a meaningful impact."

— Carl Gruden, IT architect

PRAISE FOR ANDY JAMES' WORKS

"Another highly inspiring book written with great clarity and broad scope by Andy James who, in addition to his mastery over Tai Chi Chuan and Qigong, received a complete training under my instruction and guidance. After reading *Ageless Wisdom Spirituality*, I am given a new perspective regarding the synthesis of Religion and Science, the effects of technology, our common ground on genesis, spirit, and the evolution of consciousness."
— Dhiravamsa, Foreword to Ageless Wisdom Spirituality

"In this book, Sifu Andy James gives us the true history and evolution of the Shaolin, Daoist, and Chan (Zen) Buddhist systems and disposes of misconceptions and widespread cultural distortions surrounding these disciplines. James's in-depth understanding of the Chinese integral mind-body training stems from his thirty-five years of personal internal martial arts experience. A master instructor internationally recognized by his peers."
— Professor Jerry Alan Johnson, Executive Director of the International Institute of Medical Qigong, in the Foreword to *The Spiritual Legacy of Shaolin Temple*

"I just finished your book Ageless Wisdom Spirituality. It is so fine. For more than 30 years, I have been saying, teaching, breathing Wisdom's connecting consciousness. You are a master of this connecting of all of life and your insights are a gift."
— Georgene Wilson, OSF (Franciscan)

"Andy James is a profound thinker whose writing transcends the individual, weaving together threads of philosophy, psychology, and Vipassana meditation with politics, culture and the human experience. I find myself returning to his books often for inspiration."
— Cindy Stone, M.A., Reg. Psychotherapist, author

HEAD ON FIRE

The Path to Personal and Collective Transformation

NOW

A Memoir By

ANDY JAMES

IGUANA

Copyright © 2025 Andy James
Published by Iguana Books
720 Bathurst Street
Toronto, ON M5S 2R4

All rights reserved. No part of this publication may be reproduced, stored in a retrieval system or transmitted, in any form or by any means, electronic, mechanical, recording or otherwise (except brief passages for purposes of review) without the prior permission of the author.

Publisher: Cheryl Hawley
Editor: Amanda Feeney
Front cover art: Avery Snelling
Front cover design: Jonathan Relph

ISBN 978-1-77180-715-9 (paperback)
ISBN 978-1-77180-716-6 (epub)

This is an original print edition of *Head on Fire*.

To my wife, Nicola, who has always actively and lovingly encouraged me, especially in the writing of this book.

To my daughters and their children, who will face a rapidly changing, challenging, and volatile world over the next few decades: Shuwen and her daughter, Emmie; Shuwei and her sons, Bodhi, Grey, and Indie; and Hana and her son, Nolan, and daughter, Riley. May this book help them be part of a clear-headed and compassionate solution to our shared problems.

To my senior students, especially Donna Oliver, who have accompanied me on this less-traveled path, in some cases for decades, helping to bring much-needed light into the world through their mind-body efforts and teaching skills.

CONTENTS

PREFACE	IX
FINDING THE BUDDHA	1
North-South, East-West	1
An Unexpected Twist of Fate	7
Commitment: Teachers and Marriage	15
A Plunge into the Unknown	26
OUR MOMENT OF TRUTH	51
The Promise of Progress	52
Is There an Alternative to "Progress"?	66
Our Ageless, Often Forgotten, Wisdom	71
BUDDHA'S SIMPLE AND PROFOUND WISDOM	81
The Four Noble Truths	83
Vipassana and Mindfulness Meditation	87
Meditators' Questions and Challenges	92
Belief versus Beginner's Mind	111
PATHS TO SELF-REALIZATION	121
The Major Paths: Devotion and Wisdom	123
Karma Yoga	125
Raja Yoga	128
Qigong	130
A Self-Realization Diagram	137
Moving to the Center: A Journey in Consciousness	138

    Upper-Left Quadrant: Non-Attachment
    and Vipassana   145
    Upper-Right Quadrant: Wisdom and Self-Inquiry   147
    Lower-Right Quadrant: Compassion and Service   151
    Lower-Left Quadrant: The Power of Love   152
    Emptiness or *Sunyata*   153

CONDITIONING AND PERSONALITY   157
    What Is Conditioning?   157
    The Enneagram of Personality   161

REALIZING A DREAM   179
    Another Wake-Up Call   181
    Building with Green and Subtle Energy   183
    Harmony Dawn   187
    A New Life Stage   194

CONCLUSION   211

ACKNOWLEDGMENTS   229

PREFACE

If we are able to set aside our invested beliefs and opinions for a brief moment, most of us would agree that we — individually and collectively — seem to have lost our sense of joy, purpose, and meaning. We are compulsively driven by our entrenched system of free-market consumerism and technology to strive and compete with each other ever harder just to keep afloat. We feel more stress than satisfaction. Life often seems a struggle, and a growing number of people are being left behind since wealth and income inequality has been growing for decades in many countries. In the United States, where inequality is very high compared to other developed countries, the top 1 percent hold over 30 percent of the country's wealth while the bottom 50 percent own under 3 percent. The sight of people living on the streets in the United States is no longer shocking to many.

In addition to our individual concerns, there seems to be a constant drip of alarming news and research concerning many facets of our collective lives, including the economy, health, pollution, and the accelerating existential threats of climate change, nuclear war (of which many younger people are ignorant), and widespread replacement of humans by artificial intelligence and robots. What will society do with unproductive or unemployable people? That question is understandably being avoided by our leaders.

Not surprisingly, research and polls show that many are reacting in accordance with Dr. Hans Selye's widely accepted general adaptation – or stress — syndrome theory, the first stage of which is alarm, popularly known as the fight-or-flight response. Most of us choose "flight" by stuffing our already-busy lives with entertainment, drugs, alcohol, gambling, social media, travel, and more. The smartphone is always at hand. Many summarily dismiss "negative-seeming" but persuasive scientific evidence, even if soundly based, as a conspiracy or political ploy; others place their trust in hope and a positive attitude, assuming an ever-open time window for meeting our challenges. Many of us do not want to think about or are just too stressed to think about other people, other countries, or the future itself. We do not want change, even though it is taking place anyway.

Those who choose "fight" are more obvious and seem to be increasing in number. They look for others to blame and then demonize them on the grounds of political ideology, religion, race, and more. This, of course, creates more generalized stress through increased conflict. Stress is usually made up of several non-specific factors, so choosing one target, even if successful, will not fix the total systemic threat. We cannot successfully tackle our problems one at a time, as we currently attempt to do, since our problems — and indeed life itself – are constantly changing and are interconnected. They do not exist in isolation in the separate conceptual boxes we have created.

The stress syndrome theory predicts that if underlying stress factors are not promptly resolved, then the second stage of accommodation, or adaptation, begins, wherein we try to find various ways to live with our stressors and threats. This may initially seem an easy way of avoiding our problems. But in the longer term, it drains or depletes our energy and coping systems since we are in fact consciously allowing toxins to keep operating within us. Our problems steadily worsen under the surface of our attention.

The third and final stage of the stress syndrome theory is exhaustion and collapse, wherein our mind-body system begins to rapidly deteriorate, as we have no energy or time left to fight or resist. Collapse ensues. I would guess that many of us have observed these stress dynamics in friends, family, or perhaps even ourselves. These stress stages also seem to be manifesting collectively, and signs of exhaustion are evident. People are increasingly impatient, angry, and violent; polarization and conflict are increasing, often justified on the basis of race and religion; walls are going up around countries to keep out foreigners; a global pandemic has recently killed over seven million people; and the planet is experiencing record-breaking heat and climate extremes. The year 2023 was the planet's hottest year since records began in 1850. The ten hottest years have all occurred in the last decade, which should be a loud wake-up call, but apparently many have hit the snooze button. A 2022 *American Psychological Association* poll found that 27 percent of respondents were so stressed and overwhelmed that on many days they could not function.

We need urgent and meaningful change, but no practical solutions are being proposed in the public sphere. Our leaders, including political, business, and religious, persist with flawed strategies, tinkering with individual problems and hoping for a radically different result. Logically, we cannot change by holding on to our old patterns, albeit in superficial permutations and presentations.

However, drawing on my observations as a Vipassana-Mindfulness meditation teacher for forty years, this is precisely what most people do. Letting go is difficult (for reasons which will be examined later in this book), but especially for those already invested in positions of power and influence. The present system, warts and all, suits them, and they are better equipped than most to survive hard times since power is usually accompanied by wealth. As we shall later see, rapidly growing inequality, especially in the United States, has for decades been concentrating great wealth into the top 1 to 5 percent of citizens. In the insightful words of Lord Acton, "Power tends to corrupt, and absolute power corrupts absolutely."

The good news is that there actually is something we can all do to bring about real change, and we can start now with ourselves! Collective actions and behaviors are the result of individual ones, which in turn arise within each of us and are therefore accessible if we choose to skillfully inquire. Together, we have created our present life situations, and we can change them if we have the necessary will, skill, perseverance, and wisdom. We also need a sense of urgency, as in the Buddhist adage, "Practice as if your head is on fire."

Conventional society is very poor at understanding the nature of the "self" or "I" since almost all attention is focused on exploring and navigating the external world. We are taught, if fortunate, by parents and caregivers how to behave in various social situations; schools try to teach us skills necessary for earning a living. Behavior is usually only examined in cases of unconventional or antisocial behavior, and even then, the solution comes from outside — punishment, therapy, or perhaps strict religious rules. We pray to an external god for happiness and salvation; we alternately vote for one political party and then the other despite repeated unfulfilled promises. Many now view technology as the new messiah, expected to solve all our problems, while ignoring the fact that we ourselves have created those problems and will continue to do so if we do not change ourselves. We are addicted to the promise of the external "quick fix," which does not require effort on our own part, a tendency demonstrated by our fondness for pills, drugs, surgery, and the like.

It seems not widely known that deep self-knowledge has long been advocated by the world's greatest spiritual teachers, starting with the so-called Axial sages, who emerged between 800 and 200 BCE, bringing a more profound form of religion and spirituality to the world. These include Confucius (Kong Fuzi) and Laozi in China, the Buddha and the authors of the Upanishads in India, Socrates and Plato in Greece, and others. The Buddha advised, "Be a refuge unto yourself," pointing out that we are the result of what we have thought and that we can free ourselves from suffering (and reach enlightenment) by learning how to become aware and let go of our attachments and compulsions. Laozi's classic work, the *Daodejing*, states, "He who knows others is wise; He who knows himself is enlightened. He who conquers others is strong; He who conquers himself is mighty."

While the concept of the Axial Age points to certain common features between the major religions, the related idea of a perennial philosophy, popularized by thinkers like Aldous Huxley, asserts that there is a universal core of wisdom and truth shared by all the major religions at their highest levels. The metaphor of the spiritual mountain is often used to explain that while religions may come to the same point at the very peak of the mountain, at its wide base, there may often be separation and conflict between the religions, as is currently evident. I remind my students that not all chosen paths on the spiritual mountain lead to the summit, and even if a path does lead there, it takes persistence, courage, and skill to reach the top. An experienced guide in the form of a "spiritual friend" can also be most helpful.

Sometimes perennial philosophy is known as the "ageless wisdom." Huston Smith also called it the "forgotten truth" because it has to be rediscovered by each new generation through personal realization. Study and thinking are not enough because thought itself generates the fragmentation, complexity, division, and conflict from which we suffer. Thought is our most evolved conventional human faculty, but it is not omnipotent as presumed by many, which, at one time, included me. That perception (and my entire life) changed around the age of twenty, when I first started reading about Buddhism. I was suddenly struck by the crystal-clear realization of the truth of the Buddha's teaching that all manifestations of life are conditioned and ever-changing, including thought! Thought is not omnipotent because it is conditioned by all the experiences, beliefs, studies, and cultural background of the thinker, whom we know as "I." No matter how powerful artificial intelligence becomes, it is conditioned by its human creators, who incorporate their assumptions and beliefs (largely unexamined) about humanity and what is "good" for it. AI is nearing the point of being able to make decisions without humans, but it will still be conditioned.

It may be an initially shocking statement to most, but we are not our thoughts! Our extremely powerful identification with our thoughts makes it difficult to free ourselves of their compulsion over us. As will be explained later in this book, thought is not the highest form of human consciousness. In addition, it is commonly distorted and overturned by our emotional and instinctive brains, within ourselves and by others who want to manipulate us, including marketers, politicians, swindlers, and cult leaders.

I write this book because, based on decades of personal practice and teaching experience, I know that there is much that we can do to change ourselves and, therefore, our world at a much more profound level than is common at present. We all share a beautiful and relatively small planet, and the fact of our interdependence grows more evident by the day, if we take the time to look and listen. Society presently does not reward individuals who lead balanced, responsible, and caring lives, but such people are invaluable in a win-win sense. They personally enjoy contentment, mind-body health, and fulfilling relationships. They do not burden society and instead enhance our collective lives through their relationships, lifestyles, decision making and actions, whatever their specific positions or abilities. They are a much-needed light in darkening times. Neglect and complacency by us now mean more difficulties and crises for our children and grandchildren in the future.

This path is not my creation, but a perennial, spiritual path trodden by others in each age and on each continent. It is not based on belief or intellect but on open-ended, unconditional exploration of our inner world and dynamics. Everything must be open to examination with nothing hidden or protected. The Buddha advised that if we are making progress on the path, we will demonstrate both increased wisdom (the head) and compassion (the heart). I think a more evolved consciousness and deeper spiritual realization will enable us to see life in harmonizing "both/and" rather than "either/or" terms, especially separate and connected, Left and Right (politically), secular and religious, East and West, North and South, complex and simple.

This book will describe how I came to discover Buddhism and Daoism (especially as manifested in *taijiquan* and qigong), and how and why those paths radically transformed my life and impacted those around me, especially family, students, and the many guests at our green Harmony Dawn retreat center. Life is always now and challenges us to flow with it. The experiences, insights, and practices offered in this book are the best that I can offer to my grandchildren … and also to the children of the world who may be searching for meaning, clarity, love, and joy.

FINDING THE BUDDHA

I never intentionally set out to discover Buddhism or spirituality as a personal path or way of life. The Buddha's wisdom came to me as a sudden and unexpected realization, which has taken hold of and radically transformed my life from that moment, around the age of twenty. The most basic definition of a Buddhist is one who takes refuge in the Three Jewels, a practice also known as the Triple Refuge. The Three Jewels, or Gems, are the Buddha, the dharma (the Buddha's teachings), and the sangha (the Buddhist monks and nuns or, more broadly, community). Several eminent teachers have pointed out that the Three Gems are not only external, but also internal, especially awakening the Buddha mind within. Although I am not a member of a formal Buddhist organization, I take de facto refuge in the Three Gems through my life. In finding the Buddha, the Buddha found me.

North-South, East-West

In many ways, I grew up as a citizen of the world, and so perhaps I was more open to the notion of universal wisdom and principles that include all people. I was born and spent my early, idyllic life in British Guiana, or "BG" as it was commonly known then. BG was a British colony culturally aligned with the West Indies but located on the north coast of South America, being the only English-speaking colony on the continent. It was not a rich colony, and when I lived there, it would have been regarded as being similar to a third-world or developing country. It gained independence in 1966 and became known as Guyana. It was historically composed of five ethnic groups: Indigenous, East Indian, African, European (mostly Portuguese immigrants and British administrators), and Chinese. A sixth ethnic group has since emerged— those of mixed races. Although we were obviously aware of our racial differences in BG, they were the subject of light banter and jesting, not animosity. I felt completely "Guyanese" and did not realize then that the Chinese in BG made up less than 0.5% of the population. I was racially Chinese but did not speak any Chinese dialect and felt no real connection with China, except through the food and some inherited customs and words. Nevertheless, I felt somehow different from everyone else, probably because my features were so different and because, sometimes, I would be teased on the street by people mocking the Chinese language. I could not escape my Eastern heritage.

Our family was Church of England (Anglican), and we went to church every Sunday, sitting in the front pew. I guess my father, a business owner, was a major donor. I attended a Roman Catholic (RC) primary school because my parents heard that the teachers were good. Classes there were big (up to thirty students), and discipline was harsh. In my first year, our nun teacher locked one of the students in a cupboard in eighty-five-degree Fahrenheit heat. Welt-raising caning on the hands and buttocks was not uncommon throughout the various grades, or standards as they were called then.

During my years at the RC primary school, I gradually became more introspective, which I now know is common for my personality type. Prior to that, I was a "loveable rascal," causing mindless mayhem wherever I went. I was now in a more threatening world, away from the family cocoon, where students were older and bigger than I, and playground fights and bullies were common. I was sometimes caned by teachers, which I felt was not always justified, so my feelings as well as my body were hurt. I had a fiery temper, which I knew I had to tame somehow if I were to fit in with others. For the first time in my life, I began to seriously inquire into the role of religion beyond just attending Sunday services. Adjoining our school buildings was an RC church and I found myself going there during my recreational breaks at least once a day. I was fascinated by the statues, especially the Stations of the Cross, the candles, and the rituals. I caught the attention of the local Jesuit priest, who thought I would be good Jesuit material in the future.

During my daily visits to the church, I sincerely prayed to Jesus to help me deal with my anger and fears. I also prayed at home and even got my whole family to say grace before each meal. After a year or two of this practice, I began to question the prayer process and, more broadly, religion as I had been taught. What if nothing happens even though I pray to Jesus? If I do not pray to Jesus, would I be damned to hell and, if so, why, since Jesus is supposed to embody love? Did the nuns, priests, and teachers embody love? Did they embody wisdom in always making the right decision? I decided to be more proactive and created a process for myself that I would now describe as affirmation-awareness, almost unknown at that time. I repeated to myself, especially in times of stress, "I will not get angry," and "I will not be afraid of anyone, even bullies and teachers, since we are all equal human beings." Over time, it seemed to work since my anger and fear lessened. At the age of ten, I won a national scholarship to the secondary school of my choice.

The late 1950s and early 1960s were probably the peak of the global, anti-colonialist movement, which especially impacted the many colonies of the British Commonwealth, formerly the British Empire. The leaders of the two biggest political parties in BG, representing the largest ethnic groups — those of East Indian and African descent — decided to campaign along racial lines despite being early anti-colonialist allies. That abruptly ended the idyllic, fun-loving, joking BG. Things quickly got ugly, resulting in a general strike in February 1962. Rumors suggested that the CIA provoked the strike and was supporting Forbes Burnham, the leader of the People's National Congress (PNC), which drew most of its predominantly

Black supporters from the capital, Georgetown. They were protesting against the ruling government of Cheddi Jagan, leader of the People's Progressive Party (PPP). Jagan and Burnham had founded the PPP together in 1950.

On February 16, 1962, now known as Black Friday in Guyana, riots broke out in Georgetown, and the mobs started looting, burning, and attacking people, mostly of Indian descent, on the streets. Few knew what was really happening, but word on the street spread that a British warship with troops was on its way. My personal recollections of that day were a mixture of excitement, fear, and chaos. I was three days short of my thirteenth birthday, and my older brother, Brian, was five years older with his own car. We heard that our family business was being attacked. When we got there, we found a line of a few employees and friends facing up to the mob in front of the business premises. Brian and I joined the thin line, and someone gave me a machete. It was a very tense and volatile situation, but the tension suddenly broke when one of the mob leaders shouted out that Andrew James (my father) was a "good man." The mob moved on. Brian and I drove around Georgetown checking up on friends and relatives and running into several hot spots where rioters and police were clashing. As we were returning home after dark, both of us somehow heard a distinct metallic "click," and Brian instantly braked. In our headlights was a British machine-gun crew getting ready to open fire. We did not know that a curfew had been imposed. Our neighborhood housed some prominent people, including government ministers, foreign consuls, and the Anglican archbishop. In hindsight, I have wondered how different my life would have been if the mob had chosen to attack us or if the British soldiers had fired. In such moments, a life may turn.

Black Friday was a traumatic shock for most Guyanese, my family included. We had never witnessed such anger and violence. My parents decided to move our family to England as soon as possible, since it was our "mother country" and was seemingly stable and safe. We started hunting for warm clothing to buy, but there were few items to be found.

My family arrived in London on March 3, 1962, about two weeks after the riots. It was a physical and cultural shock. Everything looked gray, dark, and smoky as we touched down at the airport and made our way into central London. The damp cold was penetrating, and we shivered constantly, even with English clothing; we piled newspapers and carpets atop our blankets when we slept. I so longed for the heat, greenery, and gentle lifestyle of old BG.

After a few weeks, our family found a house in the outer suburbs, and I was enrolled in a grammar school, which is a publicly funded secondary school in the more academic stream. I was not obviously shunned or discriminated against, but I felt a complete outsider and a bit of a curiosity. In a school of several hundred, there were fewer than ten non-white faces, including mine. I was self-conscious about my looks and my accent, which was West Indian and unusual for a Chinese-looking person. I was also surprised and intimidated by the sexual advances of a couple of my more mature female classmates. I felt overwhelmed in so many ways.

In September 1962, the beginning of the English school year, I was enrolled by my parents as a boarder (live-in student) at Mill Hill School, a London public school. English public schools are actually private schools and form a de-facto "old boys' (and now girls') network," which not only offers quality education, but also valuable social and business connections. Several of my fellow students at Mill Hill are now "movers and shakers" in current UK society. Public schools also took pride in upholding "traditional values" and "toughening" students. Even in the winter, we played outdoor sports in skimpy clothing; I was astonished that mud could freeze on my exposed legs. During my first winter, a glass of water left on our dormitory windowsill started turning to ice.

During my time, Mill Hill School consisted of a cluster of main buildings housing administration, classrooms, gyms, various racquetball courts, and an infirmary. Although there was a residential "house" in the main building, most students lived in houses a few hundred meters away. Each house contained students of all ages and was hierarchical, with the senior boys/prefects supervising the younger ones. The youngest students were still called "fags" then and were expected to serve the seniors. I was a fag in my first year.

Mill Hill proved to be a far greater cultural shock than Downer Grammar School, even though the racial demographics were about the same. For a start, I was living away from my family for the first time in my life, in a cold, alien environment. I felt great loneliness, even though I was surrounded all the time by fellow pupils. There was an institutional school hierarchy, and the older students seemed to have been given the leeway to dictate to or even bully younger ones. Even in my very early days of experiencing English culture, I detected a class bias that did not exist in Guyana. As in the iconic book *Lord of the Flies,* the bullies picked on the weak and the outsiders. The "fat" and "goofy" students were the first targets, but I knew my turn was coming since I was an obvious outsider. I was also the target of subtle pressure and discrimination from the older prefects.

Fortunately for me, at the age of thirteen, I was almost the same size that I am now — about 150 pounds and five feet seven or eight inches. Unfortunately, I did not get any bigger from that point on. When the bullying gang eventually targeted me, I told the leader that if they were to beat me up, they should take me out completely, because if I survived, I would then surely ambush them one by one and severely hurt them, leaving no incriminating evidence. I was persuasive enough that they got the message and left. I do not know what I would actually have done if beaten up, but I was outraged by the stupidity, senselessness, and, indeed, cowardice of bullying the weak. Curiously, the leader of the gang sometime later decided to befriend me.

At Mill Hill, my interest gradually turned from religion to politics, and I found myself generally agreeing with Karl Marx's statement, "Religion is the opiate of the masses," although, of course, there were exceptions. In 1962, there was the Cuban Missile Crisis, and a year later, President Kennedy was assassinated. One of my best school friends at that time was American, and I began to share his interest in and concern for what was happening in global politics. In my free time at school, I would go for solitary walks in the parks or people-watching in London's busy West End. I was fascinated by people's behavior and began to notice recurring patterns of behavior, including facial expressions, gestures, and tones of voice. In 1967, at the age of eighteen, I won a place at the London School of Economics and Political Science (LSE), which I chose because of what they taught and their academic reputation. Their past students included leaders of several newly independent colonies. I was pleasantly surprised not long ago to discover that LSE now trails only Oxford and Cambridge in UK university rankings.

An Unexpected Twist of Fate

During the years 1968–1970 (when I was nineteen to twenty-one years old), I experienced a series of unusual, interconnected events that fundamentally transformed the arc of my life. In the summer of 1968, a Guyanese friend (of East Indian descent) and I were traveling through Scandinavia on holiday and checked into a Helsinki student hostel. At dinner, we met an East Indian man from Africa who was with a young Finnish woman, and we invited them to sit at our table. I noticed a huge (over six feet tall and muscular), shaven-headed Finnish soldier glaring at us from across the room. He eventually walked over and sat himself at our table, belligerently scolding the woman in Finnish and calling our new acquaintance "a black monkey." In order to diffuse the situation, we told him that we were going back to our rooms, but he insisted on coming as well! As we walked across the lawn to our rooms, he started pushing and slapping our African friend, who was short and very slight. That blatant bullying caused something in me to snap, and I grabbed the soldier, pushing him away and yelling at him to stop and go away. I immediately realized that I was now his target! He started bellowing and charging at me like a bull. Time suddenly slowed, and in the two seconds I had before possibly being smashed, a stream of thoughts ran through my head: *This was a serious situation, and I could get badly injured. Kick him in the groin, my only seeming choice? What if I really hurt him and the other hostel members come out, judge me as the foreign aggressor, and I go to a Finnish jail?* I kicked him in the groin with all my might. To my astonishment, he was still standing and then issued a challenge to fight my two friends and me all at the same time. Yikes! However, he was hurt and soon found an excuse to leave.

The experience was truly shocking and traumatic to me. It was my first real, adult fight and, so far, my last, although over the years I have been sorely tested and threatened many times. I realized that my stature of five feet eight inches was not intimidating to most and may even be an invitation for attack. I also learned that speed and maybe technique could possibly overcome brute force and size. When I returned to London, I enrolled in Japanese karate and judo classes, which I had seen advertised in some London Underground (metro) stations. I was surprisingly enthralled with my discovery of the Asian martial arts! I practiced every day and attended classes whenever they were available. I wanted even more. This was me at a very deep level! It seemed somehow much more than sports, athletics, or even self-defense. I was fascinated and started reading about the history and philosophy of the Asian martial arts and yoga, which, at that time, was not well known.

The second life-transforming event occurred one year later, in the summer of 1969. Having disembarked from the car ferry from England, I was speeding through the Norwegian countryside on my way to a summer job in Stockholm, Sweden, passing many local cars on the way on a hot and dry day. All of a sudden, the forest on either side of the road disappeared into open sky and the paved road became a ninety-degree slippery gravel turn rightwards downhill. To my left was a long drop into the fjord, and on the right was a steep rock wall that became a rock dead end 200 to 300 meters downhill. The only option was a ninety-degree turn to the left, which, if I got that far, I was unlikely to survive since I was going so fast. My options seemed either to plunge into the fjord or smash into steep rock downhill. I skidded right and left downhill and hit the only tree on the fjord side, which carved deep into my engine block. I was physically okay, but mentally and emotionally shaken up, in a state of shock. Soon all the other drivers I had overtaken passed by, smirking, and not stopping to offer any assistance. It took me over an hour to get a ride to the nearest village, about thirty minutes away, and I waited there almost two days to get a plane ride to Stockholm while my car underwent repairs.

In those two days, there was a lot of empty space and time for me to focus on myself and my actions. In hindsight, it was a spontaneous meditation retreat. I felt stupid, arrogant, and immature. Yes indeed, death may be only a fraction of a second away at any given time; there is no guarantee of a happy life or even a long life. I could have been badly injured or permanently disabled. What is the purpose of life anyway? No one seemed to know the answers, even though we can all repeat trite sayings and adages. I started to do yoga postures I could remember from a book I had recently bought. In the enforced stillness and aloneness, I started observing my thoughts in a crude, instinctive Vipassana-Mindfulness meditation way, even though I had not heard or read of such a practice. I felt that maybe I needed to somehow change my beliefs and perspectives on life, but how and in what way?

Towards the end of my three years at LSE, I stumbled on to Buddhism, which forever and fundamentally did change my life. In my early days at LSE, I was very anti-religious and hung out with the socialists and anti-colonialists, especially the few West Indians and Guyanese at LSE. On one of my visits back to Guyana, I even had the opportunity (at one of my parents' dinner parties) to engage in a spirited political discussion with Forbes Burnham, who was then prime minister of Guyana.

October 1968 saw the student occupation of LSE in solidarity with the global anti-Vietnam War movement. I was mostly sympathetic with the movement but became increasingly put off by the self-aggrandizing posturing of the student "leaders" and the growing, dogmatic groupthink mentality. The leaders wanted to be somebodies, which seemed to me disappointingly predictable and not much different from the establishment figures and politicians they were criticizing. In June 1969, I witnessed the radicals going after Frank Zappa on stage at LSE while he was previewing his new movie. They asked him what the (political) "message" of the film was and what he was personally doing to stop America. He explained that he was a musician and much of his material is deliberately absurd. He famously and colorfully retorted that he was not responsible for stopping America, which is a polite paraphrase. There can be bigots on the left as well as on the right. Bigots presume that their unexamined belief is truth, which is common but misguided, and the source of much human suffering as the Buddha explained 2,500 years ago.

I started researching Zen because it was being touted as a "cool" and different religion, and I was anti-religious at the time. I wanted to learn about it so that I could debunk it. I discovered that "Zen" was a later Japanese version of "Chan," a novel form of Buddhism that originated at the Shaolin Temple in China around 500 CE, approximately 1,000 years after the original Buddha. I was surprised and intrigued, since my early research into the Asian martial arts also pointed to the obscure Shaolin Temple as the source of most of the Asian martial arts, not only those in China. Decades later, I wrote a book for Wisdom Publications, *The Spiritual Legacy of Shaolin Temple: Buddhism, Daoism, and the Energetic Arts*, on this remarkable temple and its historical and spiritual legacies that are still influential.

Like a dog following a scent, I eagerly tried to find out more about the Buddha's original teachings, which are known as Theravada Buddhism. Zen is regarded as belonging to the later Mahayana Buddhism. I was, of course, familiar with Buddha statues and depictions, which seemed to suggest serenity or even passivity. I was shocked that the Buddha was against belief/faith, which is the basis of most popular religions, East and West, including present popular Buddhism. He plainly stated that he was not a god, but a perfectly enlightened human being, which is within the potential of everyone. He stressed individual experience and responsibility, "Be a refuge unto yourself," pointing out that even Buddhas could only point the way. The Buddha was certainly not passive and indeed advocated the necessity for urgent self-transformation: "Practice as if your head is on fire!"

His main insight into the nature of life was that everything — all manifestation — is impermanent and conditioned, because every "thing" depends on multiple, interrelated, ever-changing factors. Nothing is substantial, fixed, and unchanging, including our "I" or self. The notion that the universe is in a constant state of change and conditionality is one that modern science now largely (and very belatedly) recognizes. The Buddha regarded life as suffering since we generally try to hold on to it, especially the good and pleasant, which is an impossible endeavor. His solution to ending suffering and attaining enlightenment was simple and profound: stop holding on (being attached) and grasping so that we can flow with life in the ever-present now. Simple but not easy, as we shall see.

My personal eureka moment in understanding the Buddha's teachings was the sudden, crystal-clear realization that the thinking, intellectual mind is not all-powerful! Like everything else, it is also conditioned and programmed, much as a computer's functioning depends on its programming and hardware, which in turn depends on its human creators' conditioning, including subjective notions about "what is good" for humanity. I had previously assumed that the thinking mind was the ultimate tool or weapon, but I was mistaken at a fundamental level. After being struck by this realization, my world was never again the same. I began to understand how people, including respected and brilliant academics and experts, could make persuasive logical arguments about society, yet be deluded at a deeper level, since their arguments were based on their own basic assumptions — largely unexamined because those assumptions were presumed to be "obvious." In my later teaching years, I would ask my senior students, "What is the difference between a bigot and the Buddha?" They both seem persuasive and convincing and can sway people. However, all statements are not fifty-fifty in terms of deeper truth or quality. As Aldous Huxley pointed out, the "divine reality" can only be apprehended by those who "fulfill certain conditions, making themselves loving, pure in heart... making certain psychological and moral experiments." This requires far more than intellectual reasoning and manipulation. It calls for conscientious, skillful, vulnerable, open-ended, and ongoing spiritual practice. Life itself is ongoing; we cannot stop. We can only ever act in the now.

The clear realization that I made, around the age of twenty, of the Buddha's teaching was momentous and life-changing. I knew from that moment that Buddhism would always be part of my life, but I did not know in what way and to what extent. After my BSc (Econ) degree at LSE, I had, at the urging of my father, committed to undertake professional training in the City of London to be a chartered accountant. This meant a few years of working nine to five as an articled clerk, visiting various clients around London and sometimes England to audit their books and systems. Articled clerks then were also expected to complete accounting correspondence courses during their own time in order to sit final exams.

I enjoyed my ongoing research and readings on Buddhism and related subjects like religion, spirituality, mysticism, and occultism. I also tried to incorporate Buddhism into my life to the best of my understanding at that time. I consciously refrained from filling my time with unnecessary activity and sought to build moments of quiet into my busy day. During my long daily commutes to and from work, I would sit with my eyes closed rather than read the newspapers; during my lunch breaks, I would seek out one of the many old churches in the City of London to sit quietly in one of the empty pews.

Like many on the factory floors and in offices, I found "work" repetitive and boring, and the decisions of many "superiors" suspect and generally self-serving, which made our work efforts seem largely meaningless. I stretched out my coffee and lunch breaks as long as I could and kept thinking about the end of the workday, the weekends, and annual holidays. Eventually I began to realize, in a Buddhist way, that the resistance to and non-acceptance of my work situation was actually causing me pain — a negative form of attachment or holding on. The more I resisted work, the harder it was for me to do it. I decided to try to attain what Buddhists call "clear comprehension of purpose." I asked myself whether there was anything better, more productive, or more enjoyable that I could realistically be doing? I loved Buddhism and the martial arts but had to earn a living, and I was also aware that perhaps my infatuation with Buddhism and the martial arts might fade in the future. After considering many alternatives, the answer was "no," there was no realistic alternative. I then consciously accepted my work situation and let go of my frustration and resistance. Almost magically, my work life became easier and free of stress. I did not change my work circumstances, I just changed my mind and thinking, which was such a powerful, enduring lesson for me! Prior to this experience, I would never think of letting go. I would try to find some strategy to fight, control, or evade.

Once I fully accepted doing my job, even though it was routine and seemingly of no great importance, I began to see opportunities and lessons in it. As an auditor, I investigated systems and people from the factory floor up to the directors' boardroom all across the United Kingdom. I realized that this was a rare and valuable opportunity to gain insight not only into corporate dynamics and politics, but also into many personal life stories, replete with hopes and disappointments, which were fascinating from my new Buddhist perspective. I could get honest opinions on how people from differing backgrounds really saw and lived their lives, for better or worse. It was clear that their pain or discontent came not only from their surroundings, but also from how they chose to respond to them. It saddened me that many spent most of their lives doing jobs they hated just so they could have a happy retirement, only to have that often evade them through ill health, rising prices that eroded their savings, or death soon after retiring.

In 1970, I reconnected with my Chinese and Eastern heritage in another surprising and unexpected way. My father's distant cousin from Singapore had asked if I would keep an eye on his daughter, Yolind, who was three years younger than me and just beginning boarding school in England. I happened to mention this to the only other Singaporean I knew — we met at a local discotheque — and he told me he actually knew her very well! I invited them both to my twenty-first birthday party and, after a few months, we started dating. She was beautiful, bubbly, and intelligent, and we shared a similar, and at that time rare, background in that we were both "English-Chinese." She was racially half-Chinese and half-English, had grown up in a Singaporean, predominantly Chinese, culture, and was able to speak the Cantonese dialect. I was racially Chinese, but culturally Western with no Chinese language skills and little knowledge of

Chinese culture and customs. Another coincidence that linked us was that her parents met while her mother was studying at LSE. Since both Guyana and Singapore were tropical British colonies when we were growing up, Yolind and I had become literal citizens of the world, in the sense of East and West, North and South.

Yolind's ability to speak Cantonese opened up a new avenue for me to explore both Chinese culture and the Chinese martial arts, then called "kung fu." The only martial arts classes being publicly taught in London at that time were Japanese and Korean, mostly karate, judo, jujitsu, aikido, and tae kwon do. I longed to learn more about the Chinese martial arts, which were the original source of all the other Asian martial arts. Yolind (Yo) helped me explore London's Chinatown to root out obscure Chinese kung fu magazines and also attend the first kung fu movies, which were just arriving from Hong Kong and were in Cantonese. It was like a secret source of martial arts knowledge for me.

When Yo entered London University's School of Oriental and African Studies (SOAS) to study the more common Mandarin form of Chinese in both speaking and writing (which are now standard throughout China), I was able to meet and socialize with her teachers and professors, who specialized not only in language, but also literature and philosophy. I got to chat and even debate with intellectual heavyweights like Professor D.C. Lau, who translated a book on the *Daodejing* or *Tao Te Ching* by Laozi. All of this was an unexpected gift and boost to my efforts to deepen my understanding of Chinese culture and philosophy. After SOAS, Yo went to Cambridge to pursue a PhD in classical Chinese poetry.

Yo also joined me in my searches throughout "alternative" London for any and every piece of information on spirituality and martial arts, which was not readily available in those pre-internet times. My favorite place for spiritual books was the Theosophical Society bookstore in London, where I discovered books on Hinduism, occultism, spirituality, mysticism, and more. I was especially drawn to the works of Jiddu Krishnamurti. The Theosophical Society bookstore opened my eyes to a whole new world of thought, ideas, and practices. Their present international mission statement on their website reads: "To serve humanity by cultivating an ever-deepening understanding and realization of the Ageless Wisdom, spiritual Self-transformation, and the Unity of All Life." Reading that in 2024 is surprising to me because that could also be my personal mission statement, even though I was never a member of the Theosophical Society and shied away from some of their more occult teachings. My 2004 book was entitled *Ageless Wisdom Spirituality: Investing in Human Evolution*.

Commitment: Teachers and Marriage

The year 1974 has so far proven to be the single most momentous year of my life. Not only did Yo and I decide to marry in the following year, but I met my main teachers. Dhiravamsa, a former Thai Buddhist abbot, was to be my meditation and spiritual teacher. Miss Rose Li would teach me the "internal family" (*nei jia*) disciplines of the Chinese martial arts, including *taijiquan* (tai chi chuan), *baguazhang*, and *xingyiquan*. As an unexpected bonus, I was also introduced to an esteemed Shaolin master in Singapore, Tan Choo-Seng. In hindsight, the four years of searching and experimenting after my life-changing experiences eventually led to life's doors suddenly opening for me in many ways.

My decision to propose to Yo after four years of being together was a monumental step for me in terms of relationships and love. Before her, I always sought to be in control of my relationships, and I was never committed; marriage never entered my mind. I sensed something special and different in her, but I did not know how she really felt about me in terms of long-term commitment and marriage. I remember one particular moment in our volatile early relationship, when I was about to literally walk away forever, but an image of someone killing a baby flashed into my mind. I then remembered the Buddha's teaching on letting go and nonattachment, in this case concerning my suspicions, doubts, and fears. I decided to stay in the relationship and be open to all eventualities rather than deliberately cutting it off. We got married in 1975 and now share three great, beautiful daughters and six delightful grandchildren.

Committing myself to a non-controlling, open-ended, loving, unconditional relationship was a profound step for me. It was a deep letting go that allowed me to flow with the uncertainties of life, including the possibility of the eventual loss of love. It seemed to me that marriage simply must be based on love and wanting to be together. I did not want a relationship based on co-dependence, mutual benefit, or conditional bargains, which are often present but unspoken in relationships. My relationship with Yolind lasted twenty-three years.

After experimenting with yoga, occultism, Zen, and more, I decided to return to the form of spiritual practice that resonated with me at the beginning: Vipassana-Mindfulness meditation, first taught by the Buddha in his *Satipatthana Sutta* (*Discourse on Establishing Mindfulness*) about 2,500 years ago. I had sat in meditation a few times with some London-based Buddhist monks but felt that I needed more experienced guidance and intensity. I looked for a Vipassana meditation retreat and eventually discovered a Cambridgeshire retreat center founded by Dhiravamsa, who had come to England in the 1960s as part of a royal Thai mission to bring Buddhism to the West. In 1966, he became the *Chao Kun* (chief incumbent monk) at the Buddhapadipa Temple in London. In 1971, at the age of thirty-six, he gave up the "robe" and ceased to be a monk. He commented, "Robes are a symbol, a form, and when we put them on, we live in a certain role where we try to conform to an idea or to rules without looking into all aspects of life." He first became a novice monk in Thailand at the age of thirteen.

My first intensive retreat with Dhiravamsa was in the summer of 1974, fifty years ago as I write this. I retreated intensively with him for ten days or more at a time in England for several consecutive summers, which seemed to speed up my body-emotion-mind-spirit processing and evolution. It seemed that during every retreat a major life issue came up for my conscious attention and I would then spend the next year digesting and processing that meditation retreat experience.

Even during those early retreats, I experienced spontaneous energy movements. Some mirrored what I would later discover to be traditional Chinese medicine channels, meridians, and *dan tians* (energy centers), but others were very specific and defined, almost like blips on a radar screen, tracing a path through different areas of my body, almost pointing to what areas needed my attention or what was subtly happening in my mind-body system at that moment. At times during retreats, all thinking stopped, not only during formal meditation, but a few times while walking or sitting outside during our breaks. I could see and hear people and nature, but there was no internal comment. It just was. During that period, Dhiravamsa was a pioneer in expressive meditation, so there could be deep (and loud) emotional expression — shouts, crying, heaving, flailing, and more — from meditators punctuating the long periods of silent sitting. Dhiravamsa explained the reasons for this non-traditional Vipassana practice in his book *The Dynamic Way of Meditation*. I will also touch on this subject in my chapter on Buddhism and Vipassana meditation.

I later discovered a 1978 book by Ann Bancroft called *Modern Mystics and Sages*. It included a chapter on Dhiravamsa as well as pieces on Aldous Huxley, Alan Watts, Thomas Merton, Pierre Teilhard de Chardin, Meher Baba, Jiddu Krishnamurti, Maharaj Ji, Ramana Maharshi, the Maharishi, Chögyam Trungpa, Martin Buber, Rudolf Steiner, Mother Teresa, George Gurdjieff, Carlos Castaneda, and others. In hindsight, her book was certainly insightful and forward looking, opening a window for me into other forms of deep spirituality and the teachers who were emerging, many channeling Eastern wisdom. Dhira mentioned to me that he and Trungpa were very close friends while in the United Kingdom together. I was already familiar with Krishnamurti, and I also resonated with the works of Huxley, Watts, Merton, Trungpa, Ramana Maharshi, and, later, Gurdjieff through the Enneagram of Personality. During my U.K. retreats, I developed a personal relationship with Dhiravamsa. He subsequently invited me and Yo to stay with him in Berkely, California, where he was living and where one of his then Vipassana students was Claudio Naranjo, who is now seen as the father or founder of the modern Western Enneagram Personality Types.

In addition to Dhiravamsa, my other main teacher was Rose Li, whom I also met in 1974. My early research into the Asian martial arts pointed to the Shaolin Temple, founded around 500 CE in rural China, as the original source of them all. In the early 1970s, an English language book, first published in 1969, by Donn Draeger and Robert Smith caught my attention and interest. It was called *Comprehensive Asian Fighting Arts* and seemed well-researched, detailing the history and fighting methods from many Asian countries, but acknowledging China as their birthplace and source. Smith was particularly intriguing to me, since he had studied Western boxing and wrestling from an early age and had spent time in Asia as a member of the American CIA. He met and trained with martial arts masters from a variety of traditions and countries.

One thing about Robert Smith's books that stood out for me was his reference to and distinction between the Chinese "internal" and "external" martial arts, which was new to me. The former, which Smith seemed to favor as superior, included *taijiquan* and were subtler, emphasizing mind or intention, subtle energy (qi), circularity, and yin-yang principles. Could gentle-seeming *taijiquan* really defeat fearsome looking Shaolin, karate, or tae kwon do in combat? Smith described the internal system as follows:

> What is called the Internal System derived from exercises (kung-fu) explicit in early Taoist writings. Lao Tzu's *The Way and the Power* (*Tao Te Ching*), though it does not mention boxing by name, is quite opposed to horn-butting (*chiao ti-shi*) of that period: Show me a man of violence that came to a good end and I will take him as my teacher.

Smith then quotes extensively from the *Daodejing*, which explains how the soft and pliable can overcome the hard and rigid. I subsequently bought two of Smith's other books, *Pa-Kua Chinese Boxing for Fitness and Self-Defense* and *Hsing-I: Chinese Mind-Body Boxing*. In addition to the more well-known *taijiquan*, these were the other two members of the internal system, or family, of martial arts, now commonly written as *baguazhang* and *xingyiquan*. In both of these books, Smith made a brief but glowing reference to a "Rose Li" as one of the few genuine internal family masters in the West, since she had an impeccable lineage and had learned from some of the great masters in China. She was living in the United States at that time.

In early 1974, I was browsing through an alternative London bookstore, as was my custom, when I noticed a small, handwritten card pinned to its notice board saying "RL" was starting tai chi classes in London. I called and was shocked to discover that it was indeed Rose Li, who had just moved to England because, as she later told me, she did not want to be part of America's "melting pot" and be boiled down to an American stew. Both Dhiravamsa and Rose Li shunned personal publicity, but the latter took it to a greater degree.

Rose Li was an extremely knowledgeable teacher and had a compelling manner. However, she had an unusual teaching style in the sense that she seemed to deliberately avoid explaining things in straightforward terms, such as philosophical principles as well as actual physical postures and movements. She preferred to tell "stories" instead. I mostly understood what she was getting at and did not mind, but some students became frustrated at her approach. She said that she did not want to be a "performing monkey" for her students to try to imitate. Much later, I reflected that this approach was not dissimilar to the Buddha's; he said, "Even Buddhas can only point the way." Whether *taijiquan* or Buddhism, we each have to find a way to realize or embody wisdom, of whatever tradition, and not just to copy superficial mannerisms or sayings.

Miss Li and I (and subsequently Yolind) developed a personal relationship, which was unusual between her and her students. A factor may have been that I was Chinese and somewhat understood "Chineseness," and Yolind by that time could speak fluent Mandarin with her and was brought up in Singapore, where most of the population is ethnically Chinese. We invited her over to our flat for dinner many times, and we even went on a brief holiday together to south-west England and Wales. Her personal history was fascinating. She was the only girl child from a Mandarin family as the communist revolution was taking place, resulting in her family house eventually being taken over by a commune. She related how even after her father had lost his lands and official positions, some of his former rural tenants would bring produce for their now impoverished landlord and his family. Around 1949, she undertook an arduous trek across China to try to come to America. Her Christian missionary friends facilitated her trip and eventual entry into the United States.

Miss Li's classes during the late 1970s included fellow students who were at the cutting edge of exploring alternative ways of being and living, including sustainable living and energy, vegetarianism, organic foods, and especially traditional Chinese medicine (TCM). One of my best friends in Miss Li's classes was Chow Manxing, an acupuncturist born in Thailand. Her partner at that time was Giovanni Maciocia, who has now written a comprehensive and acclaimed English-language textbook on TCM. Other students introduced us to macrobiotics, which was a modern Japanese version of TCM and yin-yang herbalism-based eating and cooking principles.

Miss Li invited Robert Smith as an honored guest to one of her weekend workshops. I was able to spend some personal time with him when Miss Li invited me and two other senior students to join her and Smith for dinner afterwards. In 1981, as Yolind and I were preparing to emigrate to Canada, Rose Li informed me that I was qualified to be a *taijiquan* teacher within her tradition and system.

My final 1974 life gift was meeting the Singapore Shaolin master, Tan Choo-Seng. I had accompanied Yolind on a few of her summer visits to her family in Singapore, and I appreciated the great food stalls and the shopping, but I wanted more, especially to explore its rich martial arts tradition. My soon-to-be father-in-law sensed my boredom and introduced me to his veterinarian, who he thought had some vague connection to kung fu. It turned out that his vet was a senior official in the *Hua Tiong* martial arts organization, which I had recently noticed in the local Singapore newspapers. They had swept both the forms and fighting competitions in nearby Malaysia, which boasted a high standard in martial arts. Even before being introduced to Master Tan, Yolind and I had visited one of his schools and were impressed by the skill and welcoming nature of the practitioners. I usually checked out Chinese martial arts organizations wherever I went, and most were far from welcoming. In Boston, a group used their German shepherd dog to escort us out!

Even though, at that time, I wanted to focus on the internal martial arts, I was determined to test myself against external, athletic fighters. Master Tan asked me to show him my *taijiquan* form, even though it was very young (immature or novice) at that time. He accepted me as a personal student, and I trained with him individually, and bare-footed, every morning on the burning-hot concrete of his backyard. In the evenings, I attended his group classes and tested my forms and combat skills with his students, some many years younger than me. It was exhausting but very instructive and stimulating.

One summer, I was asked to be part of the *Hua Tiong* dragon dance team during Singapore's National Day celebrations. Competing martial arts groups, some gang-related, strutted menacingly in their uniforms and colors. I was assigned the dragon's tail, which was only slightly lighter than the head. Both the head and tail were heavy, requiring strength, and had metallic adornments, which could cut, especially within the close confines of a crowd. Each section of the twelve-person dragon had to be held aloft on a pole, which required a hand change (switching top and bottom hand positions) every time the dragon changed direction. Each section had three backups who would (hopefully) take over on the fly when someone tired in the ninety-degree Fahrenheit sun. Like a snake or a dragon, the lower body and tail moved much more than the head, sometimes whipping with speed. The dragon was not allowed to be still after it was ceremonially awakened. It was a unique and rich experience rooted in age-old traditional lore ... and not unlike a kung fu movie.

Two decades later, I met Master Tan in Baltimore during the World Wushu Championships. He was the head coach of the successful Singapore team, and I was a judge and a member of the Canadian masters' demonstration team. I demonstrated *baguazhang*, which is not a common art.

In 1976, Yo and I went on a month-long trip through northern India, traveling hippy style by long-distance buses and trains and staying in the cheapest hotels. I wanted to experience the country that gave birth to both Hinduism and Buddhism. The impression that has stayed with me was one of timelessness, simplicity, and earthiness, especially in the countryside. The rural people were welcoming and generous, even offering us meals when they themselves probably had so little.

We managed to visit the Taj Mahal, the (Sikh) Golden Temple in Amritsar, Srinagar in Kashmir, and the holy cities of Haridwar near the source of the Ganges, Varanasi, and Sarnath, where the Buddha gained enlightenment and gave his first discourses. During the trip, I had discussions with several Hindu holy men but heard nothing to divert me from my commitment to Vipassana.

In the late 1970s, I started offering an exploratory kung fu class. I felt that judo and karate, in which I had black belts, were somewhat limited, and I wanted to explore further and share what little I had gathered from Miss Li and Master Tan. Classes seemed to go well, except when we socialized afterwards. To my surprise, the working-class members of our group were uncomfortable with the middle class, which apparently included me. That was a shock to me, as I sought to include everyone, which I thought all would deem a good thing. I did not think of myself as belonging to any particular English class. The English class-privilege system endures, for better or worse, and it is not only top-down, but also bottom-up. However, class seems rarely to be openly discussed in a critical manner. This was a major factor in Yolind's and my decision to move from the United Kingdom to Canada.

Having visited Toronto for several enjoyable summers, and after my father had sent me numerous newspaper clippings about the lucrative job opportunities available to qualified chartered accountants, Yolind, pregnant at that time, and I emigrated to Toronto, Canada, in October 1981. Our first daughter, Shuwen, was born in Toronto in February 1982. Canada was not perfect, but it was more forward-looking, expansive, and welcoming. I recognized that I needed more personal space in which to express myself, and Toronto offered me that possibility. An additional bonus was that many in our extended Guyanese and West Indian family had also moved to the Toronto area. My mother had ten siblings! It seemed like a good place to raise a family and to open a new and exciting chapter in our lives.

I immediately started working for my family business but was surprised that I was being treated and paid as a bookkeeper rather than as a more qualified chartered accountant. I revamped our family company's accounting and administrative systems, which would have cost a lot if I was paid as an outside consultant. I felt somewhat let down by my father and my older brother, Brian, who made the family business decisions. I had a newborn child and mounting bills to pay. My younger twin brothers, Michael and Ray, also worked in the family business at that time.

My other life kept tugging at me. Soon after our arrival in Toronto, one of Brian's real estate acquaintances learned that I was experienced in martial arts and introduced me to his Wing Chun teacher, Sifu Steven Law, who ran a closed-doors, or private, club out of his home basement. Wing Chun is a Chinese martial arts style that was popular in Hong Kong and was the style Bruce Lee first learned. Sifu Law and his teacher were considered older Wing Chun "brothers" of Bruce Lee. I attended all available Wing Chun classes at Sifu Law's and continued my daily practice of the styles I already knew. I was also consistent in my daily Vipassana meditation practice.

In early 1983, Dhiravamsa announced that he had moved from Berkeley, California, to San Juan Island, Washington, and was building a retreat center there to offer Vipassana meditation. I eagerly signed up for his first ten-day retreat in the summer of 1983, as I had not been on a long retreat for a few years. It turned out that Dhira's building plans were behind schedule and his beautiful, geodesic meditation dome was only half built when retreatants arrived. Dhira, as usual, was not stressed, but many participants were upset because there was no space for formal meditation sessions and there was noise from the ongoing construction of the dome. Most rebelled and sat separately in meditation in the main house. I and a few others completed building the dome, sometimes in pouring rain, which made the rafters slippery. Even though I could not meditate in the formal sense, sitting quietly, I was determined to get the most out of the retreat and "meditated" in doing what physical work was necessary with awareness, moment by moment. The meditation dome was covered with giant tarps for the last few days of the retreat and all participants were able to finally meditate together.

Shortly after the retreat, Dhiravamsa unexpectedly called me in Toronto and invited me to train with him personally on San Juan Island as a Vipassana teacher, which was a rare opportunity and privilege. It is not something he usually does, if ever. I was surprised and flattered since I never thought about my meditation attainments or about teaching, which would be a radical departure from my expected life arc. After a day or two of checking our bank accounts and how much we might be able to get from renting out our Toronto house, the financial news was not good. However, in my heart I knew it was a unique opportunity and adventure that I could not pass up. Yo seemed fine with it. I said "yes" to Dhira and broke the news to my family. I heard that my father and Brian thought I was joining a cult, and the idea of disinheriting me was discussed. We went anyway in October 1983, expecting a second child around April 1984. As a chartered accountant, I knew that I was taking an undue financial risk, but I felt a strong pull or call that took us to the West Coast.

Our days on San Juan Island were idyllic, especially given its exquisite beauty and moderate temperatures and precipitation levels, in the protective shadow of the Vancouver Island Mountains. We made many colorful local friends on the island, and when I took our first daughter, Shuwen, out for our walks, it was on the beaches where orcas frolicked nearby or on hills where bald eagles nested and deer roamed. Two-year-old Shuwen and I climbed high up pine trees and ran down steep, rock-strewn hills. We went to Vancouver — a ferry ride and about a two-to-three-hour car drive away — every month to monitor Yolind's pregnancy because we could not afford a local U.S. birth, which would have cost us US$15,000 then. In Canada, medical care, including childbirth, is free.

It was not always easy with Shuwen on the island, even though we dearly loved her and she loved us too. Indeed, she loved us so much that she demanded to be with us and be entertained by us all the time, which became exhausting. She did not like to be restrained in any way, which made car rides and even strollers a battle of wills with much prolonged crying and screaming.

On one of his visits to our house for dinner, Dhira observed her behavior and suggested that in the Enneagram Personality Types, she might be a Type 8 personality, The Boss. Dhiravamsa had learned the modern Enneagram personality system from its founder, Claudio Naranjo, who was one of his Vipassana students in Berkeley, before the publication of any books on the subject. He found it to be very useful, especially in understanding relationships. Dhira explained that a Type 8 personality values power and, therefore, responds to power, not placation, which would be seen as weakness and an invitation to push further. He suggested standing up to her and bargaining with her. Both Yo and I were shocked at the suggestion that we should engage in a power struggle with our loving two-year-old daughter. However, when we eventually tried standing up and bargaining, Shuwen's behavior was immediately transformed, seemingly like magic! We could now speak her language of power without being mean or aggressive and she responded positively. Our relationship with her quickly became much smoother and easier.

Yo and I set out to learn more about the Enneagram and especially our own personality types, as well as those of family and close friends. It was a major and almost shocking eye-opener. However, knowledge of the Enneagram Personality Types did not replace Vipassana or Buddhism. It described a very deep form of personal (perhaps universal) conditioning, which the Buddha pointed out as a factor in making our lives seem solid and permanent, when, in fact, they were not — hence why we suffer. A powerful tool, but not in itself a way to enlightenment and maybe, if misunderstood, a way of deepening conditioning.

My personal routine on San Juan Island with Dhira started before dawn. I would drive a half hour from our rented house to the retreat center, and Dhira and I would meditate for an hour or more before making and eating breakfast together. After breakfast, we had an open-ended session, which included his dharma talks, my meditation and Buddhist questions, and broad-ranging discussions on current teachers, books, and other spiritual paths. It was uniquely instructive, revealing, stimulating, and inspiring. On one memorable post-breakfast session, neither Dhira nor I had anything to say, so we kept staring into each other's eyes for about thirty minutes, then got up and silently parted. Perfect!

A Plunge into the Unknown

In early 1984, I briefly returned to Toronto to attend my Wing Chun disciple graduation ceremony with Sifu Law, which was held at a huge Chinese restaurant. In April, my second daughter, Shuwei, was born in Vancouver, and she has always somehow felt a special connection to San Juan Island and to Dhiravamsa. I finally found the self-confidence to start working on the first rough drafts of a book, which would eventually become *The Conscious I: Clarity and Direction through Meditation*, published in Toronto in 1992. Approaching the autumn of 1984 and after one year of being with Dhiravamsa, money was running out, despite an unexpected and much-appreciated monetary gift from Yo's mother, Anne. She was the only one of our four joint parents to offer us any financial assistance while we were on San Juan Island.

One thing was absolutely clear to me: My heart would no longer allow me to go back into the business world on a full-time, nine-to-five basis, and maybe not even on a part-time basis. Both Miss Li and Dhiravamsa had given me permission to teach what I loved: Vipassana, *taijiquan*, *baguazhang*, and *xingyiquan*. I was also now really deepening my understanding of the Enneagram system, which I regarded as a very valuable, additional source of self-knowledge. We decided to move back to Toronto, where there was a bigger population base than the West Coast and where we had family, who we hoped could offer some support. Yolind seemed to be in supportive agreement that I should "follow my heart," although, in hindsight, I do not know how whole-hearted that statement was. Maybe at that time it was indeed one hundred percent. Driving a small Dodge Omni and dragging a U-Haul trailer with our belongings, we arrived in Toronto from the West Coast after nine days and with two small children in tow.

My father graciously offered us one of his rental houses in the suburbs for our temporary accommodation. Our initial trips into downtown Toronto were surprisingly stressful after a full year on peaceful, sleepy San Juan Island. There was so much noise, stimulus, and aggressive driving. How and where would I even start trying to be a teacher in Toronto? Where would our income come from?

The answer to our questions and doubts appeared shortly after we arrived in Toronto. We spotted an advertisement that an alternative magazine, called *Common Ground,* was just being launched, and one of its founders was Ron Rosenthal. It seemed a surprising coincidence, since Ron ran the local health food store in the Beaches neighborhood, where we bought our first Toronto property in 1982. Ron told me that he was not only offering ads in his magazine, but was organizing the very first, upscale "body-mind-spirit" convention in Toronto. He offered me a deal on a small booth, which I accepted. It seemed the perfect opportunity to present myself to Toronto.

All I had to display at my booth was a small, simple, foam core sign stating, "Tai Chi & Insight Meditation," and brief, amateurish video footage on a small TV of me doing my *taijiquan* form on San Juan Island. I sat with Shuwen on my lap, not knowing what to expect. I tried my best in a few sentences to try to explain to passersby why meditation and *taiji* were beneficial and how they were connected, which was a difficult task that eventually took me decades of polishing. How to simply explain the complex-simple-profound? To my surprise, about eighty people signed up over the weekend as "interested," which gave me a core of about twenty to thirty students for initial classes. Suddenly, I was a teacher!

The only negative aspect of that initial weekend was an unexpected and shocking threat by a self-styled black magic practitioner to launch psychic attacks and spells at me, apparently for no particular reason. During my time as a teacher, I subsequently experienced a few more such threats, which can be very alarming, especially if mounted by several people. I knew from experience that subtle mind-body energy (qi) was a fact and that it could be projected. I also guessed that such people were probably just trying to create fear, which weakens you and makes you more vulnerable. I was admittedly disturbed by the threat but did not react; I just stayed mindful and aware. The person issuing the threat probably wanted some kind of reaction from me, and I declined to oblige him.

I was not specifically taught by Miss Li or Dhiravamsa how to respond to psychic attacks. I guess neither they nor I deemed such attacks as high, or even likely, on our teaching-learning agenda. A much earlier experience I had in England, probably around the mid-1970s, immediately came to my mind after the incident with the black magic practitioner, which I saw as an early test. I had awakened from a terrifying dream of the Devil himself approaching me — not just any devil or negative entity! My fear was extreme, beyond a nightmare. I went to the window of the suburban bedroom to look out on the street to assure myself of waking, familiar reality. However, in this case, the Devil continued to approach me, even in my waking, conscious state. It was terrifying. For some reason — this was even before meeting Dhiravamsa — I thought of the Buddha's Four Noble Truths and especially the statement that all phenomena and manifestation were conditioned and, therefore, "impermanent and insubstantial." My only weapon-response was to recall and repeat as a mantra the Buddha's teaching that all phenomena-manifestations were insubstantial and impermanent. To my surprise and relief, the Devil gradually faded away. My present response to any kind of attack is to stand in quiet, present awareness, looking at what is, guarding against fear and overreaction, but pushing back energetically and even physically if appropriate. Such moments of challenge can be volatile and unpredictable.

The first few years of teaching in Toronto were difficult. *Taijiquan* was little known and mostly associated with elderly Chinese people in the park. The only form of meditation most people had even heard of was Transcendental Meditation (TM), famous mostly because of the Beatles. Almost no one had heard of Mindfulness meditation, much less Vipassana. No one in Toronto knew me as a teacher. In short, there was not then a big market for what I had to offer. But I was sure that it would eventually happen because these arts were invaluable in improving mind-body health and self-knowledge. I aimed for quality not quantity in terms of students. There was very little income at the beginning, which was stressful for Yolind and me, especially with a young and growing family.

In an attempt to bring in some additional income, I agreed to join someone I had met at Dhira's retreat on a business venture, which was flying fresh fish and seafood from Vancouver Island to Toronto. He had promises from specific fishing boats to sell him their catch. My part was finance, administration, and physically helping with the weekly deliveries. I managed to persuade my father to invest in what seemed to be a profitable venture, since we made modest profits on each shipment. My friend and I would unload our shipment at the airport, about 10,000 pounds at a time, and then drive around to wholesalers and retailers in a rented truck, sometimes air cooled and sometimes not. Time was of the essence. It was hard, sometimes smelly work, but I enjoyed the physical challenge and the extra income.

The seafood business went well for over six months, but then disaster struck in late summer. The airline shipping our cargo left it out in the stifling heat and subsequently refused to compensate us, resulting in thousands of dollars in losses. My business partner then disappeared with what remaining assets we had. I felt a deep sense of betrayal not only by my business partner but by the universe and life itself! After all, I was trying to do the right thing by following my heart in being a teacher and working two jobs to support my family. I was devastated and discouraged and started doubting my decision to be a teacher. Maybe all those who thought me an idealistic dreamer were right?

I decided to follow the Buddha's example when he resolved to sit under the bodhi tree until he found enlightenment, clarity, and truth. I sat in meditation, watching my thoughts and fully feeling my emotions without any agenda. I remember sending out a silent message to all divinities, saints, or enlightened beings from any tradition, East or West, to appear to me and give me guidance. After about two hours, clarity came to me, although not in any miraculous visitation or vision. I clearly saw that in wanting to be a teacher, I also subtly wanted some assurance, success, comfort, or safety net. I did not fully trust my own decision to become a teacher and perhaps doubted my own abilities. From that moment onwards, I decided to give all of myself to being a teacher, whatever the consequences or outcome.

After a while, Yo found a job as a chef at a health food store to add to our income, which meant I had to take care of our daughters during the day, since I taught in the evenings. At that time, I was the only stay-at-home dad at the local kindergarten and, later, primary school. I ferried them to and from their classes and took them, sometimes with friends, on urban adventures to the parks, beaches, and petting zoo. I also cooked for them. Looking after our daughters and bonding with them was important and especially rewarding for me. However, it also meant far less personal practice time, which I had to mindfully surrender after over a decade of consistent daily practice.

The only advertising I could afford in the early days was a small magazine ad, placement in the Yellow Pages, and local flyers that I delivered door to door myself. Agreeing with Miss Li's and Dhiravamsa's eschewing of self-promotion, I did not mention or try to market my links to my lineage teachers except if specifically asked. In my ads, I focused on what I personally knew and could offer students and did not promise more, including quick fixes. I understood that charisma, credibility, and perhaps a redemption story of recovery from addiction or tragedy were effective attention grabbers, but I deliberately declined to play any Marketing-101 games. I avoided wearing Asian-style robes or costumes, except for formal demonstrations and occasions, because I did not want to sell the image of being Chinese or Asian, which I thought was irrelevant to the practice itself. I recalled Miss Li's "I'm not a performing monkey" and the Buddha's "Even Buddhas can only point the way" statements. My rationale then (as now) was that serious students would listen to and observe what I had to offer, which was guidance in self-investigation and self-knowledge, rather than be persuaded, impressed, or charmed. The latter is often a form of belief, authority, and reassurance, adding to, not subtracting from, ego identity.

Starting with one initial class in a rented downtown Toronto studio, I gradually added a few other classes around the Greater Toronto Area (GTA), renting small studio or office spaces, church halls, and community center or public library rooms. Student numbers slowly grew, but all the traveling was exhausting, especially during the Canadian winters. After two to three years of driving all across the GTA, I had enough of a student base and some name recognition to rent a small office space in mid-town Toronto as a permanent studio. In addition to increasing my income, I got to teach more classes, which meant more personal practice for me — a win-win situation. In hindsight, my personal practice greatly matured through my teaching, even though I spent less actual time practicing alone. In explaining to others and practicing with them, I was also explaining to myself and practicing for myself.

After a few years of teaching, I noticed an interesting trend in the composition of my classes, which was to endure for some time. Women accounted for consistently more than half the classes; most students were white and middle class; and there were very few minorities, including Chinese. This latter fact did not surprise me, but it did disappoint me, since our teaching organization was near a local Chinatown. Living as part of a visible minority in three countries, I was used to, mostly subtle, discrimination. Canada seemed to be the best of the three countries in terms of discrimination. However, many Chinese discriminate against other Chinese because they are not "Chinese" enough. This is an absurdity shared by other nationalities but is particularly strong among Chinese.

I had long understood that most Chinese born and brought up in Asia thought that you were only genuinely Chinese if you spoke Chinese, although, ironically, many Chinese speakers could not communicate with each other since they spoke different dialects. Even Miss Li looked down on Cantonese-speaking Hong Kong self-styled

"Chinese experts," since they did not live in mainland China and did not speak Mandarin, which is now the universal Chinese language, the result of an early initiative within communist China. The derogatory term "banana" — meaning yellow on the outside but white inside — is becoming more widely known. It is ignorant and prejudiced, but it is even now a significant cultural factor. I admit that my name, Andy James, did not help in this regard. My Chinese name, bestowed on me by one of Yolind's professors, is Wu An-Dao. The latter means "way of peace." Wu is our family name in Mandarin. In Cantonese, it is Ng, which was ditched by my grandfather because of local Guyanese prejudices and constant ridicule. In many British colonies in the past, an immigrant's whole Chinese name was assumed by British authorities to be the surname and an anglicized first name was given to him or her. My grandfather's formal name was Henry James Ng-a-yow, and he eventually changed it to Henry James.

I first experienced this form of prejudice in the 1960s in London's Soho Chinatown. A waiter in a Chinese (Cantonese) restaurant scolded me, a customer, because I could not speak Chinese. It would not be the last of such incidents in my life. Fast forward to 2015. A Canadian Chinese facilitator for a Chan-Zen meditation group based in New York was trying to organize a Chan retreat in our meditation center, Harmony Dawn, in rural Ontario. She visited our premises to check them out and, as an aside, said to my face, "How can you teach Buddhism if you don't speak Chinese!?" I usually have words to respond, but I was speechless and bit my tongue. That group proved to be an unpleasant experience for me and my second wife, Nicola, mostly because of the organizer and the teacher, who was probably new to teaching and trying to assert herself, which is not what I would have expected from a Chan-Zen teacher. The actual participants, local Chinese from the Toronto area, were great, being friendly and appreciative of our hospitality.

Fortunately, in 2024, I finally see encouraging signs of improvement in this regard. In just recent years, our organizations have attracted and maintained as students a few China-born young women living in Toronto, which in itself is an unprecedented accomplishment. Although respecting Chinese traditions and culture, they could see how some aspects caused difficulties for them and their families in adapting to life in the West. They see the necessity of respecting and integrating East and West, not only in relationships and the particulars of modern life, but in the great wisdom traditions that both East and West have to offer. They see me as a pioneer and even a sort of father figure in this important East-West integrating process.

On the other side of this "Chineseness" issue was non-Chinese, Canadian prejudice. In 2002–2003, SARS was a health scare amplified by the United States, which associated it mostly with China and Chinese. Our Yellow Pages telephone calls rapidly dropped from around sixty a month to zero, which torpedoed our Tai Chi and Meditation Centre teaching organization. As I have mentioned, we actually had very few Chinese students, but that did not matter to most Torontonians, which greatly disappointed me as a Canadian. Simple prejudice and knee-jerk reaction, which is an almost universal human failing, is avoidable and a focal point of my overall teaching. As I write, racial prejudice against many peoples, including Asians, has been inflamed by self-serving demagogues in North America, mostly in the United States, and this has been spreading to other Western countries. History continues to repeat itself in a senseless, cruel, and destructive way, its lessons seemingly unheeded.

During the late 1980s, the Tai Chi and Meditation Centre eventually got local and national radio, TV, magazine, and newspaper coverage, including in *The Toronto Star*, one of the biggest newspapers in Canada. This added to our popular media profile and our student numbers gradually increased but remained relatively limited since our real work required ongoing personal commitment. We openly pointed out that we were not offering any miraculous quick fixes but guidance towards real transformation and mind-body health, which was more like a lifestyle change.

In early 1990, I noticed for the first time that Chinese martial arts (kung fu or *wushu*) competitions were being organized in the United States, dictating their own standards and formats, rather than just playing a minor part in the more popular Japanese karate and Korean tae kwon do competitions. I was excited at the prospect of testing my skills and knowledge, but also, at the same time, fearful of participating, lest my hard-earned "knowledge" and "teaching" be proven to be sub-standard or even illusory. Precisely because of my acknowledged fear, I made a pledge to myself to submit to competition and judgment by others for one year only, whether the actual results were good or bad.

I enrolled as a competitor in the U.S. All-Taijiquan Championships in Virginia and in the U.S. National Chinese Martial Arts Championships in Houston, Texas. My competition results were very good, considering that I had never even witnessed any such tournaments and that my "forms" and style were unfamiliar to the judges, since it came from an individual teacher, albeit with an undoubted lineage, rather than a big school or system. Also, I was not a student of a famous U.S.-based teacher as were many of my fellow competitors and, thus, I had no name recognition. Nevertheless, I returned to Toronto encouraged, inspired, and invigorated by my competition experiences.

Although I personally competed for only one year, my students competed for several years subsequently and garnered many medals in different competition categories, not only in the United States, but also in Canada. My senior student, Donna Oliver, who presently heads the Tai Chi and Meditation Centre following my retirement, was the most successful competitor, especially in tai chi push hands (*tui shou*). *Tui shou* is a two-person training exercise used in the internal martial arts (*nei jia*) — *taijiquan, baguazhang,* and *xingyiquan* — to introduce hands-on martial interactive skills, which, in the *nei jia*, means sensitivity, listening, sticking, and more, rather than brute force. The *taijiquan* classics say, "Four ounces deflects one thousand pounds," which I have actually experienced as a fact in various ways. Donna, at about 110 pounds, was the Lightweight Push Hands Champion at the U.S. All-Taijiquan Championships for four consecutive years, from 1995 to 1998, despite intense, highly skilled competition. In 1997, she also became the Push Hands Grand Champion, going against the Middleweight and Heavyweight champions. The latter was about seven inches taller and about sixty pounds heavier, which is a lot to overcome, both mentally and physically. Her competitors were not only much taller, bigger, and stronger, but also skilled in push hands. In Western contact sports such as boxing and wrestling, weight is considered to be such a decisive factor that weight categories span only about ten pounds or less.

An unexpected benefit of my decision to engage in these *taijiquan* and *wushu* competitions was meeting with esteemed fellow teachers. I particularly connected with Chung-Jen Chang from Taiwan, who swept the awards at the 1990 U.S. All-Taijiquan Championships at which I competed. His flexibility and flow were amazing. Chung-Jen subsequently shared with my students and me his beautiful yang-style *taiji* sword form and his unique Chen-style *taijiquan* forms. He has been a regular visitor to Toronto, staying with me and my students and conducting various *taijiquan* workshops. He has also become a very good friend.

I met with Master/Professor/Doctor Jerry Alan Johnson at the first North American meeting of *baguazhang* teachers in 1991. He generously invited me to visit and train with him at his home near Monterey, California, which surprised me since most masters want to guard their kung fu secrets from strangers. Traditionally, high-level, secret teaching was only passed on to senior, trusted disciples. We focused on *baguazhang* and martial qigong. He was both a renowned fighter as well as a healer who subsequently pioneered the establishment of separate qigong faculties in traditional Chinese-medicine teaching institutes in the United States. Dr. Johnson visited us in Toronto several times to share his knowledge with me and my students. He introduced us to medical qigong, which required TCM theory and energetic healing skills. In 1997, I went on my first trip to China, joining a group organized by Dr. Johnson, to study medical qigong at the China Beijing International Acupuncture Training Centre. He was recognized in China as a qigong TCM doctor according to Chinese medical establishment standards. When I first checked into my Beijing hotel, I was shocked to hear that Princess Diana had died in Paris, which made my experience there seem all the more surreal.

In the evenings after formal qigong classes, I learned Chen-style *taijiquan* from Master Zhang Yufei in Beijing's famous Temple of Heaven park. During the Mooncake Festival, he insisted I have dinner with him and his family, as it was a time to be with family. He rode me to his home through the dark back streets of Beijing on the back of his bicycle. It was another surreal experience, as if I was dreaming or watching a movie. I was finally actually experiencing life in China after reading about it for so long. My paltry language skills even enabled me to pass as a local during brief encounters. Yet, I remained a citizen of the world, neither wholly Eastern nor Western.

Master Liu Yu-Zeng, who is a formal disciple of both the original (Buddhist) Shaolin Temple as well as the (Daoist) Wudang Temple, stayed with me in Toronto when we were both judges at the 1998 Pan American Wushu Championships. He invited me and my students to train with him in China in the lesser-known Wudang martial and energetic arts, a rare opportunity. My senior students and I went to China later that year, with my three daughters joining us. They learned Wudang-style qigong. Master Liu arranged a personal meeting for us with the Patriarch of the Shaolin Temple, in his humble personal cottage outside of the main public temple areas. We felt the greatness and weight of the past as we walked the grounds of the Shaolin Temple. The Wudang forms are very old and their *baguazhang* form reminded me of Miss Li's. Master Liu is a member of China's Martial Arts Hall of Fame and has trained the police force in combat methods.

Amid all of these positive developments in my teaching life, including the 1992 publication of my first book, *The Conscious I: Clarity and Direction through Meditation*, my personal life was suddenly upended in April 1993. Without previous warning signs or arguments between us, Yolind announced she wanted an immediate separation! My daughters and I all spontaneously burst into shocked tears. A couple of months earlier, I had sensed something was amiss, but when I asked her if everything was all right with her, she said it was. I trusted her because we had a long-standing agreement with each other to talk about "issues" before they became "problems," and we did so for a long time. After initial resistance to Buddhism in our early years together, she had attended several meditation retreats with Dhiravamsa and, of course, knew about the Enneagram of Personality from our time on San Juan Island. She had the tools for deep self-inquiry and honest communication.

Not for the first time in my life, coincidence/happenstance/destiny and Buddhism played a role in a pivotal life moment. About two to three weeks before Yo's bombshell, my daughters got into an unusually heated and prolonged argument. I threatened ever-longer time-outs in their rooms, which eventually reached about two hours. I then remembered Dhira's San Juan Island advice about bargaining with Type 8 personalities, and I offered a deal: stand in silent, motionless meditation for ten minutes and escape any time-out. I was surprised that they all enthusiastically accepted the proposal and, even more, that they could actually stand motionless in silence for ten minutes in a qigong ball-holding posture. I cheated by not calling time at the ten-minute mark, because they seemed so still and serene, but ended the session after about fifteen minutes. They all reported feeling great and calm, and indeed they could not even remember what they were originally fighting about. I saw an opportunity and suggested that we should all sit in meditation together as a family for a short period every evening. They enthusiastically agreed and we did. At that time, they were quite young, aged six, nine, and eleven.

I had never previously tried to pressure my daughters into formal meditation practice, so our starting to sit together in meditation every evening proved extremely timely and invaluable for them in dealing with the ensuing parental separation and divorce, both in the short and long term. Meditation afforded them space and quiet, wherein they could examine their thoughts and, more importantly, as I advised, the condition of their hearts. They instinctively knew what this meant and could ascertain whether their hearts were open or closed and sometimes the color of the heart. They could also distinguish between the true inner voice coming from the heart as opposed to, for example, from the throat, which they observed could be misleading. These were their own observations, not something I had told them. Meditation also helped them speak honestly to each other, even on subjects that were contentious. In time, it became something that they instinctively took refuge in when life became stressful or difficult, even when I was not physically present with them or when they themselves were apart.

After a couple of awkward months with Yolind — seeking conversation, reasons, and resolution — I simply asked her if she still loved me. She said, "No." At that time, I let go of her and our relationship, since love was a necessary foundation for me. I still do not know the reason for her request to divorce, but for me, it did not and does not matter because it takes two to have a partnership or marriage relationship.

An unexpected fallout from my separation and divorce was the impact it had on our original core group of senior students at the Tai Chi and Meditation Centre. We were very close and often socialized outside of classes. Maybe the illusion of the "ideal couple" was shattered or maybe students started taking sides, which surprised me since I did not initiate the separation and since taking sides seemed to be an immature reaction. For the first time, I began hearing views from them, which were apparently arising at that time in academia and the media, that all relationships and views were fifty-fifty. I rejected that belief or theory as illogical, arbitrary, and unsubstantiated at that time, and still do now. I pointed out that if someone is walking down the street and is randomly attacked (which happens), how can blame be apportioned fifty-fifty? I instead recommended paying careful, objective attention to actually "what is."

In the late 1990s, several of our original core group of teachers left, some to try to be teachers on their own. I did not discourage them from teaching but suggested that we should stick together as a mind-body family, supporting each other, as our work was difficult enough to communicate and establish. A handful of that original group still supports our organization, the Tai Chi and Meditation Centre, and teaches. Donna Oliver is now the chief instructor following my retirement. She has been my student for thirty-six years.

In 1998, I met my present wife, Nicola, who would soon co-create the next major chapter of my life. She had contacted the Tai Chi and Meditation Centre to learn *taijiquan*, which she thought would help ground her for her acting classes. Nicola was born in London, England, and had emigrated to Canada at four years old. Having lived in England for twenty years, I could easily relate to her and her family and banter in Brit-speak. She was very open to learning about and embracing my unusual background and experiences and also participating in the disciplines that I taught. We have lived in great joy and harmony ever since. In 2003, we hosted the grand opening of our rural, green retreat center, which we named Harmony Dawn as a hope, refuge, and beacon for our children and future generations. The last twenty-year period at Harmony Dawn has been a very different, fulfilling, and joyful chapter in my life, which I will describe later on in this book.

Looking back over my decades-long journey of discovering, exploring, practicing, and eventually teaching Buddhism, the interplay between East and West has been a recurring theme. This applies not only to my personal experiences, but also to global interactions in different spheres, including political, cultural, economic, and spiritual.

The fact of being of Chinese descent and growing up and living in the West, albeit in three very different countries and cultures, has of course been a major East-West factor in my life. It became more prominent in England, where various events I have already described led me to the discovery of the Asian martial arts and Buddhism, and where I met my first wife, Yolind, who was from Singapore and of English-Chinese descent.

At that time, I was not aware of the perennial philosophy or that scholars like Joseph Campbell were writing about the very real and impactful differences between the mythologies and religions of the West (Abrahamic) and the East, especially Hinduism and Buddhism. I was personally discovering and experiencing those differences and trying, in my own way, to reconcile them, which seemed to be the only win-win solution. I was not aware of Huston Smith's observation that perennial wisdom may be regarded as the forgotten wisdom or truth, since each new generation is required to (hopefully) rediscover and relearn its lessons. At present, there seems to be great tension between this essentially Eastern notion of circular rediscovery and, in a way, rebirth and the Western notion of linear, historical progress, which seems to be approaching perilous, global tipping points.

The East–West dynamic continues through the generations of my family. All of my daughters have Caucasian husbands and partners. My second daughter, Shuwei, who lives in Singapore, got married in Istanbul because she and her husband, Leon, have many friends in both East and West and because Istanbul is the ancient and historic Constantinople, which has traditionally been regarded as the dividing line between East and West. Their views on world politics reflect their experience in and respect for both East and West, which I find refreshing and hopeful. My eldest grandson, Bodhi, who has always lived in Singapore, plays ice hockey and supports the Maple Leafs.

Since the end of the Second World War, the West's export of its technology to the East through global trade has dramatically raised global standards of living. This is especially obvious in the massive and populous countries of India and China, which, in the process, have become world powers. The West, of course, also exported its culture, including consumerism and its views on the family, especially the role and rights of women. The latter has been met with great and often violent resistance in countries where patriarchy is still strong. The East is still in the complicated process of digesting Western culture.

In a less conscious and obvious way, the East has been exporting its spirituality to the West for a long time, going back to at least the latter part of the nineteenth century through the Theosophical Society, Swami Vivekananda, Emerson, and many others. This movement has accelerated over the last sixty years with the most high-profile moments perhaps being the Beatles studying with Maharishi Mahesh Yogi and the West's discovery of Bruce Lee movies and the Asian martial arts. When I first started teaching in 1984, yoga and tai chi were equally popular forms of exotic, Eastern exercise, but now yoga reigns supreme, primarily because of its celebrity endorsements. My early hopes that this broad infusion of Eastern spirituality might facilitate an urgently needed shift in popular consciousness have diminished over the ensuing decades. I still have hope because what is urgently needed is not necessarily full enlightenment, but just more attention, care, compassion, sharing, cooperation, and recognition of connectedness between all peoples. Many verbalize similar vague aspirations but neither walk the talk nor have any idea of how this transformation can actually be achieved.

From my experience as a teacher, I can think of a few reasons for the so-far underwhelming impact of Eastern spirituality on the West. The first and most obvious is that there are a substantial number of people in the West who are not (and probably never will be) interested, as it is deemed un-Western, un-American, un-Christian, and the like. These people are also highly unlikely to be aware that the higher levels of each major religion share similarities and commonalities, as in the image of the spiritual mountain where all paths converge at the top.

Among those open to trying or experimenting, many treat spirituality and mind-body disciplines like other consumer items. If you pay money and invest time, then you expect quick, tangible, measurable results — "bang for your buck." In response to this common expectation, many teachers use standard, proven marketing strategies: focus on a particular selling point; promise tangible benefits; try to make it fun, exciting, and beautiful; encourage rewards and signs of progress; and avoid negativity. It is often argued that a little of these practices is better than none. It can also be argued that their true depth, meaning, and potentiality are often ignored or bypassed through the attitude of "been there and done that" or just another item crossed off one's lifetime bucket list.

As many in the East became more preoccupied with attaining a Western lifestyle, they often neglected or belittled their own forms of religion and spirituality. This has encouraged many Eastern teachers to come to the West, where the demand for their teaching has slowly grown. This has generally benefited the West, but many teachers brought not only their core religious and spiritual teachings, but also their cultural adornments or even impediments. Costumes, robes, rites, chants, gurus, and lineages are exotic and alluring, but for me, they have little to do with self-transformation, which is an inner practice, often seemingly ordinary. The Chan-Zen tradition advises:

> Before enlightenment, chop wood and carry water. After enlightenment, chop wood and carry water…
>
> The finger pointing to the moon is not the moon itself…
>
> If you meet the Buddha on the path, kill the Buddha.

Society does not celebrate and value the wisdom and compassion of enlightenment and, indeed, may not even recognize it. Reading books and listening to teachers or watching their videos is not transformation itself (the moon), but the finger pointing to the moon. Our ideas about the Buddha are not the real essence of the Buddha and so must be destroyed so that we can keep mindfully walking the path or way until we realize (in other words, make real) our own Buddha nature in ourselves.

James family circa 1956: Left to right, Brian, Michael, Andrew, Beryl, Ray, Andy.

Andrew meets the Queen during her 1966 Guyana visit.

The historic Georgetown City Hall, Guyana.

Two very different groups of fellow students. Above: Ridgeway House, Mill Hill School, London 1966. Below: Hua Tiong Pugilistic Art Institute, Singapore, 1977.

Andy trains in Singapore 1977

1976 Dhiravamsa retreat, Cambridgeshire, UK. Andy and Dhira are in front, at right; Yolind is in the middle of the standing row.

Rose Li's 1992 weeklong Tai Chi seminar in Yorkshire, UK. Miss Li is center back of group. Andy is center front.

Dhiravamsa and Andy on San Juan Island 1984.

1984, Andy graduates as one of Sifu Steven Law's Wing Chun disciples.

1984 Andy presents himself as a Tai Chi and meditation Teacher.

Andy leads his first Vipassana meditation retreat circa 1988.

First Students' Christmas party circa 1990.

Andy helps Grandmaster Yang Zhen-Duo demonstrate circa 1991.

Andy coaches his medal-winning students. Donna Oliver is center with medal. Master Chung-Jen Chang is far right. Circa 1993.

Andy with Professor Jerry Allan Johnson circa 1991.

Andy's daughters Shuwen, Shuwei, and Hana in standing meditation 1993.

Yolind, Andy, Shuwei, Hana, Shuwen and Chung-Jen Chang 1992.

Andy with the Abbot of the Shao Lin Temple, China 1999.

Professor Liu Yu-Zeng (third from right in front) in China with Andy's students and daughters 1999.

Senior disciple Donna Oliver 1995.

OUR MOMENT OF TRUTH

Everyone who is seriously involved in the pursuit of science becomes convinced that some spirit is manifest in the laws of the universe, one that is vastly superior to that of man.

We must never relax our efforts to arouse in the people of the world, and especially their governments, an awareness of the unprecedented disaster which they are absolutely certain to bring on themselves unless there is a fundamental change in their attitudes towards one another as well as in their concept of the future. The unleashed power of the atom has changed everything except our modes of thinking.

—Albert Einstein

I have long told my daughters and my students that it is not necessary to analyze yourself for possible problems just for the sake of it, because if something from the past is urgent enough, it will arise for your attention sooner or later, and that is the time to deal with it. In that way, you can meet whatever challenge life throws at you in each moment as you journey through life, without accumulating ever heavier burdens.

As I mentioned in the preface, individually and collectively, we are facing great, perhaps unprecedented, challenges — our moment of truth — and are showing signs of buckling or even collapsing under their constant pressure. Our leaders are not providing any innovative solutions to our problems; they are content to tinker and kick the proverbial can down the road.

Many brilliant minds in various fields of expertise, including Einstein, have warned that although science and technology have brought us great prosperity and power, our ability to use that power wisely is questionable at best. We tend to think that we just need greater power to solve our problems, ignoring the fact that almost all our problems have been created by us. There is a big difference between power and the wisdom to use it wisely.

This brings to mind the Buddha's distinction between the two main streams of meditation: one-pointedness, focus, or *samadhi* and wisdom or jnana/Vipassana. Focus brings concentration and power, like a fire hose or laser beam, but by itself does not generate the wisdom and insight necessary for enlightenment and the ending of suffering. Power is blind and may be used for both constructive and destructive purposes or may simply magnify the consequences of error. History (and yin-yang theory) tells us that rulers, countries, and empires rise and fall. Nothing or no one stays in power forever, or even a long time, since circumstances are constantly changing. It is futile to resist change, as the Buddha pointed out. However, we can learn to ride the waves of change, like a boat, knowing when to stay or change our course. This ability is deep, transformational wisdom in the spiritual sense, not just intellect or cleverness.

The Promise of Progress

The main promise of modern society is that material progress and prosperity will solve our problems and make us happy. This is not a universal or timeless notion but largely the result of the industrial revolution, which began around the middle of the eighteenth century, about 250 years ago, a proverbial blink of an eye in terms of human history. Up until then, even in the West, life for most was a struggle just to survive, as it still is in several parts of the world. The invention of new machinery, together with harnessing new sources of power, including coal, gas, and oil, dramatically increased productivity not only of food but also of all kinds of products and inventions. This sparked rapid rises in the standard of living and in population growth. Open sewers gradually disappeared, and houses were connected to water and power. Economic historians generally agree that the industrial revolution was the most important development in human history since the domestication of plants and animals. The world's population reached one billion for the first time ever around 1800. It is eight billion now and growing fast.

The industrial revolution was given great early momentum and direction by the birth of modern capitalism and of the founding of the United States of America. Indeed, 1776 was the year of both the American *Declaration of Independence* and the publication of Adam Smith's *The Wealth of Nations*, long regarded as the "bible of capitalism." Smith saw human nature as basically self-serving but, in the end, reasonable. He believed that by bettering themselves, people also bettered society. He theorized that, as we compete with each other out of self-interest in a free market (both domestic and foreign), the "invisible hand" of the market will optimize various forces, especially production, for the overall good of society. Smith advocated the division of labor and specialization to make production more efficient, and his advice has been duly followed. We have long placed a high value on productivity, which is the amount of output relative to input, including human labor and creativity. Smith discouraged government interference in the free market, suggesting its function be limited to national defense, civil order, infrastructure, and some public works, like education. Machines, robots, and AI substantially raise productivity because they enable ever fewer workers to achieve greater levels of output.

The *United States Declaration of Independence* in 1776 has also shaped modern aspirations and perspectives. It stated that "all men are created equal" and have the right to "life, liberty and the pursuit of happiness." The right to life and liberty were associated with the preservation of democracy. Happiness became associated with the ability to access and consume goods and services in an economy that was to be powerfully shaped by Smith's vision of free-market capitalism and competition. Not long afterwards, Thorstein Veblen's

1899 *The Theory of the Leisure Class* described a novel phenomenon spawned and nurtured by the unprecedented and widespread prosperity of the capitalist industrial revolution — consumerism and conspicuous consumption. This related to the acquisition of goods and services far beyond what was necessary for survival, in large part to demonstrate social superiority and status.

James Truslow Adams, writing 155 years after both Adam Smith and the *Declaration of Independence*, coined the widely inspiring term "the American dream" in his 1931 book, *The Epic of America*:

> That dream of a land in which life should be better and richer and fuller for everyone, with opportunity for each according to ability or achievement... It is not a dream of motor cars and high wages merely, but of a social order in which each man and each woman shall be able to attain the fullest stature of which they are innately capable, and be recognized by others for what they are.

Free-market capitalism, the American dream, consumerism, and technology have long molded modern civilization and still do. They have undoubtedly and impressively raised overall standards of living across the planet, and especially in the West. However, this socioeconomic system has consistently also brought about social and economic inequality, destabilizing boom-and-bust economic cycles, environmental damage and pollution, and depletion of scarce resources. Voters seem to think that this instability is the fault of the last government administration, so they try the alternative political party without realizing that instability is part of the system itself. Free-market proponents constantly repeat the persuasive but deceptive slogan "the rising tide lifts all boats" to justify tax benefits to the rich, but evidence is clear that this particular "tide" lifts the rich much more than the poor, widening inequality.

Many have a sense of being better off yet somehow never seeming to get ahead, always having to pay some kind of price for our gains, never fully satisfied or happy. For example, even something as obviously good as medical advances that prolong life have resulted in increases in old-age diseases like dementia, loss of mobility, and more. This also requires those living longer to need more long-term care, which many cannot afford because their life savings are inadequate. Even those who can afford long-term care often live unfulfilled lives, akin to being "warehoused" apart from their busy families.

This dynamic reminds me of the first law of thermodynamics, or the law of conservation of energy — energy is neither created nor destroyed but merely changes form. We cannot get something from nothing. This circular interconnectedness reminds me even more of yin-yang principles, examples of which were profoundly and poetically expressed over two thousand years ago in the *Daodejing*:

> When all in the world understand beauty to be beautiful, then ugliness exists. When all understand goodness to be good, then evil exists. Thus existence suggests non-existence; easy gives rise to difficult...

As early as the beginning of the nineteenth century, the intellectual and artistic Romantic movement raised concerns about the obvious, rapidly spreading degradation of nature due to industrialization, including the increase in chemical, water, and smoke pollution. William Blake's famous poem and hymn "Jerusalem" mourned the despoiling of "England's green and pleasant land" by the spread of "dark satanic mills."

Although scientists and activists have kept us informed about the increasing degradation of the environment and the depletion of scarce resources, remedial measures have been late or totally inadequate, for reasons which will be explored later. The planet seems to be approaching a tipping point, which some see as Mother Earth crying out in pain. I will not go into a detailed description of all our environmental ills because information is readily available for those moved to investigate. I think it pertinent, however, to list a few major ones as a reminder of their cumulative and interconnected impact on the planet and, therefore, ourselves.

One of the most obvious and present threats is climate change, which used to be aptly called "global warming," but was renamed under President George W. Bush on the advice of leading Republican strategist Frank Luntz because "global warming" sounded too alarming. A leaked 2002 memo from Luntz sheds much light on how this global issue became deliberately politicized and reframed as a Left–Right issue rather than a global threat backed by overwhelming scientific evidence. This is yet another example of leaders prioritizing immediate personal and partisan interests over the collective (in this case global), thereby casting more doubt on the wisdom of Adam Smith's trust in people's "better nature." Luntz wrote:

> The scientific debate is closing against us but not yet closed. There is still a window of opportunity to challenge the science ... should the public come to believe that the scientific issues were settled, their views about global warming will change accordingly... Therefore, you need to make the lack of scientific certainty a primary issue... A compelling story, even if factually inaccurate, can be more compelling than a dry recitation of the truth.

The science was settled even back then, but the inaccurate, compelling story spun by the Republicans and the fossil fuels lobbyists still carries much weight within right-wing parties and supporters. Ironically, many of those followers are bearing the brunt of global warming effects as, for example, in the southern United States. Scientists first noticed a connection between global warming and carbon dioxide (CO_2) as early as the 1930s. Now, almost one hundred years later, astonishingly many still doubt it even as they are overwhelmed by increasing heat waves, droughts, floods, storms, hurricanes, wildfires, and more. The inaccurate but compelling story successfully stonewalled the "dry recitation of truth," and for that both leaders and those being led must take responsibility.

Global deforestation, especially in the Amazon, not only reduces natural habitats for many species, but also increases CO_2 emissions and, therefore, global warming. The reason for much tropical deforestation is the clearing of land for cattle raising, since increasing prosperity commonly translates into more conspicuous consumption of meat as a status symbol. Factory farming of animals also generates lakes of effluent and chemicals, which make their way into rivers and eventually oceans, as other pollutants from agriculture and garbage dumps do. Unsurprisingly, so-called forever chemicals and microplastics lodge in our bodies for the long term with as yet undetermined consequences.

Human activities damage not only humans but all other species. Many scientists claim we are now experiencing the onset of the planet's sixth, or Anthropocene (caused by humans), extinction. Current rates of extinction of species are estimated to be one hundred to one thousand times higher than natural "background extinction rates." It is not just tigers, polar bears, and elephants that are under threat. The fifth mass extinction of species, including, of course, the dinosaurs, occurred sixty-six million years ago when a large asteroid crashed into the Earth. All our activities are interconnected; we are interconnected with other humans, other species, and the planet itself. The air that we breathe and the water in our bodies have passed through other bodies. The pervasive evidence of our interconnection should be obvious but is widely ignored or denied. Evidence is now emerging that trees exhibit a form of intelligence in exchanging nutrients with each other and communicating about insects and other environmental threats, no doubt including massive clear-cutting and deforestation.

Most people, including politicians and leaders, do not seem to realize or will not openly admit that boom-and-bust cycles, income and wealth inequality, endless competition, and replacement of humans by machines are inherent aspects of free-market capitalism rather than unfortunate aberrations. Adam Smith's *The Wealth of Nations*, regarded as the first comprehensive system of "political economy," is not just about productivity but contains his philosophy and views on human nature and how individuals and society interact, mostly featured in his earlier work, *The Theory of Moral Sentiments*.

Like other philosophers and spiritual and religious leaders, Smith recognized the universal conflict within individuals between the reasonable, objective "inner man" and a more basic instinct for self-preservation and self-interest. This conflict will also be discussed later in this book. Smith's particular chosen solution was to try to make individuals' self-interest (presumably including greed) work for the greater good of society through regulation by the "invisible hand" of the free market, including the up-and-down movements of supply and demand and boom-and-bust cycles. He frowned on government or other intentional direction or regulation, hence the laissez-faire description of his brand of capitalism:

> By pursuing his own interest, he frequently promotes that of society more effectually than when he really intends to promote it. I have never known much good done by those who affected to trade for the public good.

Without going into a detailed analysis of Smith's theories, I will just make a few observations. Firstly, and perhaps not surprisingly, he did not foresee the scale and rate at which capitalism and technology would transform not only the newly independent United States but also the entire world. He, and certainly many followers, seemed to assume that productivity and consumption were boundless. As previously mentioned, the world population reached one billion for the first time in 1804 and is now eight billion, doubling in ever-shorter time spans. The U.S. population in 1776 was 2.5 million and is now 341 million. There is now an unprecedentedly large number of people to feed, house, transport, and pamper, which, as we have seen, is literally eating away at the planet and its finite resources.

Smith acknowledged that his system would likely lead to disparities in wealth and power through the necessity for capital accumulation ("money makes money"), boom-and-bust cycles, wherein people would lose their jobs, and the fact that employers usually had more power in wage negotiations than workers. However, he presumed that, in the long term, the invisible hand would somehow provide new jobs and that the government might provide public education to help displaced workers retrain and broaden their outlook, even though he was generally not in favor of government, except for defense, civil order (police), and infrastructure.

We now know that U.S. governments, despite generally embracing non-regulated free-market policies and small government, have nevertheless been historically strong on defense spending but not so much on education, much less safety-net programs and health care. The U.S. military defense budget in 2022 was US$877 billion, greater than the next ten biggest spenders combined! China was second at US$292 billion. Defense accounted for about twelve percent of the total U.S. budget, or just under half of discretionary spending.

American income and wealth inequality is the highest amongst developed nations and has risen for much of the last sixty years. The Organisation for Economic Co-operation and Development (OECD), using the Gini income inequality coefficient, found that in 2017 the U.S. had the highest inequality among the G7 developed nations. According to the U.S. Census Bureau, in 1970 the top one percent of income earners accounted for just under ten percent of national income, but by 2019, the top one percent earned over twenty percent, more than doubling their share. The bottom fifty percent earned twenty-two percent of the national income in 1970 and just fifteen percent in 2019. In terms of wealth, the top ten percent of Americans own a stunning seventy percent of total national wealth while the bottom fifty percent own only 1.5 percent. Inequality is an important factor in our sense of well-being because people compare themselves, especially to those seemingly better off. In absolute terms, the poorest Americans are much better off than the poor in many other countries, but they take no comfort in that statistic because they compare themselves to fellow Americans, especially the celebrated "rich and famous."

In his *Ten Lessons for a Post-Pandemic World*, Fareed Zakaria titled Lesson Seven "Inequality will get worse." He noted:

> Inequality in America looms worse than ever, the worst in the Western world, even after accounting for taxes and government transfers...
>
> Racism's contribution to inequality goes back centuries, but structural shifts are also fueling it. For one thing, the

> financial benefits of a college education have risen steadily as the economies of the industrial world become more digital and service-oriented…
>
> The story of inequality is not just about nations but about companies as well. The retreat to safety and security will manifest itself in corporate life, where the big will get bigger.

Smith could not have foreseen how much unregulated free-market competition would turbocharge the development of technology. Not only do workers compete for jobs and wages, but so do companies and countries to get or maintain a competitive advantage. For decades now, the areas of most competition have been nuclear energy, information technology, robotics, artificial intelligence (AI), genetics, nanotechnology, and more. Because of the power of technology, the world has seen not only new benefits but also new dangers on an unprecedented scale. Many younger people are unaware of (and some older ones complacent about) the dropping of atomic bombs by the United States on Hiroshima and Nagasaki in 1945, but the danger of a nuclear war is still very much a possibility. Recent reports suggest that Russia is planning to launch nuclear weapons into space, which would be capable of destroying most satellites in orbit and, therefore, disabling most infrastructure systems.

AI is evolving so fast that self-sufficient, decision-making AI and robots are close. Artificial intelligence could replace humans in different ways, many already featured in sci-fi books and movies. Much of "sci-fi" is no longer fiction and no longer in the distant future. In May 2023, the most prominent AI leaders and developers, including Sam Altman, CEO of OpenAI, which developed ChatGPT with Microsoft backing, and Geoffrey Hinton, so-called Godfather of AI and formerly of Google, issued this public warning:

> Mitigating the risk of extinction from AI should be a global priority alongside societal-scale risks such as pandemics and nuclear war.

"Risk of extinction" is clear, authoritative, blunt, and straightforward. However, as I write more than one year later, development of AI speeds ahead unchecked and unregulated despite government hearings and committees and, of course, passing news cycle media coverage. Urgent warnings soon evaporate amidst our distracted busyness and short attention spans. It seems to me that many non-technical societal leaders do not really understand AI's nature and vast potential. As usual, they prefer to look at potential benefits rather than risks, congratulating themselves that they are being "positive." In October 2024, Hinton, a Professor at the University of Toronto, was awarded the Nobel Prize in Physics.

Technical and non-technical leaders alike are not yet asking the bigger, underlying questions like, "What is a human being and human purpose?" or even more simply, "Who am I?" These questions are at the core of this book, since knowing the nature of one's self and purpose should logically direct all our aspirations and actions, individual and collective. Many tech leaders justify their work on the claim that it is "for the good of humanity." How would they know that? How is humanity defined? What research into human nature have they done outside of their own technical specialization? From their behavior and actions, many do not seem to know much about humanity or themselves, exhibiting personal volatility, inconsistency, and, of course, ambition and vanity. It brings to mind an old adage that perhaps younger people might not even understand, "putting the cart before the horse."

Many tech leaders' theories and speculations about the future of AI are appalling and alarming to me. Unless there is radical societal change, many expect the eventual, perhaps imminent, arrival of "technological singularity," or simply singularity. This is the point in time when technological (especially AI) growth becomes irreversible and uncontrollable — the point of no return — resulting in radical and unpredictable consequences for humanity, including extinction. Artificial intelligence is evolving at an explosive rate compared to human intelligence, which has not appreciably evolved over the past centuries. Indeed, many people seem to be regressing as they deliberately dismiss reason and embrace wild conspiracy theories.

Some tech leaders suggest a solution for humans to survive is to upload their minds to computers or develop mechanical, biological, genetic, or nanotechnological enhancements — the cyborg of sci-fi literature.

The basic questions "Why?" and "How?" remain. If the free market continues in its present form, competition will make it difficult to control, much less stop, the projected developmental path of AI. In 2023, after AI leaders issued two separate warnings about the dangers of AI, they subsequently intensified their competition in pushing ahead with its development. Even before human beings are totally replaced by AI and robots, there will be the question of what to do with those people who become unproductive or even redundant. The invisible hand of the free market rewards productivity with resources and discourages outside, especially governmental, intervention. If self-determining robots are more productive and efficient, will they not demand more resources? Who or what will deny them, especially if they control most elements of human life, including food and water supply, infrastructure, the military, police, hospitals, power systems, transportation, and more. Even if some humans want to become cyborgs, how many can afford to pay for this transition? In most scenarios, the future looks especially bleak for poor and powerless humans ... unless we change now!

Einstein, perhaps facetiously, opined, "Two things are infinite: the universe and human stupidity; and I'm not sure about the universe." On a more serious note, he observed, "The measure of intelligence is the ability to change. It is not that I am so smart, but I stay with the question longer."

Einstein's observation of intelligence is both pertinent to our times and agelessly profound. We live in an era of unprecedented change, driven by technology, and many are already overwhelmed by it, frightened, and lashing out. This not only creates more division but, of course, also makes vital cooperation in meeting our shared challenges much more difficult. A 2017 *Scientific American* article by Edmund S. Higgins on mental health in the United States reported:

> The mental health of the nation may have even declined in the past 20 years... Suicide rates per 100,000 people

increased to a 30-year high. Substance abuse, particularly of opiates, has become epidemic. Disability awards for mental disorders have dramatically increased since 1980, and the U.S. Department of Veterans Affairs is struggling to keep up with the surge in post-traumatic stress disorder (PTSD).

As has happened many times in the past, when people feel threatened, they look for others to blame, usually foreigners or outsiders. In the developed Western countries, the middle class is shrinking, and this is especially true in the United States with its large wealth and income inequality gap. As we have seen, this is primarily due to free-market, laissez-faire capitalism, with the actual major threat to jobs being robotics and AI. However, the growing number of white nationalists or supremacists clearly direct their fears of being replaced to immigrants, non-whites, and non-Christians. The first time most Americans heard of the term "replacement" was in August 2017 at the Unite the Right rally in Charlottesville, Virginia. Torch-carrying participants marched and chanted, "You will not replace us. Jews will not replace us." A white supremacist drove his car into a crowd of counter-protesters, killing one and injuring several others. Europeans would have been more familiar with the term "great replacement" from the writings by the French philosopher, Renaud Camus. His focus was on European civilization and identity being threatened by mass migrations, especially from Muslim countries.

In the United States, fear of immigration often merges with unresolved issues from the past, primarily the legacy of (Black) slavery and, of course, gun rights, which, not surprisingly, results in gun deaths, in which the United States is a statistical world leader. Here are a few excerpts from a 2022 *Science* magazine article by Rodrigo Pérez Ortega on the results of a survey of more than 8,600 adults on violence in the United States:

> One in five Americans believes violence motivated by political reasons is, at least sometimes, justified. Nearly

half expect a civil war and many say they would trade democracy for a strong leader…

Firearm deaths in the United States grew by nearly 43% between 2010 and 2020, and gun sales soared during the coronavirus pandemic…

Conspiracy theories, some rooted in racism, are helping shape views about political violence. They found roughly two in five agreed with the white nationalist "great replacement theory," or the idea that native-born white voters are being replaced by immigrants for electoral gains.

The solution to gun deaths in America proposed by the gun lobby and a substantial minority of Americans is even more gun ownership, including military-style automatic weapons. They blame America's high gun death rate not on gun ownership but on mental health, which is factually no worse in America than other developed countries. Ironically, most Republicans do not support government funding for issues like mental health, in line with Adam Smith's free-market advice. All is interconnected.

A 2018 University of Washington study reported the U.S. gun death rate as 10.6 people per 100,000 population, the highest of any developed country. The next highest was France at 2.7 per 100,000. The highest global gun death rates were to be found in Central and South America, with El Salvador at 39.2 and Venezuela at 38.7. Gun ownership in America is about 1.3 guns per person, or 434 million firearms in total. The next highest gun-owning developed country is Canada at 0.34 guns per person.

Easy gun ownership in America also facilitates the formation of private militias. In a 2021 article for the Brookings Institution, William Gale and Darrell West wrote:

"Several-hundred private-militia groups now exist around the country, and they have proliferated in recent years." Current militias generally are made up of right-wing white men who worry about changing demographics, stagnating wages, and how the shift to a multi-racial and multiethnic America will affect them. These groups create the potential for violence because they tend to attract radicalized individuals, train members for violent encounters, and use social media to reinforce existing beliefs. They openly talk about armed rebellion and some members of these organizations already have engaged in violence.

Einstein's quote, "The measure of intelligence is the ability to change. It is not that I am so smart, but I stay with the question longer," reminds me of the Buddha's teachings from 2,500 years ago. The Buddha described life as constantly changing, interconnected, conditioned, and insubstantial — nothing is really solid. Since life is change and, in reality, there is nothing that we can truly grasp and hold, we suffer if we try to do so, which we invariably do. The Buddha's answer to ending suffering and attaining enlightenment (absolute truth) is letting go. Flow with life and change instead of fighting a constantly losing battle to control it. In Vipassana meditation, I counsel my students that if they learn to pay bare attention without control or judgment, eventually doubtless clarity and insight will arise, leading to "right action," which seems akin to Einstein's advice to "stay with the question longer."

Einstein, probably the most brilliant mind of modern times, giving the same advice as one of the world's greatest spiritual teachers, the Buddha, should logically merit attention and deep consideration by many, including our leaders and thinkers, but presently it does not. As already mentioned, we tend to look at our issues and challenges as separate boxes without acknowledging their actual interconnectedness; we also seldom question our underlying assumptions about life, society, and self, including fundamentals like purpose, meaning, and truth. This approach has not and will not work, no matter how often we attempt it.

Is There an Alternative to "Progress"?

We can create a more caring, compassionate, and sustainable world if we have the collective wisdom, heart, vision, and will to do so. Mahatma Gandhi correctly observed, "The world has enough for everyone's need but not enough for everyone's greed." Right now, even without new technologies or greater production, we can waste less and share more, as several countries are already demonstrating.

In our instant gratification, throwaway society, we generate enormous amounts of waste, at present just over two billion tons a year globally. Experts predict this figure will increase seventy percent in the next thirty years to 3.4 billion tons. Our garbage is composed mainly of everyday items like packaging, clothes, bottles, papers, electronics, batteries, and, of course, food, which amounts to 1.3 billion tons, or one-third of all food generated for human consumption. Less than twenty percent of waste is recycled annually, with the balance going to landfill sites that invariably leak and emit a variety of toxins and pollutants. The more waste we generate, the more resources we have to expend to get rid of it and minimize its toxicity. It does not take much effort to organize our lives to reuse rather than throw away. For example, we can buy classic, long-lasting clothing items that never go out of fashion rather than the throwaway, aptly called "fast fashion" that fills our dumps. We can buy multi-use containers and household products and food that can be stored, like grains and beans, so we can avoid unnecessary packaging. Pressure can also be put on manufacturers to pay a penalty for waste disposal if their products intentionally generate waste or toxicity. The practice of "built-in obsolescence" must be stopped. Durable products like appliances and cars should be built to last longer and be more easily repaired rather than becoming obsolete by design, being junked, and forcing consumers to buy new replacements.

One major source of waste that is not usually classified as such is arms production and wars. Global spending on arms is about 2.3 percent of countries' budgets. The United States is the biggest military spender at about 12 percent of its budget, which, as mentioned before, is more than the next ten biggest spenders combined. The best usage of arms is that they are not used and just junked — more waste. Unfortunately, there are always armed conflicts taking place across the world. In 2012, the economic impact of war and violence cost 11 percent of gross world product. This does not consider the human suffering and necessary remedial care for those killed, injured, and disabled, long-term environmental damage from toxins like depleted uranium and Agent Orange (both used by the U.S.), the destruction of hospitals and schools and resulting damage to health care and education, and more. Most wars can be avoided.

In terms of sharing, we can look to current quality of life indexes for guidance rather than just for bare financial data like income and output. These measure essential and desirable factors like safety, health care, affordability, education, pollution, and transportation. Nations that consistently rank in the top brackets include the Scandinavian countries, Switzerland, Canada, Netherlands, and Australia. Yes, tax rates in those countries are higher than in the United States, but such social services cost money and, in the long term, are cheaper than individuals paying for their own education and health care, even if they get taxed marginally less. The more we share overhead costs, the cheaper the product or service is for individuals.

Probably the most comprehensive and high-profile analysis and report on sharing and cooperation between countries was the 1980 "Independent Commission on International Development Issues," called "The North-South Report" or sometimes "The Brandt Report" for short. It was chaired by Willy Brandt, former chancellor of West Germany, and commission members included former prime ministers of the United Kingdom and Sweden, Edward Heath and Olof Palme; publisher of *The Washington Post*, Katharine Graham; and other global luminaries. The commission advocated the "principle of mutual interest" between the world's nations, which could be served by a sharing of power and resources rather than dominance and monopoly. It recommended "human solidarity and a commitment to international social justice" and reported on specific issues, including development, poverty, hunger and food, population, disarmament, energy, the world monetary order, transnational corporations, and more. Brandt's summary of the commission's recommendations was hopeful but pointed out its success depended on the necessary "collective will" by the peoples of the world.

Whether we want changes within countries or between countries, we need the collective will to do so and this, of course, depends on the will and cooperation (rather than self-interest and conflict) of individuals. This, in turn, brings us to questions about the nature of "self-interest" (as Adam Smith pondered) and, therefore, to the nature of "self" or "human," including its purpose and meaning. Technology and AI are also asking us these questions from a different perspective. Is our main purpose "productivity," and if so, who among us are entitled to its consumption? Is a human brain downloaded into a machine a human? Is a variously implanted and enhanced cyborg a human? Will there be levels of humans and cyborgs with different rights and entitlements?

The eighth edition of the *Concise Oxford English Dictionary* defines "self" as "a person's or thing's own individuality or essence; a person or thing as the object of introspection or reflexive action; one's own interests or pleasure." It is clear that as soon as there is awareness of an individual self, then there is separation from others, or non-self. Individuality is both exhilarating and threatening at the same time. We get to explore and express ourselves but are also aware of the many threats from the external (and internal) environment. Most of us emphasize our individuality and separateness, thinking of ourselves as islands within our skins. Many feel entitled to individual "rights." Apart from close personal relationships, we generally are not aware of or we ignore our interconnections and interdependence with our greater environment, whether human, artificial, or natural. However, the global economy, communications, politics, climate change/global warming, and more increasingly impact our daily lives in a real and urgent way. Smartphones, to which many are addicted, are relatively recent examples of our interconnectedness and interdependence.

Our ideas about our self and its relationship to the world have long been molded by the Western Abrahamic religions — Judaism, Christianity, and Islam — which are so called because they all recognize the same lineage of prophets who go back to Abraham, originating with Adam. These beliefs are not universal, as many in the West assume, since they differ with the major Eastern religions in significant ways, as we shall see. However, Abrahamic religions presently make up more than half of the world's religions in sheer number, with Christianity at thirty-two percent and Islam at twenty-three percent. There are not as many Jews as most seem to think; they number just 15.7 million, or 0.2 percent. The Abrahamic religions are also influential because they are the religions of the powerful, industrialized, and developed Western countries.

The one God of the Abrahamic tradition is the omnipotent and omniscient creator and ruler, and humanity is the creation and the ruled, as described in the Book of Genesis, the first book of both the Hebrew Bible and the Christian Old Testament. Both Jesus and Muhammad are included in the lineage of biblical prophets, but Islam and Judaism do not accept the popular Christian beliefs about Jesus' incarnation and the Holy Trinity. In the Old Testament Book of Deuteronomy, which followed Genesis, God declared the Jews his chosen people. Both Christians and Muslims claim that they have now inherited the designation of being the "chosen."

The Book of Genesis opens with the familiar creation story, "In the beginning…" God created a perfect world, including Adam, the first human whom God made "in his own image." Adam was given dominion over beasts, fowl, and all other living creatures. God subsequently created Eve from one of Adam's ribs, to give Adam a "help mate" or helpful companion. Eve was encouraged by the wily serpent to eat from the tree of knowledge of good and evil, which God had, for some reason, specifically forbidden. Eve gave the fruit to Adam, and he also ate it. This act brought sin and pain into the world for the first time, and God expelled Adam and Eve from the hitherto perfect, painless life in the Garden of Eden. "And the Lord God said, Behold, the man is become as one of us, to know good and evil; and now, lest he put forth his hand, and take also from the Tree of Life, and eat, and live forever. Therefore, the Lord God sent him forth from the Garden of Eden to 'till the ground from whence he came.'"

The creation story established many attitudes and beliefs that are still apparent today. God is in charge, and sin and suffering can only be mitigated by following God's directions (usually interpreted by the leaders of various churches or sects) and praying for forgiveness and salvation. God can become very angry at humanity's sin and wickedness, as was demonstrated by the great flood that wiped out all living creatures except those on Noah's ark. Of course, there is also the ever-present threat of eternal damnation in hell for those who sin. The creation story also seems to give Adam and his descendants the right to do whatever they want with other living creatures; it suggested that Eve was not quite Adam's equal, having been created from one of his ribs; Eve is also seen by some believers as gullible and sly, having been tricked by the serpent.

Huston Smith, author of the bestselling *The World's Religions*, points to significant differences between Western and Eastern perspectives on history, time, and God's role. He reminds us that most Hindus see the world of the senses as *maya* or illusion and believe that the individual soul or atman goes through a series of rebirths as it purifies itself in order to unite with the greater, eternal Atman. The Greek philosophers see life as archetypal recurring processes. The Bible is quite different in describing God as being involved in the unfolding events of linear time.

Looking back over the last 250 years of rapid, transformative change since the start of the industrial revolution and birth of capitalism, we can observe both circular recurring cycles and a linear progression through time to what appears to be finite tipping points. As we shall see, humans function from different levels of consciousness, so "both/and" thinking is possible. We can move beyond apparent "either/or" conflicts existing only on one particular level of consciousness.

Regarding our sense of separateness, there are also differences between Eastern and Western spirituality. In the West, separation is an accepted fact since God created us so. Swami Vivekananda, who is credited with bringing Hinduism to the West in the late-nineteenth century, observed:

> This is another great theme of Vedanta, this Oneness of life, this Oneness of everything. We shall see how it demonstrates that all our misery comes through ignorance, and that this ignorance is nothing but the idea of manifoldness, of separation between man and man, between nation and nation, between earth and moon, between moon and sun ... but Vedanta says that this separation does not exist; it is not real.

In contrast to the above, Genesis tells us that humans are not part of God but God's separate creation. We are not part of the oneness that Vivekananda describes above.

Our Ageless, Often Forgotten, Wisdom

As mentioned in the preface, there is a substantial body of prominent religious scholars and philosophers who propose that the differences between East and West disappear if the followers of different religious or spiritual paths reach the uppermost levels or even the very peak of the so-called spiritual mountain. Among the widespread foothills of this mountain, there have consistently been and still are wars fought over conflicting religious beliefs. At this lower level, adherents want to believe their God is the right one and the most powerful so that their wishes and hopes will be rewarded or, at the very least, they will be in the right place in the afterlife or on Judgment Day. They are identified with their beliefs so any questioning or doubt is felt as a personal attack that must be repelled. Most do not question the source or validity of their beliefs.

There are many views about what the top of the mountain represents, and I will mention a few of them as examples. However, in this book, I will describe in detail only the paths that I personally have explored, experienced, and taught, principally Buddhism and Daoism.

There have been mystics within all major religious traditions, East and West, over millennia, and their experiences point to a common (non-geographical) ground. The *Concise Oxford English Dictionary*'s definition of a mystic is "a person who seeks by contemplation and self-surrender to obtain unity with or absorption into the Deity or the Ultimate Reality," or, more simply, becoming one with God or the Absolute. Evelyn Underhill, whose 1911 book *Mysticism* greatly influenced modern Anglican-Catholic spirituality, wrote:

> Mysticism, in its pure form, is the science of ultimates, the science of union with the Absolute, and nothing else, and that the mystic is the person who attains to this union, not the person who talks about it. Not to know about, but to Be, is the mark of the true initiate.

More recently, Wayne Teasdale, a lay monk, wrote in his 1999 book, *The Mystic Heart*:

> This mystical tradition, which underpins all genuine faith, is the living source of religion itself. It is an attempt to possess the inner reality of spiritual life, with its mystical, or direct, access to the divine. Each great religion has a similar origin: the spiritual awakening of its founders to God, the divine, the absolute, the spirit, Tao, boundless awareness.

Huston Smith wrote that the goal of the Sufi mystics, who are regarded as part of Islam, is "fana" or extinction. This does not refer to the extinction of their being or consciousness, but their sense as being separate from God. When this separation disappears, all is God. Karen Armstrong, a former Roman Catholic nun, also mentions "fana" in her best-selling, *A History of God*:

> The systematic destruction of the ego led to a sense of absorption in a larger, ineffable reality. This state of annihilation ("fana") became central to the Sufi ideal.

Armstrong pointed out that "fana" was subject to an extreme interpretation by some and later mystics, known as "sober" Sufis, like Al-Junayd of Baghdad, elaborated on what "fana" entailed:

He taught that "fana" must be succeeded by "baqa" (revival), a return to an enhanced self. Union with God should not destroy our natural capabilities but fulfill them.

In his introduction to *The Perennial Philosophy*, Aldous Huxley explains the ancient, global wisdom that has long recognized a common ground of being or divine reality shared by all:

> Philosophia Perennis ... the metaphysic that recognizes a divine Reality substantial to the world of things and lives and mind; the psychology that finds in the soul something similar to, or even identical with, divine Reality; the ethic that places man's final end in the knowledge of the immanent and transcendent Ground of all being ... immemorial and universal. Rudiments of the Perennial Philosophy may be found among the traditionary lore of primitive peoples in every region of the world, and in its fully developed forms, it has a place in every one of the higher religions.

The Upanishads (800–200 BCE), which are the final section of the Vedas and called the Vedanta, are regarded as the most important part of the Hindu scriptures. The Isha Upanishad states:

> The Self is one. Unmoving, it moves swifter than thought. The senses do not overtake it, for it always goes before. Remaining still, it outstrips all that run. Without the Self, there is no life... He who sees all beings in the Self and the Self in all beings hates none. To the illumined soul, the Self is all. For him who sees everywhere oneness, how can there be delusion or grief?

And in the *Daodejing*, which is one of China's greatest classics, we find the following:

> The Dao (Way) that can be expressed is not the eternal Dao; The name that can be defined is not the

unchanging name. Non-existence is called the antecedent of Heaven and Earth; Existence is the mother of all things. From eternal non-existence therefore, we serenely observe the beginning of the Universe; From eternal existence we clearly see the apparent distinctions (Yin and Yang). The two are the same in source and become different when manifested.

Plotinus (205–270 CE), the founder of Neoplatonism and regarded as the most influential Greek philosopher after Plato and Aristotle, emphasized that the One or Good (in other words, the Supreme or Absolute) was beyond the reach of thought or language and that his descriptions only pointed the way, which appears remarkably similar to the Buddha's advice, "You yourself must strive. The Buddhas only point the way." Plotinus observed:

> If we were to think positively about the One, there would be more truth in silence … the One is Everything and Nothing; it can be none of the existing things, and yet it is all.

Plotinus's "nothing" has parallels with the emptiness (*wuji*) of Daoism and *sunyata* of Chan-Zen Buddhism, which will be discussed later.

Considering the above descriptions of the Absolute, the One, the supreme identity, or the divine reality, it is clearly different from what is advocated in popular religions, which is an external, transcendent, mostly personalized God whom we hope will somehow take care of us. In the former, there is an emphasis not on belief, study, discussion, conventional prayer, churches, or temples, but on personally finding a way to be, in union with the One or the Divinity.

Not doing, emptying, and self-surrender are an important part of the path or Dao. We must get out of our own way in order to stop muddying the waters and sabotaging ourselves; we need to switch our personal radio sets from broadcast to receive; and we have to put aside our opinions and beliefs to which we are so attached. Most of us find this extremely difficult to do since we are encouraged by society to do the opposite — always be active and busy (fill space and time), strive, buy, excel, compete, achieve, become "someone." "Just do it" (whatever "it" may be), as the famous Nike slogan advises. Indeed, we largely identify our "selves" with our activities and the designations or plaudits they may bring.

"Being" rather than "becoming" implies and requires immediate attention and awareness of the present moment, or now. It means that we are beginning to be aware and take responsibility for the consequences of our own thoughts and actions, rather than relying on some outside entity to do so, whether church, state, the free market, or technology. Being in the now also implies urgency, because we realize that the ability to respond to life is always now, never the past or future. Thinking that we are slowly improving and progressing often becomes an excuse for complacency and inaction — always approaching God but never reaching and achieving union with God; constantly improving destructive behavioral patterns, but they somehow remain compulsive; and trying to help humanity, but self-interest, corruption, greed, ignorance, and conflict keep dragging us backwards. The Buddha counseled that progress on the path required practice with an urgency akin to your head being on fire! We cannot change in the future, only the now. The first step and next step is now.

Success on a true mystical or spiritual path should result in transformation or real, deep change, not just feeling less stressed, feeling happier, or having unusual or exciting experiences. Huston Smith pointed out, "The goal of spiritual life is not altered states but altered traits." The Buddha said that progress towards enlightenment manifests the twin virtues of wisdom (head) and compassion (heart), and I have personally found this a useful measure, check, and guide for myself and others. After transformation, we may look the same to those observing us, but the source of our action will have shifted. We see the world in a different light and, thus, act according to our new direct insights, understanding, and compassion in spontaneous "right action" as the Buddhists term it. "Right action" takes into account not only individuals but also their greater environment.

Knowing ourselves at a profound level also increases understanding of others at a deep level, since the deeper we go, the more we come to a common ground of internal dynamics, like basic software and hardware in a computer. Our personal "input" — experiences, genetics, education, culture, and more — will produce output different in its particulars. However, all things being equal, fundamental human issues and processing are universal. In modern parlance, we can increase our emotional intelligence, except this process involves more than just the emotions, as we shall see. The *Doadejing*, millennia ago, alluded to this phenomenon in the statement, "Without going out of the door, One can know the whole world. Without peeping out of the window, One can see the Dao of Heaven."

A transformed or evolved consciousness is capable of seeing life in "both/and" terms rather than the conventional "either/or," which, therefore, eliminates many conflicts that presently seem intractable. The seeming opposites are interrelated and part of a bigger whole, which is exquisitely and simply depicted in the famous yin-yang symbol, more properly called the *taijitu* or the Supreme Ultimate diagram. The circle enclosing the interaction of yin and yang represents both totality and emptiness.

Perhaps the most fundamental and important example of "both/and" is that God is transcendent and all-powerful yet immanent in all beings, including humans, of course. The Buddhists say that we all possess the Buddha Mind, and it is in our potential to awaken and realize it. The present Dalai Lama wrote in his foreword to *Mystics, Masters, Saints, and Sages: Stories of Enlightenment* by Robert Ullman and Judyth Reichenberg-Ullman:

> As Human Beings, we all want happiness, peace, and release from suffering. We often think that the enlightened ones are somehow special, different from us, with a state of mind that is unattainable to an ordinary person. And yet, each human being has an equal opportunity to attain wisdom, happiness, and enlightenment by cultivating a correct motivation — a

sincere aspiration to benefit all sentient beings — and engaging in diligent practice.

Another important example of the "both/and" perspective is that we are separate individuals and, at the same time, interconnected with all humans and living beings. Science and technology are demonstrating the fact of interconnectedness in ever-increasing ways, but for too many of us, it remains a remote and unimportant concept. The full and direct realization of this fact can come to us through both deep compassion and wisdom (as will be subsequently explained), and when it does, it will have a much more powerful and direct impact than any theory, logical argument, or ideal. Such insight just is. Clear insight allows direct seeing into the cause-and-effect of our interactions in all contexts, whether personal relationships, politics, the environment, or other. It is beyond the deceptive and specious argument that every conflict is fifty-fifty and beyond the political and marketing spins and manipulations that work so effectively on the present conventional level. A transformed and evolved consciousness, like a sharp sword, cuts through these common deceptions with direct and penetrating insight.

Underlying all of the current challenges we have discussed above — including climate change, ecological devastation, global inequality, political and religious polarization, wars, AI, and more — is conflict, which, at a deeper level, is based on the feeling of being separate and vulnerable. We are actually not separate and if we accept (let go of) our fears, they disappear, as the Buddha pointed out. Change need not be stressful if we accept it for what it is — a constant and integral part of life. Yet we persist in trying, and failing, to control or stop change.

Other aspects of "both/and" that will be unpacked later in this book include emptiness and fullness/completeness, doing and not doing, active and passive. Modern society is heavily tilted towards doing, activity, and positivity, but those are just aspects of yin-yang, more specifically yang. Often not doing is far better than doing, especially in reactive circumstances, like someone cutting you off on the road or suddenly insulting or threatening you for no apparent reason. The pause and space of not doing gives you time to consider the wisdom and appropriateness of your actions.

This dynamic also applies to public life, with the most obvious and consequential recent example being President George W. Bush's reaction to the 9/11 terror attacks on New York City in 2001. Just to show he was doing something "strong" and getting revenge, he cherry-picked intelligence information to justify attacking Iraq, which had nothing to do with 9/11. This action not only consumed hundreds of thousands of lives and massive resources and finances, but it alienated the Muslim world, which had sympathized with America immediately after the attacks. Instead of building on this spontaneous support and solidarity, he chose to tout revenge and American military might. This folly was so obvious to me that I wrote about it as it was unfolding in my book *Ageless Wisdom Spirituality*, and I was subsequently proven correct by the unfolding of events over the ensuing years.

The blame for this debacle must be shared not only by the American people, but also by the mainstream media, which did little to speak out when there were obvious red flags. Several non-American media outlets were reporting that there were no weapons of mass destruction in Iraq prior to the U.S. invasion, yet there was little or no coverage of these dissenting but credible sources in the U.S. media. These sources included Canadian media as well as the BBC and *The Guardian* in the United Kingdom. In life, it is better to pause and observe, both yourself and others, before reacting in a knee-jerk manner. That pause is space, emptiness, stillness, and non-doing.

People may ask why, if the perennial wisdom has been known by sages across the continents and centuries, so few people are aware of it, especially in our present age of widespread knowledge, internet, and AI. I myself have pondered that question. Probably the most obvious and pragmatic answer is organized religion, which exists to promote and expand its own interpretation of and beliefs about God or the Absolute. They usually assert that their interpretation is superior or even exclusive in its monopoly of truth. The notion that all religions share a common ground and that the best way to realize union with the divine is through your own efforts, jettisoning beliefs and rituals, is seen by many in organized religion as a direct contradiction of and attack on their purpose and existence. It is bad for the business of religion. However, there always seems to be a popular demand for it. There has long existed a Buddhist "religion" with millions praying to the Buddha, even though he himself clearly stated that he was not God, but a perfectly enlightened being. He also said that each of us must take refuge in ourselves, as even Buddhas can only point the way.

Transformational spirituality will probably not soon, or ever, attain the number of adherents boasted by popular religion since it takes understanding, commitment, perseverance, and self-surrender or, in other words, personal exploration, practice, and realization. However, whoever manages to successfully walk this path will be an invaluable embodied light in times of creeping darkness. Huston Smith wrote a book called *Forgotten Truth: The Common Vision of the World's Religions* because he saw that each new generation needs to rediscover it though personal realization. I would add that even if you rediscover this truth, you must keep doing whatever you did to achieve it, as it is easy to forget and slip back into old patterns. The thousand-mile journey is traveled one step at a time, beginning now. Life is always lived now. Alan Watts, in his book *The Supreme Identity*, observed:

> The story of "lost and found," of death and resurrection, of self-forgetting and self-discovery, is perhaps the most common theme of mythological and religious symbolism.

One present hopeful sign is that 22 percent of Americans regard themselves as "spiritual but not religious." I think more public discussion of what this means or can mean would be very helpful, including demystifying words like "mystic" and "enlightenment," which seem remote and beyond the reach of the average person, as many sages have noted. If a spiritual practice results in less compulsive behavior and more wisdom and compassion (altered traits), then that is already a powerful transformation of both our individual and collective lives. If the process works, then trust it and keep walking the path.

BUDDHA'S SIMPLE AND PROFOUND WISDOM

I have previously described how, at around the age of twenty, I came to discover the Buddha's wisdom and how that discovery took hold of and transformed all aspects of my life. Since that moment of realization, I have spent the rest of my life, as a student and subsequently as a teacher and parent, continually exploring, deepening, living, and testing the validity of the Buddha's insights and teachings. So far, in my seventy-fifth year, I have been unable to find any reason to contradict them. They have served me extremely well and I am grateful, not only for the dharma, but for life itself.

The same year I committed myself to the Buddha's teachings, I also committed myself to the practice of *taijiquan* along with the other internal Chinese martial arts, which in turn led me to Daoism, qigong, and traditional Chinese medicine. I instinctively recognized several commonalities between these two paths, although from different countries, India and China, and different in superficial expressions. To many, meditation seems passive and mental, while *taijiquan* and *nei jia* martial arts seem active, physical, and even aggressive. In reality, human beings are always interconnected in terms of body, qi, emotions, mind, and spirit. These do not exist in separate boxes, as many conceive them to be. *Taijiquan* loosely translated means yin-yang fist, so it is indeed a martial art — one based not on aggression and attack, but on responding to the movements and challenges of the environment, human or not. This challenge may be physical, but it may also be emotional, mental, or a combination of elements. I see *taijiquan* as a personal, lifelong work of art, embodying yin-yang principles on all levels and situations, especially in relationships.

When I started teaching in 1984, I offered an unusual combination of disciplines, principally Buddhist Vipassana meditation and *taijiquan*. After forty years, it still is an unusual if not unique combination. Most students at our Tai Chi and Meditation Centre in Toronto have been attracted to *taijiquan* because it seems graceful, peaceful, and easy, which it is not. However, I have always regarded Vipassana meditation as the soul of our teaching organization because it illumines intent on all levels. The Buddha pointed out that we are the result of what we have thought. In *taijiquan* it is said that the *yi* (intention) leads the qi (subtle energy), which leads the *li* (physical strength). If serious students want to become teachers at the Tai Chi and Meditation Centre, they must show a degree of understanding and embodiment of all disciplines we offer, including Buddhism and Vipassana meditation practice.

Over time, I learned about the perennial wisdom, Axial sages, and mystics from different global spiritual traditions, which gave me a feeling of great fellowship and support. In the following two chapters, I offer descriptions of the practice of Vipassana meditation because I know it is effective in the process of transformation and ending suffering. I know how it works and am aware of the many pitfalls that may sidetrack us. We *can* fundamentally change the course of our lives, individually and collectively. This is the most valuable contribution I can make to our shared, interconnected, precious planet. I find the Buddha's teaching straightforward and clear in explanation and immediately accessible through personal practice. It does not require money, equipment, prior knowledge, or belief, so it is open and available to all.

Over fifty years ago, Alan Watts declared in his book, *The Supreme Identity*, that modern civilization was disintegrating because it had no principle of unity, enduring meaning, or purpose. He pointed to the necessity for spiritual leadership based on the realization and actual experience of the Ultimate Reality. He saw no essential difference between the truest practices of Zen Buddhists, Sufis, Vedantists, and Christian Trappist monks. Watts's many accomplishments included a master's degree in theology and a committed Zen practice. His 1957 *Way of Zen* was one of the earliest English language bestsellers on the subject of Buddhism.

The Four Noble Truths

Tradition says Siddhartha Gautama became the Buddha, the "Enlightened One," after he set out on a quest to find how to end suffering. He was brought up in secluded luxury as a prince of the Shakya clan, which was part of the Kshatriya or warrior caste in northern India. His father trained him to be a warrior king. Around the age of twenty-nine, his curiosity led him to explore outside his palace surroundings, where he was shocked and dismayed to discover the facts of sickness, old age, and death, from which he had been shielded. He was so shaken by his discovery that he left the palace and his wife to wander India as an ascetic and seek out the greatest teachers to learn what they had to offer.

After six years, which included extreme self-mortification, he found the middle way between the pleasures of his palace and the self-denial that had left him just skin and bones, too weak to move. He sat under the bodhi tree until he found total enlightenment and then subsequently sought to help others reach this state through his teachings, or "dharma." The Buddha's first and most essential set of teachings are his Four Noble Truths. When I first read them, they caused an immediate and permanent shift in me, and I still turn to them as reminders to myself and my Vipassana students. The Buddha's teachings for me have been transformative, directly simple, and complete. I see no real contradictions between them and the discoveries of modern science and psychology. They were and are remarkably insightful and prescient.

The Buddha lived until the age of eighty, forty-five years after his enlightenment, and left for humanity many sutras and teachings, which are now known as Theravada Buddhism, being based on the Buddha's original teachings. Theravada Buddhism is presently found mainly in Sri Lanka, Myanmar, Cambodia, Laos, and Thailand, the birth country of my teacher, Dhiravamsa.

Nearly one thousand years after the Buddha's death, a new form of Buddhism called Mahayana arose. Mahayana was more accessible to the lay person, since the Theravada teaching was aimed at establishing the community of monks; there was also more focus on compassion. The Theravada ideal was the arhat who has gained enlightenment and the ability to enter Nirvana and, thus, freedom from rebirth. The Mahayana ideal was the bodhisattva who is also able to enter Nirvana but postpones it in order to help save sentient beings from suffering.

Mahayana has long been practiced in China, Japan, and Korea, with the most famous example being Chan Buddhism, which originated in the Shaolin Temple in China around 500 CE. Many scholars see Chan as an intermingling of Indian Buddhism and native Chinese Daoism. Six hundred years later, Chan took root in Japan and became known as Zen, the religion of the samurai. Astonishingly, the small and obscure Shaolin Temple in China became the birthplace not only of a major new form of Buddhism, but also of the martial arts of the Far East, both of which are now practiced globally. I wrote about these unique traditions in my 2004 book *The Spiritual Legacy of Shaolin Temple: Buddhism, Daoism, and the Energetic Arts*.

The third and most recent branch of Buddhism is Vajrayana, which became established in Tibet about the eighth century. It is regarded as an offshoot of Mahayana, with its most distinguishing feature being the inclusion of various esoteric Tantric practices including mantras (sounds), mudras (hand gestures), visualizations, and subtle energies, which appear similar to the Chinese concept of qi. This should not be surprising since Tibet has been considered a part of China, on and off, over many centuries. Suffice it to say that there have long been complex connections between the two countries.

The first Noble Truth is that life is *dukkha*. Although popularly translated as "suffering," its real meaning is impermanence, insubstantiality, and emptiness caused by the conditionality of all manifestation. Everything depends on something else, and all are in the process of continual change. There are three forms of *dukkha*: ordinary suffering, which most people would perceive as such; suffering produced by change; and suffering as conditioned states. Conditioned states refer to the fact that there is no real or solid individual or "I," just a combination of changing physical and mental phenomena or energies called the five aggregates: matter, sensations, perceptions, mental formations, and consciousness. The latter in Buddhism is a generalized awareness likened to the banks of a river between which water and its diverse, ever-changing contents flow. Consciousness is not its contents.

The second Noble Truth is the origin or arising of *dukkha* (called *samudaya*), which is desire, thirst, craving, becoming, holding on, attachment (*tanha*). In other words, we suffer because we try in vain to hold on to what is always changing, whether relationship, family, job, health, youthfulness, or eventually life itself. Objects of attachment also include our ideas, opinions, hopes, expectations, and beliefs. We can neither really grasp the "positive" nor avoid the "negative" but are constantly trying to do so. I see the common, compulsive "monkey mind" in meditation as a deeply ingrained example of craving and thirst — something deep within us wants more or other; it wants to move, do, continue, expand, and become, and if it cannot, that feels like a kind of pain and suffering.

The third Noble Truth is the cessation of *dukkha* (called *nirodha* or Nirvana), being the extinction of thirst, holding, and attachment or, in other words, non-attachment and letting go. This leads to freedom from suffering or Nirvana or absolute truth, ultimate reality. If the arising of *dukkha* is caused by thirst, craving, and attachment, then its cessation happens when we let go of (surrender) thirst, craving, and attachment.

The fourth Noble Truth is the Noble Eightfold Path *(magga)* leading to the cessation of *dukkha*: right understanding, right thought, right speech, right action, right livelihood, right effort, right mindfulness, and right concentration. The Noble Eightfold Path may be broadly subdivided into ethical conduct (*sila*), mental discipline (*samadhi*), and wisdom (*panna*). Over the years, I have reminded myself and my students that even though the Eightfold Path may seem complex, its main purpose is the third Noble Truth — simple non-attachment and letting go, which we can only do in each moment, now.

Many scholars link the Four Noble Truths with the Buddha's teaching on dependent origination or conditioned genesis (*paticca-samuppada*). The latter elaborates on aspects of the former, especially conditionality, the five aggregates, and anatta, which is the doctrine of no soul or self. Anatta is implied in the first Noble Truth — all is *dukkha* or, in other words, impermanent, insubstantial, and conditioned. This includes the notion of self or "I."

Anatta is probably the Buddha's most obvious doctrinal difference with the Hindu scriptures, which acknowledge an individual atman (innermost essence or witness consciousness) seeking eventual unification with the supreme, universal Atman. This has given rise to endless debate, which will not be entered into in this book.

Conditioned genesis explains the conditionality, relativity, and interdependence of all life, including human existence. It lists twelve factors that explain how life arises and falls away in a continuing cycle, commonly called "The Wheel of Life." The factors turning the Wheel, numbered from 1 to 12, are: ignorance, volitional actions or activities, rebirth consciousness, mental and physical phenomena, the six senses (the five common physical senses plus mind), contact (*phassa*), sensations or feelings, craving or thirst, attachment or clinging, becoming, birth, decay, and death. The Four Noble Truths and conditioned genesis give background to the Buddha's famous sayings in the *Dhammapada*:

> All we are is the result of what we have thought…
> Whoever speak or act with evil thoughts, pain pursues them as the wheel of the wagon follows the hoof of the

ox that draws it... Whoever speak or act with pure thoughts, happiness pursues them like shadows that never leave... Whoever have thoughts in their minds of retaliation, in them hatred will not cease.

I counsel my Vipassana students that the above sequence in conditioned genesis is probably best broken by letting go when contact (*phassa*) and sensation arise, before desire and thirst. In a later chapter, I will explain the Buddha's profound insights into the process of conditioning and conditionality in current terms, individual and collective.

Vipassana and Mindfulness Meditation

Although the Four Noble Truths awakened me to the truth and importance of the Buddha's teachings, it took me a few years of searching and experimentation to find the specific Buddhist practice that I felt I could maintain for the long term. From my martial arts training, I knew I had the necessary self-discipline, but the teacher, the group, and the philosophy needed to feel right for me to make such a commitment. I tried sitting with some Theravada monks from Sri Lanka and also a Zen group. I found the latter a bit too rigid and structured for me, and I also noticed these qualities in a friend who practiced Zen, even though he was not with the same group I was visiting.

Eventually, I joined a Vipassana weekend retreat, not because it was Vipassana, but because Buddhist meditation retreats at that time (1974) were hard to find in the United Kingdom. I knew little about Vipassana at that time, but the retreat leader, Tew Bunnag, Dhiravamsa's senior student, exuded both strength and compassion. Like me, he had practiced karate and *taijiquan*. I found the practice of bare attention difficult and, at times, frustrating, but I recognized it was fundamentally different from the conventional way of being, which is actually always a form of "doing." Visualization, chanting, praying, body scanning, and affirming seemed to me all forms of intentional, directed doing. I had always been accustomed to doing and achieving, so not doing and making myself vulnerable was difficult, but it was what I instinctively felt I needed to explore.

I was reminded of the Buddha's teaching on meditation or mental culture (*bhavana*), which consisted of the two main streams mentioned in the Noble Eightfold Path — concentration (*samatha* or *samadhi*) and mindfulness (*sati*). *Samadhi*, which is based on concentration, focus, or one-pointedness, leads to mystic or trance states (dhyana), but these were considered by the Buddha to be still conditioned and mind-produced. *Samadhi* is not exclusively Buddhist, since it existed in Hinduism before the Buddha. Most popular forms of meditation are based on one-pointedness, as in chanting, prayer, repetition, visualization, and more. Focus and concentration practice is attractive to many because it is a source of achievement and power, as in a fire hose, a laser, a pointed weapon, or successful individuals who are single-minded in pursuing their goals.

There is some debate about the differences and similarities between Mindfulness meditation, as is now widely practiced, often in a secular manner, and Vipassana meditation. They are both based on the Buddha's famous sutra on mindfulness (*Satipatthana Sutta*). Indeed, it may be argued that this sutra is the basis of all Buddhist meditation and that both meditation streams of *samadhi* (associated with dhyana in Buddhism) and wisdom-insight always intermingle. In my experience, it depends on the specific instructions that a meditation teacher or leader gives and how each student interprets and tries to execute them. Even if one finds a "perfect" meditation balance, it may change within moments. Professor D.T. Suzuki comments on this in his renowned *Essays in Zen Buddhism*:

> When the fourth and last stage (*of dhyana*) is reached, even the feeling of self-enjoyment disappears, and what prevails in consciousness now is perfect serenity of contemplation. All the intellectual and emotional factors liable to disturb spiritual tranquility are successfully controlled … there takes place a fully adjusted equilibrium between Samatha and Vipassayana; that is

between tranquilization or cessation and contemplation. In all Buddhist discipline this harmony is always sought after. For when the mind tips either way, it either grows too heavy or too light.

In this book, I will describe the practice of Vipassana or insight meditation rather than Mindfulness, because that is what I have been taught by my teacher, Dhiravamsa, and what I have practiced and in turn taught. Vipassana is called insight meditation because its aim is to produce direct, penetrating insight (*prajna*) into all manifestation, which is necessary for deep wisdom and transformation.

Nyanaponika Thera's *The Heart of Buddhist Meditation* translates the opening lines of the Buddha's centrally important way of mindfulness sutra (*Satipatthana Sutta*) as follows:

> This is the sole way, monks, for the purification of beings, for the overcoming of sorrow and lamentation, for the destroying of pain and grief, for reaching the right path, for the realization of Nibbana, namely the four Foundations of Mindfulness [which are the body, feelings, mind, and mind-objects].

In the summer of 1974, I enrolled for my first long retreat with Dhiravamsa, who by that time was living in Berkeley, California, but returned to the United Kingdom annually in the summer to lead Vipassana retreats. He often spoke about the relationship between *samatha/samadhi* and Vipassana. In *The Way of Non-attachment: The Practice of Insight Meditation*, he contrasts Vipassana with concentration:

> Vipassana meditation is like taking a journey through life; what we come across depends on our own conditioning. If we are afraid of unpleasant experiences or if we expect only what is "positive," then we shall have more difficulties in practicing this meditation... The process of discovering what is, and accepting it as it

unfolds, is basic to Vipassana or Insight. There is an element of desire in the spirit of enquiry, in the sense of an urge to know, but this is balanced by open-mindedness and the acknowledgement of uncertainty…

Concentration can produce knowledge or power, but not insight, because insight is not "produced" — it arises naturally when passive watchfulness has allowed all veils to be fully seen through. When the conditioned mind can lose what has been accumulated and come to the Unconditioned, without having any ground, it ceases to take refuge and is open to the flow of insight, containing only what is needed at any moment. Emptiness of mind does not mean that anything is lacking. All that is needed is there, and because everything is allowed to pass according to the laws of change and impermanence, this opens the way for what is fresh and relevant to the next moment.

Dhiravamsa gives the following direction on Vipassana practice in his book, *The Real Way to Awakening*:

Watch any state of mind, whether it be worry, anxiety, wandering, talking, thinking — any condition of mind — watch carefully, closely, without thinking about it, without trying to control it and without interpreting any thought; because this is very important when you come to the deeper level of meditation. Naming is the main obstacle to coming to the deeper level, because the moment you give identity to what you are watching, ideas come into being. Then you have to work with ideas again and you come back to the superficial level. You fail to remain deep down in the reality of what you are watching. In this deep state, all concepts and all names or words must be given up completely.

Dhiravamsa's clear and straightforward Vipassana advice and instructions are still fresh and relevant to my personal practice and teaching many decades later. No matter how long one has meditated, each moment is a new moment and a new challenge. This applies not only to meditation, but also to life itself.

It should be pointed out that although Dhiravamsa was a Thai Theravada monk for over twenty years and was eventually chosen to help introduce Thai Buddhism to the West, his teachings (and subsequently my own) are not conventionally Theravadin. His piercing wisdom and open heart and mind eventually could no longer be confined to monastic life or the hierarchies and politics of organizations. In 1971, at the age of 36, he gave up the robe to be an independent Vipassana meditation master. He later wrote in his book *The Middle Path of Life*:

> Robes are a symbol, a form, and when we put them on we are in a certain role where we try to conform to an idea or to rules without looking into all aspects of life. It therefore fragments life, creating a division between the holy and the ordinary… In reality the holy is very ordinary, very simple. When we overlook simplicity, we shall not find the holy, but instead the idea of holiness and worship this, in a religious way.

I have found Dhiravamsa to be more Mahayana than Theravada in spirit, since he was eager to explore all aspects of life without being confined to tradition. When I studied with him in the early days, he asked Tew and me to teach *taijiquan* and qigong as meditative bodywork; he would invite psychotherapists to lead certain sessions and would allow spontaneous expression of emotions during meditation; and he himself would share folk and fairy tales, explaining their underlying meanings. All activities were undertaken in the spirit of Vipassana, simultaneously cultivating awareness of both inner and outer phenomena. He was also very much a bodhisattva in spirit, sharing his wisdom by traveling all over Europe to lead meditation retreats several times a year.

D.T. Suzuki wrote in his *Essays in Zen Buddhism* about enlightenment and bodhisattvas:

> It was the presence in every individual of a faculty designated by the Mahayanists as *Prajna (direct insight into Truth)*. This was the principle that made Enlightenment possible in us as well as in the Buddha… Thus we are all Bodhisattvas now, beings of Enlightenment, if not in actuality, then potentially. Bodhisattvas are also Prajna-sattvas, universally endowed with Prajna, which when fully and truly operating, will realize in us Enlightenment.

Meditators' Questions and Challenges

Although Mindfulness meditation is now popular in the West, it was not so when I started teaching in 1984 and for some time afterwards. There are obvious reasons for its growing popularity. Firstly, it can be taught in a secular fashion, since Buddhism does not require belief but experiential practice — "Be a refuge unto yourself." There has also been growing medical research on its health benefits, including stress relief, pain control, better sleep, and more. Finally, it is deceptively easy to teach — "Pay attention to the breath" — and is widespread within the extensive yoga community and beyond.

My Vipassana retreats at Harmony Dawn are open to all and, thus, draw participants with widely varying meditation backgrounds. Some have no experience at all. Many have some sort of mindfulness practice, usually self-taught, from yoga classes or from short, secular mindfulness courses. A few have been practicing Mindfulness meditation for twenty years or more and have attended ten-day retreats. It is relatively rare that committed practitioners of other kinds of meditation or religions attend my retreats.

At the beginning of every retreat, I usually give instructions on the basic Vipassana practice. This starts with establishing clear comprehension of purpose before each session, which is to give yourself permission to be fully present, here and now, to practice Vipassana meditation. It is then advisable to check your bodily posture, being upright, stable, and releasing any tensions. The basic practice is paying attention to the physical sensations caused by the inhalation and exhalation of the breath, wherever in the body that may manifest for each meditator. I point out that breathing is an automatic process, which requires no conscious direction or manipulation. If requested, I check an individual meditator's posture. I recommend to meditators an adaptation of the *wuji* (empty) posture used in *taijiquan* and qigong since this facilitates the flow of qi.

If or when the meditator's attention is no longer on the rising and falling of the breath, I recommend a three-stage process for returning to the sensations of the breath — acknowledge, let go, start over — on which I will later elaborate.

Regardless of background, retreatants nevertheless seem to experience certain common difficulties, which I will address below in a summarized question-and-answer format. Twenty-five hundred years ago, the Buddha pointed out the five hindrances (*Nivarana*) that those trying to cultivate Buddhist meditation or mental culture face: sensual desire, ill will or anger, sloth and torpor, restlessness and worry, and skeptical doubt. Many of these occur in my retreat groups, but for simplicity's sake, I will not try to classify each question or topic according to the five hindrances.

Questions: Why are meditation sessions so long and so often? Do we have to sit cross-legged on a cushion? Can I sit on a chair? Can I lie down and meditate? My legs get numb. I seem to be battling with my body all the time — what should I do? Should I train myself over time so I can sit longer in retreats? What is the best posture for meditation? When I feel discomfort, can I move or stand up? Why do we have to pay attention to the breath?

You should always try to have what the Buddha called clear comprehension of purpose (*sampajanna*) in any undertaking, whether entering into a new relationship, job, diet or exercise program, holiday, or other. In this case, you have enrolled in a Vipassana retreat under my guidance, so it would seem logical to keep an open mind and heart during the retreat and follow my instructions. Set aside what you have read or may have experienced in other retreats or meditation sessions. You are in a safe and nurturing environment at Harmony Dawn, and especially on a weekend retreat, it is a relatively short and precious time within which to allow yourself to be open to true self-inquiry. There are no chores for you to do and your meals are provided, so you can just be with yourself. My teacher Dhiravamsa said that "the process of discovering what is and accepting it as it unfolds is basic to Vipassana or insight." Vipassana is an open-ended and ongoing process, as is life itself. I do not tell you what to see or believe but try to give you the tools to look deeply into what is arising in yourself. Only each of you has direct access to that experience. No guru, therapist, or spiritual friend has direct experience of what is arising in each of you. Moreover, only you can change yourself by letting go of past patterns.

Paying attention to the breath is part of the Buddha's sutra, *Satipatthana's* mindfulness of the body, which is presumably simpler and more obvious to most people than mindfulness of feelings, mind, or mind objects, which are the other three foundations of mindfulness. Also, breathing is an automatic process that does not require thought, conscious control, or visualization.

Buddhist meditators usually sit cross-legged on cushions or on a wooden stool in a kneeling position because this allows the body to be stable and quiet, which in turn helps the mind to be quiet. The spine should be erect, with the gaze just below the horizontal, but the rest of the body should be relaxed. I allow meditators to sit on chairs with the same erect spine position (part of the *wuji* posture we use in *taijiquan* and qigong), but with feet flat on the ground, thighs horizontal, and body not leaning into the chair back. I personally find sitting on a cushion the most stable meditation posture, allowing my body to be naturally aligned and relaxed, which facilitates the flow of subtle energy (qi) throughout the body. Lying down to meditate causes most people to feel drowsy and fall asleep, which is obviously the hindrance of sloth and torpor.

As a retreat progresses, most meditators begin to feel discomfort and a degree of restlessness, even those sitting in chairs. Bodily discomfort during meditation sessions often includes a mental-emotional component. The intensity of the retreat, with longer and more frequent periods of meditation, takes retreatants out of their comfort zone and beyond their usual routines, habits, expectations, and control. It is not necessarily peaceful or blissful, and if that is what you experience, then that is fine. Restlessness, irritation, drowsiness, and doubt about the practice are not uncommon. I sometimes sense meditators silently screaming at me to end the session; others check their watches, which makes the time seem to pass even more slowly; some keep changing their physical postures but to no avail. All of this suggests mental-emotional resistance and internal conflict, feeling as if you are fighting your body and yourself. I would guess that if you are sitting for the same amount of time but watching an entertaining movie instead of meditating in silence, time would seem to pass much more quickly.

Over the years, many meditators have found that their pain and discomfort ease only with acceptance, when they stop resisting and fighting. A recent example involved a meditator on her second Vipassana weekend retreat with me. She had been preoccupied and tormented by physical pain during her first retreat and the beginning of the second. However, after my talk about the possibility that emotions can be the source of physical pain, she had a sudden realization that emotions were indeed the cause of her physical pains. Her meditation sessions after that were pain free and her mind calm. The day after the retreat, she went to her yoga class and found that her shoulder, which had been stiff and "frozen" for three months, was suddenly pain free and very flexible.

The purpose of Vipassana-Mindfulness meditation is the development of awareness and mindfulness, not bliss, peace, health benefits, or even "enlightenment," which in the beginning is just another idea. I am not saying that bliss is wrong if it occurs; that is just a fortunate experience that deserves attention like all other manifestations arising. The more common restlessness or battling with the body may seem pointless and frustrating, but Vipassana is about insight into whatever is arising and, thus, every experience is a learning opportunity. For example, most meditators do not realize that when they use the word "pain" to describe a sensation, it often triggers a fight-or-flight response since "pain" is commonly presumed to be "bad." It is not necessary to put a label on a sensation and it is not necessary to respond with fight or flight. We can remain in motionless silence, just paying bare attention to what is arising; this also creates space or emptiness for the arising of insight and perhaps a momentary pause before a knee-jerk reaction. Numbness is a common complaint, but it is not "pain" as such. Sometimes, physical pain is a symptom of deeper emotional pain.

Training yourself to sit longer may seem to work in the short term, but that approach is not in the spirit of open-ended inquiry. It is a desire to maintain control and predictability. It is probably not a coincidence that most meditators sit for twenty minutes since the generally recognized maximum attention span is twenty minutes. What if you manage to increase your meditation time to forty minutes, but a retreat requires fifty- or sixty-minute sessions? You will be back to fighting with yourself. Remember that the core of the Buddha's teaching is letting go, being fully attentive to each moment, whether seemingly pleasant or unpleasant. Such attention is unconditional, so the length or frequency of meditation sessions should not matter.

A very important aspect of Vipassana meditation that even experienced meditators commonly miss is what I call "I thoughts." Such thoughts separate to function as the "self," "I," or, in meditation, the "meditator" judging other thoughts or sensations. "I thoughts" are thoughts and should be the subject of awareness and mindfulness just as other thoughts. Over thirty years ago in my first book, *The Conscious I: Clarity and Direction through Meditation*, I wrote about this "blind spot in our consciousness":

> That blind spot is ourselves. All thoughts and activities flow from the center that we identify as our "I," our "self." We are the willing slaves of a host of inner voices and urges, yet we know very little about them… Our "I" seems solid and real enough, yet if we look for it, it is

nowhere to be found... Even if attention is turned inside, one part of yourself is usually looking at another, and the looker still remains hidden and separate. Thus, it is possible for meditators to encounter unusual, fascinating inner experiences and even extraordinary powers, yet learn very little about the meditator.

Vipassana is called insight meditation because its purpose is insight wisdom or *prajna*, which is necessary for true and deep change and, eventually, enlightenment.

Questions: How do you handle past and ongoing hurt and pain? Should you call up the positive to cope with the negative? Can you work with specific issues during Vipassana meditation? Isn't there a contradiction between paying attention to breathing and self-transformation? I have anger arising that seems to need expression. If you have been hurt in the past and it still arises, how can you forgive? How can you let go of emotional pain? What does letting go mean? Is letting go of the pain from the loss of loved ones not forgetting them? Don't you need therapy to deal with emotions?

My simple direction to Vipassana meditators is to pay bare attention to the physical sensations of the breath as it rises and falls. It is not necessary to visualize the breath or control it in any way. If you notice that your attention is no longer on the breath, then acknowledge where it is, briefly; let go; then start over. This direction is simple and precise, yet meditators interpret it in many different ways. Acknowledge does not mean "think about or analyze." Let go and start over do not mean "push or force the mind back through will power," as is common.

Unskillful interpretation of these instructions usually leads to internal conflict and frustration. We end up fighting ourselves and, in frustration, may even give up our meditation practice. More seriously, it could also lead to continuing the suppression of negative emotions from the past. If a meditator too rapidly and forcefully brings the mind back to the breath, subtle emotions arising from the subconscious may be missed, albeit with good intentions — trying to be a "good" or skillful meditator. The acknowledgment component is often overlooked. Over the years, I have encountered a few very experienced meditators who have missed out on acknowledging the subtle signals from the deeper levels of their being to the serious detriment of their mind-body health. They interpreted Mindfulness meditation practice as just focusing on the breath rather than the development of insight. Too strong a focus on the breath may tip the mind into concentration and *samadhi*, thereby blocking the arising of insight and wisdom. Zen Master D.T. Suzuki repeatedly pointed out the delicate balance needed between these two factors in Buddhist meditation.

In traditional Chinese medicine, our emotions affect our vital energy (qi), which in turn affects our physical organs, especially over a prolonged period of time. Often in the West, a patient suffering from long-term, repressed, or ignored emotions will only notice that something is "wrong" when physical symptoms appear, which usually means their condition has been allowed to deteriorate far too long and the whole mind-body system has become debilitated. This is akin to the final stage of collapse in Dr. Selye's stress syndrome theory.

Some Vipassana teachers think that Vipassana meditation should be augmented with psychotherapy. In my experience, skillful Vipassana practice does not suppress emotions but allows them to rise to consciousness where they can be seen, experienced directly, and let go. Teachers, gurus, and therapists may correctly interpret the causes of one's emotional imbalance or troubles but do not have direct access to them and, in the end, cannot let go of them for their patients or students. Change cannot happen by holding on to old patterns but only by surrendering and letting go of attachment to them. Remember that the Buddha described the four foundations of mindfulness as "the sole way ... for overcoming sorrow and lamentation, for destroying pain and grief, for reaching the right path, for the realization of Nibbana." He did not make an exception for emotions.

During Vipassana retreats, emotional pain usually, but not necessarily, surfaces after physical discomfort or pain. In many cases, emotional and physical pain are interconnected. When emotional pain first surfaces, I usually suggest acknowledging it and then returning to the normal practice of attention to the physical sensation of the breath, since it is a common temptation to want to explore the emotion, and this usually ends up in analysis and conjecture — more thinking. If after repeatedly returning to the breath, the emotional experiences persist, as if asking for your attention, then it might be appropriate to make the emotion the object of your Mindfulness meditation practice, using the mindfulness foundation of feelings or mind-objects.

In making emotions the object of your attention, treat them in a similar manner as you would do with your breath. Pay bare attention without thinking, analyzing, or judging. If you get lost in thought, return to just bare attention by acknowledging, letting go, and starting over again. Do not prematurely judge or draw conclusions about the source of your emotional pain (as is common), since you may end the process of inquiry and discovery before all is fully revealed and unraveled. In skillful Vipassana practice, insight eventually emerges, and this leads to clear, choiceless right action. This usually requires freeing yourself from the compulsion of negative patterns of thought and behavior through the process of letting go or non-attachment.

Letting go of old, deeply entrenched emotions, thoughts, and behavior is rarely an immediate and total process. Residual conditioning may resurface from time to time. I liken strong compulsive emotions and behavior to stormy winds that can toss you around. If you succeed in substantially letting go of them, their remnants may subsequently appear as a gentle breeze by comparison — still surfacing but not as compulsive or addictive. Some meditators describe their practice over time as an ascending spiral. It seems that they are occasionally confronted by the same issues, but they are not quite the same as before. There has been more understanding of their patterns and greater freedom from compulsion.

Twenty-six years ago, one of my senior students and an instructor at our Tai Chi and Meditation Centre, Dr. Carrie Bernard, wrote her first recollection about how Vipassana had radically changed her life, especially in terms of dealing with family emotions and behavioral patterns. She has continued to record her experiences intermittently over the years, creating an unintentional meditation diary over that time. Given our discussion above and the fact that Carrie recently wrote another update following a profound ten-day retreat, I thought it appropriate to include an abbreviated version of her sharing, in her own words and with her permission:

> Buddhism. Meditation. How did this become my one and only path? I remember sitting in the "Introduction to Meditation" group run by my teacher, Andy James. My incessant questions just kept on coming. I had to understand the logic of it all… Sometimes Andy had logical answers and I was satisfied (well almost satisfied, because each answer usually led to another question). At other times he simply told me that I would one day see for myself. That the answers would be obvious, needing no explanation or logic. This was hard for me to believe.
>
> Belief. Perhaps this path drew me because it did not ask me to believe. Simply to look for yourself. To observe and let go. Then one day (well probably not one day, but a series of moments over many different days that led to a day where the moments came together), I understood. Not everything. Maybe not even one discreet thing. But understanding came to me and it came not from a book, not from my teacher, but from meditation. I cannot explain when it happened because it keeps on happening again and again. The truth arises only to fade again and arise again later…
>
> I am fighting with my partner, but something seems wrong as I feel truly enraged. But then I see his face and something familiar comes up. I know that face because it is my face when I am fearful of my father, trying to appease him and prevent his rage. And in a moment, I see the generational patterns that I have absorbed as my

partner tries to appease me. I am just like my father, the man who had a volcano inside that erupted again and again, causing fear and violence to permeate our home. And I almost make the same mistake he made… I start to say "I will not be like my father. I will do everything possible to stop this volcano." That is what he promised himself and he did his best to keep his promise … but the promise could not be fulfilled, and so his self-hatred continued to grow… I was about to make the same promise but I see the truth — it didn't really work. Along with this wisdom comes a rush of compassion. A deep feeling of acceptance (not justification), a realization that in some ways, I am my father. There is fear and anger inside of me born from years of violence. It just is. In seeing this, I feel deep compassion for myself and for my father — and for the person he became from the violence he lived… I work on caring for my pain rather than trying to chase it away and I learn how to separate myself when I feel it arise, so I don't repeat those patterns. I grow and become less angry, and my sitting continues.

Years later I am sitting with our group. My legs hurt and my mind is busy, busy. Coming back to the breath, always the breath. The room and the people around me fade as the breath rises and falls. As the ocean moves in and out, so too does the breath. I see the ocean from a distance. The shore — a specific shore. It is beautiful. The ocean comes in and out again and again. The ocean is constant as is my breath. Suddenly I am no longer looking at the ocean at a distance. I see waves close up. And I see that there is no "ocean." Waves are made up of water and are different from one second to the next. There is no "shore." The same molecules of sand are not there from one moment to the next… There is no ocean and no shore, only movement of sand and water, nothing discreet, no actual form… And then I know. I KNOW that while we have form, we are not form. While there are discreet beings, we are not only discreet beings. Form and ego exist but they are only part of the picture. I had read about this and I had listened to my teacher speak about this. I had stretched my mind to try and understand this. But in meditation I came to know this.

Feeling bored in meditation and struggling to follow the breath as the mind is ever busy. Suddenly there is Kermit the Frog, animated and being a frog. Then the puppeteer removes his hand and walks away. There is a puppet that looks like Kermit lying on the table. Is there a Kermit? We all know of Kermit, but he does not really exist. The truth of separate selves is apparent to me in this moment. I have a self with a personality that others relate to. It seems real and constant, but it does not really exist. I can now understand the truth of this apparent contradiction.

Years later I am on a 10-day retreat and sitting in pain. It arises around my solar plexus, moves through my chest and into my throat and mouth. With each new breath the pain rises up in my chest. As I watch the pain arise, scenes from the past arise with it. Painful scenes. Times I have been terribly hurt by those who claimed to love me. The watching mind asks, "Is this the pain? Is this story the same as the pain?" The answer is No. Though events intensify the pain I see they did not create the pain. It was already there… Other earlier scenes arise and the pain intensifies … eventually still following the breath, I come to a place where there is no pain — physical just below my belly button. I know there is a place/time where there is no pain. The time is before form… It is inevitable that there will be pain with existence… I begin to weep for I understand I cannot end the pain in the way I had thought… At this point my egoic mind is impatient. Isn't this the place where I am supposed to feel connected with All, where Truth would set me free!?

All that I saw in this meditation I had come to believe previously, but I came to know it in meditation — the reality of suffering. Unfortunately, I have yet to experience the truth of the end of suffering... So I continue to sit. The pain seems less and I can sometimes follow the breath to the place of no pain for brief moments.

Years later on another 10-day retreat. The familiar pain is there again. It feels less intense and it has more clarity. Although there is the universal pain of *dukkha*, there is also my unique pain of feeling scared of something awful happening. Anxiety that I am not good enough, that I need to do something to become good enough... I watch these feelings from a distance and do not become entangled. I do not try to change them... After the retreat, I live my life with these feelings. My sitting helps me know they are always there, just below the surface. I start to see them when I do not sit — fear, anxiety, and feeling that I will fail are my constant companions. I realize that they sometimes drive me, just as my anger used to drive me. I don't despair, I just allow them to be. I can often separate the feelings from action, just as I did with my anger. They don't disappear, they simply become less potent.

I am at a low point. I have been physically unwell for a while and I am exhausted on my first day back at work. The feelings erupt as I get closer to my workplace. I begin to feel incapable, scared that I will fail, trembling with fear that I will fail and something awful will happen... I wonder if I should turn around and go home. Then at the moment of peak intensity, the wisdom to know that these feelings are not the "truth" arises. This insight is followed immediately by an outpouring of compassion. Wisdom and compassion merge to let me know that I am okay, just as I am. I can abide with these feelings knowing they arise from the past but need not affect the present. I drive to work and get on with my day.

It is time for retreat again. I settle into my sittings. They are quieter than in the past. I feel the familiar pain in my chest, but it is far less potent. It doesn't disturb my breath. It just is and I can let it be. I can sit and my legs don't hurt. I don't feel bored. I am present with what arises, and I let go of what arises. Nothing draws my attention, not even the pain. In my life, I notice change. I can talk with my father without waiting for his anger. I set boundaries with him from a place of wisdom and compassion. We can disagree without rage or fear erupting. I still feel the familiar pattern of anxious feelings, but I look upon them with kindness and understanding. And I let them go.

This is how meeting my teacher, Andy James, who introduced me to Vipassana Meditation, changed my life. I now sit every day. Sometimes there is pain, sometimes there isn't. Every sit is a good sit and I continue to let go.

I find Carrie's description of her meditation journey over thirty plus years insightful, inspiring, honest, and very instructive for those on the Vipassana Buddhist path. She has a very sharp, inquiring mind and is kind and always helpful, sometimes perhaps too helpful. Years ago, when volunteering with Doctors Without Borders in Africa, she was captured and briefly held by boy soldiers. During the Covid epidemic, she volunteered to work in ICUs because there were not enough nurses, even though she was also working as a family physician. As a friend, I am glad that Carrie is now finally making time to tend to her own needs rather than always prioritizing helping others, which has been as difficult for her as dealing with her father's rage, as she has described above.

As I write, Carrie is President-Elect of the College of Family Physicians of Canada. She will be President for 2024–2025.

Questions: How can you let go of the pain from the loss of a loved one? Isn't it natural to grieve? Should you forgive someone who has hurt you, especially if you still have to deal with them? What does forgiveness mean?

These are common and difficult forms of emotional pain made more complex by the often-conflicting advice and expectations of family, friends, culture, and society. In many parts of the world, a widow's life is still very restricted because of cultural and religious expectations and pressure. However, we have no control over others' expectations and beliefs, and any loss must be processed by the person suffering the loss, whether man or woman.

Of course, it is natural to feel emotional pain after a loss, whether it is from the actual death of a loved one or the loss of a close relationship, as in separation or divorce. People commonly advise that we should think of the good and happy times in order to stay positive. However, that could just as likely increase our sense of loss. I always return to the Buddha's basic advice about not holding on, or if we have done so, then letting go. We can still retain positive memories of someone without holding on; our memories will not disappear if we refrain from consciously activating and dwelling on them.

In Vipassana practice, always try to pay simple, bare attention to what is arising in consciousness in each moment — what is, not what could be, might be, or should have been. Emotional pain, like all manifestation, is *dukkha* and, as such, is always changing and is both conditioned and conditioning, involving many factors. Memories and thoughts tend to overwhelm and lead to all kinds of speculation. Always come back to paying attention to the physical sensations of the breath, like an anchor. If and when the mind becomes distracted, acknowledge where it is, let go, and humbly and patiently start over. Do not suppress pain or try to make it go away, as that just amounts to another layer of confusion and complexity. Pay attention to the acknowledgment phase (without thinking, analysis, or judgment) and watch the images, voices, emotions, and physical sensations that emerge, letting them rise and fall away again. All will eventually become clear if this process is not prematurely shut down, and the way to right action will emerge. Right action takes into consideration not only the individual, but also their environment, human or otherwise.

Follow your heart not your mind, which always wants to rule, speculate, and be in charge. The heart governs relationships and can be a good guide if you learn to listen to it. The heart in this sense is not the same as "emotions" generally, much of which is generated by the mind.

I am often asked how I dealt with my own divorce. It was a proverbial bolt out of the blue when my wife Yolind declared that she did not want to be with me anymore after eighteen years of marriage and twenty-three years of being together. My three daughters, then aged six, nine, and eleven, and I all spontaneously broke into tears as it was so shocking and disturbing. Yolind seemed quite calm and matter-of-fact and did not offer any reasons or explanations. We had not been quarreling and we had a long-standing agreement to talk to each other if we felt things were not right. She also had more relationship tools at her disposal than most, having attended several of Dhira's retreats, being in his company socially, and learning about the Enneagram Personality Types while on San Juan Island. Fortunately, as I have previously recounted, my daughters and I had begun sitting in meditation together about two weeks before Yo's announcement. We were able to be quiet together and look inwards, sharing and processing our feelings. This proved to be invaluable, not only in those early days, but long afterwards.

After about a month or two without any discussion about our relationship, I asked a simple question: "Do you still love me?" She said, "No," which was the answer I feared hearing. At that point, however, clarity immediately arose. She did not want to be with me, and without love, there is no meaningful partner relationship for me. I let go and most of my angst and questioning evaporated. In the longer term, I was able to work with her to do what was best for our daughters, whom I continued to envelop with love. I did my best to be a good parent but had little input on my wife's parenting decisions. In hindsight, I am pleased with how our daughters eventually turned out. They all now have children of their own. My present relationship with Yo is cordial and friendly.

It is never beneficial to hold and carry emotional pain within your mind-body system, even if you think you are the wronged or injured party, or in the case of a deceased loved one, you think it is your "duty" to carry grief. Let go of grief, resentment, grudges, bitterness, and anger, since they poison you, not the person who hurt you or the person who is gone. What has happened is in the past and cannot be erased or somehow relived. We can, however, let go of past hurt and related behavioral patterns so we can approach life anew and unburdened in the present. Letting go of pain within yourself is not condoning or justifying the wrongs that you have endured or betraying the memory of a loved one. Memories will endure. Focus on right action in the now, which is actually the best that you can ever do.

Stating the obvious, opening yourself to seeing and experiencing suppressed pain is painful and unpleasant. That is why most people commonly avoid doing so. Skillful Vipassana allows you to feel and let go of pain. That pain is already there; meditation did not put it there, you did. Every now and then, I come across an article in the popular media saying that Mindfulness meditation can lead to unpleasant and unsettling experiences. Of course it can. However, the warning tone of such articles reveals the common attitude that pleasant is good and must be grasped and unpleasant is bad and must be avoided, which, as we have seen, is impossible. In your Vipassana-Mindfulness practice, it is very useful to have an experienced "spiritual friend" to point the way, since this is a path less traveled.

Questions: How can you keep up meditation practice during busy city life? Is it possible to embrace silence in the company of others without seeming anti-social?

It is important to sit in silent meditation at least once a day for however long you can manage. I recommend at least thirty minutes a session in general, but if you can only manage fifteen minutes, that will still be beneficial. If you have the time, a one-hour session is best. Sitting with a group once or twice a week is also very helpful, even if it is a virtual meeting like a Zoom or Skype session. In-person group meditations are obviously preferable since a group's energy tends to be stronger and there is the opportunity for face-to-face sharing and interaction.

Try to cultivate mindfulness in everyday life in any way you can. Just do one thing at a time and be aware of your basic body postures — lying, sitting, standing, and walking. Notice when your posture changes. Try not to "fill space" by constantly listening to music or podcasts through headphones or scrolling, texting, and talking through your mobile phone. Your mind will not only be quieter, but more alert and aware of your surroundings, which is desirable in big city life that is often crowded, chaotic, stressful, and sometimes even agitated and angry. If you walk, walk with attention; if you sit, sit; if you are drinking a cup of coffee or tea, then drink it without attention fillers.

During a working day, you can find moments of quiet in parks, churches, or even standing in line at a bank, office, restaurant, or riding the bus or subway. People watching, without judgment, can be an instructive mindfulness exercise. You can find moments of quiet in a social setting, just observing, listening, and paying attention. It is not necessary to constantly contribute to a discussion or conversation, especially if you have nothing of consequence to verbalize. It is not necessary to either seek or avoid attention. If you find yourself being compelled to act in a certain way, pay close attention to see if it is appropriate. For example, if you feel you always have to be the life of the party, try staying quiet and see what that is like; if you are introverted, then try reaching out and engaging.

Some forms of physical activity lend themselves to mindfulness practice, for example *taijiquan*, qigong, yoga, and nature walks.

Questions: How to respond to energy moving in the body or involuntary physical movements like shaking, vibration, or swaying, which may happen during meditation sessions or even outside of them? Is it appropriate to express emotions like anger or sadness during meditation?

My teacher Dhiravamsa, in his 1982 book *The Dynamic Way of Meditation*, was one of the first recognized Buddhist teachers to write about expression in Buddhist meditation practice. I think the subject is still not much discussed. Claudio Naranjo, the "father" of the Enneagram Personality Types, wrote in Dhiravamsa's book foreword:

> Dhiravamsa's most striking contribution to the practice of meditation is his work in the interphase between classical Vipassana and expression: the spontaneous expression that is likely to occur after sufficient sitting and attention, if it is allowed, and of which he talks as a healing release ... spontaneous expression constitutes the process that Indian Tantrism conceptualizes in the wakening of kundalini — a dormant spiritual power in the body — and which it welcomes as a process of purification. This is just what Dhiravamsa advises his students to do.

Dhiravamsa himself wrote about expression in meditation:

> What is needed for this work is the trusting willingness to throw ourselves into the flame of attention, the act of simply but intensely attending to whatever arises in any moment with no idea of doing anything in particular or becoming anybody special. Then see what happens. It is by accepting ourselves as we are and recognizing facts and realities that we naturally reduce our resistances and open the doors for honest communication and sympathetic understanding to take place, without creating any distortion of reality; in this way no further conflict will be

encouraged. At this point, the act of releasing begins to operate with a surge of creative energy.

For the past nine years, since 1973, I have been learning a great deal, from those participating with me in retreats, about the expression of physical and psychic energies in different forms. This occurs mainly during the sitting meditation, and then carries over into the walking, standing and reclining meditation until the release is completed. These expressions include twitching, shaking, stretching in various positions ... sometimes sounds arise such as heavy breathing, crying, weeping, sudden screams, laughter, and angry words.

Having joined Dhiravamsa's U.K. retreats since 1974, I was one of the students taking part in this early, pioneering meditation exploration. I have observed the processes and expressions described above, not only during Dhiravamsa's retreats, but subsequently in the Vipassana retreats that I have led over four decades. I neither encourage nor discourage expression during meditation retreats because the key ingredient in meditative expression is genuine spontaneity. Any complications usually arise after an initial spontaneous expression since the egoic thinking mind may be frightened or excited by it and tries to "do something" with it. My advice, as usual, is not to interfere, manipulate, or judge what arises but maintain spacious awareness. A particular expression may be complete in itself or may be just a step in a longer process of discovery and release.

In my experience, physical and energetic phenomena during meditation often make sense from a traditional Chinese medicine perspective, demonstrating links between emotions, organs, meridians, and energy centers — *dan tians* — which share some similarities with the Indian chakras.

In *The Conscious I*, I described a dramatic example of expression and release that I witnessed during one of Dhiravamsa's U.K. retreats in the 1970s:

One of my fellow meditators noticed that he was leaning to one side during his sitting meditations with the group. Being an experienced meditator, he attributed this to tiredness and resolved to sit upright as he thought an experienced meditator should. His determination brought about an improvement in his posture although he still experienced a slight tugging sensation on one side. Following one of Dhiravamsa's talks on the need to be compassionate with oneself, he decided to let go of his image of being an experienced meditator and to let himself be taken wherever the tugging wanted to take him.

The most terrifying scream I have ever heard shattered the quiet of that English summer evening. The man fell to his side, convulsing, shrieking, coughing, and sputtering as he went into a fetal position. This went on for nearly an hour before the screaming gradually turned to laughter from relief and joy. It turned out he had relived a near-drowning experience (subsequently confirmed by a call to his grandmother) dating from before the age of two, even to the extent of regurgitating what he said tasted like seawater.

Many things fell into place for the man that evening. Many of his life-long problems with his body, with his relationships, with his jobs, and with life in general could be traced back to this single experience. It explained why, when life became difficult, he felt overwhelmed, pushed under, and suffocated. Suddenly, both his body and his psyche felt lighter and freer.

Belief versus Beginner's Mind

Buddhism, and Vipassana meditation practice in particular, is difficult for most people, especially in the West, since it often goes against their upbringing and culture. Twenty-five hundred years ago, the Buddha taught that we could end our suffering by letting go and not grasping anything in life, including ideas and beliefs, since all is impermanent — ever changing — insubstantial, and conditioned *dukkha*. Everything eventually slips through our fingers, so our efforts to grasp will fail and we will experience suffering. This does not mean we have to live a monastic life of austere self-denial. We can live a full and enjoyable life. Our suffering only arises when we try to grasp and control life, resisting and fighting against the inevitability of life's constant change. This behavior is common but not inevitable.

It is clear to me that the Buddha was way ahead of his time with his insights. Even now, millennia later, only a small minority seem to truly understand his teachings, despite the fact that concepts like conditionality, impermanence, and insubstantiality are being increasingly substantiated and illustrated by discoveries in physics, psychology, and other fields. The Buddha's teachings lead to enlightenment and the end of suffering, but there are gradations of enlightenment and realization. It is not a question of either total enlightenment or total ignorance. Any degree of enlightenment or deep wisdom is beneficial to all. The Buddha's original Theravada teachings were aimed at the community of monks, but subsequent developments, like Mahayana, made them more accessible to people living normal, everyday lives. The famous Chan-Zen ox-herding pictures, which will be explained later, make it clear that enlightenment and living an ordinary life are not incompatible.

The Buddha's teachings, not surprisingly, did not change the behavior of the world's masses, since most either did not understand or had never heard of the Buddha, especially in the West. Enlightenment may be regarded as a raising or evolution of consciousness, which does not manifest evenly throughout the population. The Buddha would not be called "The Enlightened One" if everyone else was equally enlightened.

Throughout recorded history, we see the pervasive and persistent human tendencies the Buddha described — our drive to expand, progress, enrich and empower ourselves, convert, and conquer. In other words, a striving or compulsion to grasp and to become ... something or someone different from the present. There seems to never be enough for satisfaction and contentment, even for those regarded as more fortunate in life. In this context, I use the word "become" in the Buddhist, psychological sense, as explained earlier in this chapter while describing the Four Noble Truths and the theory of dependent origination. Becoming is contrasted with "being" — living fully in the present, the now, and responding to each moment's challenge one step at a time. Of course, in a mechanical and automatic sense, children "become" adults, developing new faculties and adult bodies; we study to become engineers or accountants; and we become various types of wage earners to feed and house ourselves and our families as a matter of necessity. This is different from the psychological compulsion of "becoming" as described above.

The process of becoming manifests not only in individuals, but in groups as well, whether families, tribes, religions, races, or nations. As we have earlier discussed, once the sense of self or "I" comes into existence, there is simultaneously a sense of separation, in time and from others. We try to overcome our sense of separation by joining with others, mutually or by coercion. History is replete with never-ending examples of battles with the "other," however defined. Of course, as yin-yang theory points out, winners generate losers, who in turn retaliate, fight back, and are determined to become the winners ... and so the wheel keeps on turning. "Winners" are usually measured in terms of power, wealth, and control.

This process of becoming is invariably bolstered by a supporting and conditioning system of ideas, attitudes, and beliefs, conscious and unconscious, which creates conventional identity ("I am") and produces the feeling of "I know," often expanding into feeling "right," "righteous," "chosen," or a "true believer." The monotheistic, Abrahamic religions, which include Judaism, Christianity, and Islam, actively promote belief in their respective interpretations of God as being the "right," "true," or the "only" way. They account for well over half of the world's population and have long been extremely influential in Western, and now global, culture. Most in the West are not very much aware of Eastern religions and culture, even now, and so Western beliefs and attitudes are widely seen as universal and, therefore, largely unquestioned.

Our individual sense of identity (our "I," ego, or self) is enhanced and empowered by being part of a greater and more numerous collective entity. The more people who believe as we do, the more "right" and powerful we feel. Political and religious gatherings and interactions are common examples of this group dynamic, as are the more recent rock concerts and sporting events, replete with fans and supporters in their respective colors and uniforms. However, quantity is not quality. Numbers are no guarantee of truth. Believers, by their very existence, create non-believers and, therefore, potential conflict.

With the advent of the internet and social media, the power of group belief has become much more obvious since it can be greatly accelerated and amplified. Small groups and even individuals can amass thousands or millions of "likes" and "followers" within a very short period of time, which then might go viral across the planet. An unexceptional person can instantly become a "somebody," feeling powerful and special, even if only for the proverbial fifteen minutes of fame. People gather themselves into like-minded, social-media silos and celebrate lies, conspiracy theories, and their own "alternative" truths. Self-investigation and searching for a broad-based understanding of reality not obviously biased in favor of one's own belief system or group are avoided as signs of weakness and doubt. Being a non-believer among a group of believers is difficult and maybe even dangerous.

It should be obvious that common group dynamics mirror individual inner dynamics, since groups are made up of individuals. Once the sense of the individual "I" exists, it strives to feel more solid and permanent since, at some level, it feels vulnerable and insufficient. The thinking mind is fundamental to this process, and even novice meditators can directly witness the various strategies that it employs to keep busy and, therefore, feel more solid. Although most adults consider themselves rational human beings, those who try to meditate quickly discover that they have much less control of their thinking minds than is commonly presumed. The mind seems to have its own agenda, even in the context of a meditation retreat. It is conditioned and patterned. The "monkey mind" ventures off in its own direction, playing its games, and is difficult to restrain.

Many meditators report that they are often looking forward to the future, making mental to-do lists, planning, fantasizing, imagining, creating goals, bucket lists, and more. Some constantly delve into the past, reliving it and imagining different versions of "what if things were different." The mind commonly comments and judges, creating a body of opinion and belief. All this activity builds a (false) sense of continuity and solidity of our "I," projecting from the past to the future, but often at the expense of not paying full attention to the present, the only opportunity for action. Although we spend most of our time thinking about the past and future, we can only ever act in the now.

The feeling "I know" is in my experience the most common and subtlest obstacle to Vipassana meditation practice, the goal of which is freedom from suffering, Nirvana, and absolute truth. The thinking mind is always judging and accumulating. According to the Buddha's teachings, this process would likely be classified as one of the five hindrances — doubt, which would include anything that prevents clear understanding of truth, such as false views. The ninth-century Chan master, Linji, shockingly advised, "If you meet the Buddha on the road, kill him." This, of course, was not a literal advocation of murder. The "road" is your spiritual path. If you think you fully understand or know the Buddha or have found all the answers, you are mistaken, since as the Buddha himself pointed out, everything is conditioned and constantly changing. Get rid of your rigid beliefs and keep inquiring with an open mind. Be here now and walk the path one step at a time. Belief, even Buddhist belief, is not truth. If one really "knows" directly in a deep spiritual sense, it is not necessary to feel or say, "I know," just act accordingly. The feeling "I know" usually contains some element of ego identification, invoking authority in order to persuade both oneself and others.

The Chinese classic, *Daodejing*, which is commonly dated at about the same era as the Buddha, similarly advised:

> Not knowing that one knows is best; Thinking that one knows when one does not is sickness. Only when one becomes sick of this sickness can one be free of sickness.

The thirteenth-century Zen master, Dogen Zenji, taught his students the concept of *shoshin*, which is currently translated as "beginner's mind," to be practiced during *zazen* or "just sitting." This means sitting in meditation without goals or preconceptions, not trying to do or achieve anything, but always returning to open and accepting awareness. Even experienced meditators are warned about being complacent or feeling superior because of their experience and knowledge. However, the feeling "I know" is intoxicating. I have even had the experience of one of my Vipassana retreatants scolding me based on her experience of other retreats and teachers. I always listen to criticisms of myself in case I am at fault, but in this particular case, her views were simply misconceived, misinterpreted, and absurd. The rest of the retreatants were silently appalled but continued their practice as usual.

Beginner's mind is popularly associated with Zen, but it is also fundamental in Vipassana, as illustrated by Dhiravamsa's instructions:

> Watch any state of mind, whether it be worry, anxiety, wandering, talking, thinking — any condition of mind— watch carefully, closely, without thinking about it, without trying to control it and without interpreting any thought.
>
> Many of us find it difficult to make progress in meditation because we want to achieve an experience, or hope that something will happen so that each time our meditation will be "better." We have to work without expecting results, without focusing our minds on any

goal of enlightenment. Give up these things; don't care about success, but care about the action, the doing with awareness in every moment.

My own instruction to Vipassana meditators always includes a reminder not to judge, analyze, project, control, or direct what is arising in consciousness. In addition, I point out that "I" thoughts are also thoughts that should be viewed with bare attention, just like other thoughts. However, many meditators identify with their "I" thoughts, which then become the "meditator" judging the process of meditation. We are not our thoughts. All thoughts, feelings, and beliefs, without exception, should be brought into the light of awareness — put on the proverbial table for examination in the now.

Despite my instructions and warnings, most meditators' minds are preoccupied with physical discomfort, making to-do lists, wondering how much longer the meditation session will last, questioning the wisdom of my instructions or Buddhism in general, and much more. Some retreatants have done silent chanting and yoga mudras during their Vipassana meditation sessions, yet somehow managed to see that as compatible with my instructions. One meditator who reported having a naturally empty mind, was actually visualizing her inner dialogue as titles on a movie screen that scrolled downwards and fell into an imaginary bucket.

It takes most meditators several retreats or even years before they begin to recognize that they are not their thoughts, even their "I" thoughts. Several experienced meditators have confided that, in hindsight, during their first few retreats they were *thinking* about meditating, not actually meditating in the Vipassana way. Eventually less thinking during meditation led to greater space-emptiness and to deeper insight into their inner processes.

In almost fifty years of Vipassana practice and teaching, I have only once witnessed a clear, profound, and moving example of a retreatant acting out of beginner's mind. In 2021, we received a request from someone wanting to attend our autumn ten-day, silent Vipassana retreat at Harmony Dawn. We usually ask would-be participants about their meditative experience to make sure that they know there would be about six hours of sitting meditation a day (as well as other activities) and silence throughout the retreat. Her response made Nicola and me initially hesitant. She had absolutely no sitting meditation experience and had heard or read nothing about meditation. She grew up and spent most of her life in China and said her English was not fluent. She seemed to be a middle-aged woman who wanted to do something for herself for the first time in her life, since her daughter was just leaving home. She asked if there was anything she could do to prepare herself in the few weeks preceding the retreat. I suggested reading my book *The Conscious I* and maybe trying to sit for about half an hour at a time.

At the beginning of the retreat, she shared that she had heard somewhere the idea that all people were connected, and she felt that maybe meditation could help her understand that since it was an appealing idea. As the retreat began, I was surprised that she never seemed to move or shift her sitting position during our one-hour sitting meditation sessions, which was unusual for a totally inexperienced meditator. She never broke her silence and asked only a few (written) questions in order to clarify my instructions about the practice. At the end of the retreat, she fully and joyfully shared her retreat experience, which astounded everyone in the meditation group. Nicola asked her to write a short summary of her sharing as an inspiration for others. It is enclosed below. I have taken the liberty of lightly editing it because English is not her first language:

> I believe a certain Power must have guided me to choose Harmony Dawn for the first meditation experience in my life. I knew nothing about meditation or about any place to go, just randomly searching the internet. Among so many choices, I chose Harmony Dawn and Harmony Dawn returned to me all these precious experiences. I am so grateful and thankful.
>
> There were so many "first times" for me — first time participating in a retreat, first time practicing

meditation, first time meeting people with the same interest, and first time feeling so spoiled by deep wisdom, delicious food, beautiful environment, and sweet smiles.

The experiences were so wonderful. I could not believe I could sit for 6 hours a day for 10 days without back pain which I usually have in my daily life. The numbness in my hand has gone away and my constant chest pain went away after the guided meditation on past emotional pain. I had a wonderful experience of "emptiness" after Andy's guided meditation on emptiness and everything disappeared, only "breathe in from emptiness" and "breathe out into emptiness."

There were also other beautiful experiences such as seeing colored lights, waving a white lotus, and more, which I think might just be my imagination, so I didn't mention them in my sharing during the retreat. However, my experience on Thursday (seventh day of the retreat) was so real yet indescribable. I could not stop crying although I tried hard to hold on. The first time I was feeling that silence, that field, that warmth and calm, I think that is what we call Love ... holding everything, with everything, in everything, being everything — just there, just around me, just is me ... so obvious, waiting for me for a long, long time. How could I not have seen it!? Everything became so beautiful. The sound of the bug hitting the ceiling is music; the clanging sound of cooking from the kitchen is music; the whirring wind is coming for celebration. Everyone in the room has become so holy and beautiful ... becoming Buddha. I just want to kneel down before everyone, bow to everyone, hug everyone. Unfortunately, I could not experience this feeling again after the session, but it gave me the confidence to continue on this Way, to find Truth and Love.

Thank you so much for giving me the chance to share the wonderful experiences. Thank you and Andy for creating this magical Harmony Dawn.

PATHS TO SELF-REALIZATION

Early on during my attempts to learn more about Buddhism, I was also keen to gain some understanding about world religions in order to understand Buddhism in a wider context. I have recounted that at that time the best, or perhaps only, source of books on Eastern and esoteric religions was the Theosophical Society bookstore in London. In hindsight, it was an invaluable source of information, and its purpose was very much in line with my own eventually revealed purpose and interests. The Theosophical Society, which was incorporated in 1905, was way ahead of its time with its "Three Objects":

1. To form a nucleus of the universal brotherhood of humanity without distinction of race, creed, sex, caste, or color.
2. To encourage the study of comparative religion, philosophy, and science.
3. To investigate the unexplained laws of nature and the powers latent in man.

I was not really interested in the occultism aspect of the Theosophical Society, but I was particularly attracted to the works of

Jiddu Krishnamurti, especially his *Commentaries on Living* trilogy. His personal story also intrigued me. He was "discovered" in 1909 at the age of fourteen by one of the Theosophical Society leaders, C.W. Leadbeater, who thought he was the vehicle for Lord Maitreya, the anticipated "World Teacher" who would guide the evolution of humanity. He was educated in Madras and later in England to prepare him for his role as the leader of an organization the Theosophical Society formed for him called The Order of the Star in the East (OSE). In 1929, to the shock and surprise of many, Krishnamurti dissolved the OSE before an assembled audience of over three thousand. He explained:

> Truth is a pathless land and you cannot approach it by any path whatsoever, by any religion, by any sect. That is my point of view and I adhere to it absolutely and unconditionally. Truth being limitless, unconditioned, unapproachable by any path whatsoever, cannot be organized; nor should any organization be formed to lead or coerce people along any particular path… Truth cannot be brought down, rather the individual must make an effort to ascend to it… If you would attain the mountain top you must pass through the valley, climb the steeps, unafraid of the dangerous precipices.

I also discovered a remote personal connection to Krishnamurti in the fact that one of his closest confidantes in England was Lady Emily Lutyens, wife of the famous architect Sir Edwin Lutyens who played a major role in the design of Hampstead Garden Suburb, where I bought my first property, a flat in a Tudor-style building featuring a quadrangle, common in the Oxford and Cambridge colleges.

Through the Theosophical Society, I also discovered the millennia-old four yogas of Hinduism, which described in detail the major paths to union with the Atman, or Universal and Infinite Consciousness. Yoga literally means to join, yoke, or unite. I have found the yogas a useful template in understanding the approaches of the major world religions and describe them briefly below.

The Major Paths: Devotion and Wisdom

Most scholars recognize bhakti yoga (devotion, the heart) and jnana yoga (wisdom, knowledge, the head) as the two major paths within Hinduism. The two other yogas are karma yoga (work, service) and raja yoga (esoteric, psychophysical practices), which will be described later.

Bhakti yoga is the preferred practice of the vast majority of Hindus. At present, the world's most popular religions by number are Christianity (31 percent), Islam (25 percent), Hinduism (15 percent), and Buddhism (7 percent). Judaism, Christianity, and Islam (the Abrahamic religions) combine for 56 percent and are clearly in the devotional stream, which grows to 71 percent of the world's religions when Hinduism is added. The attraction of a devotional path, whether the Abrahamic religions or bhakti yoga, is obvious to both scholars and casual observers. It harnesses our readily available emotions, especially love and affection, and directs them to a personal relationship with an image or notion of the divine. It usually requires a structured practice, which might include prayers, chanting, the reading of sacred texts, rituals, and, most importantly, belief and faith.

In terms of the devotional path, it is necessary to distinguish between those religious followers who think God is transcendent (supernatural, almighty), as in the Abrahamic religions, and those who regard God as both transcendent and immanent in human beings, as is supposed to be the case in Hinduism. I say "supposed to be" because many bhakti followers tend to forget the immanent part

Swami Vivekananda, who 130 years ago played a major part in introducing Hinduism to the West at the first World's Parliament of Religions, wrote about bhakti yoga:

> Bhakti yoga is a real, genuine search after the Lord, a search beginning, continuing, and ending in love. One single moment of the madness of extreme love of God brings us eternal freedom…

> There is not really so much difference between jnana and bhakti as people sometimes imagine. In the end they converge and finally meet in the same point. So also is it with Raja yoga…
>
> The one great advantage of Bhakti is that it is the easiest and most natural way to reach the great divine end in view. Its great disadvantage is that in its lower forms, it oftentimes degenerates into hideous fanaticism. The fanatical crew in Hinduism, Mohammedanism or Christianity have always been almost exclusively recruited from these worshippers on the lower planes of bhakti. That singleness of attachment to a loved object, without which no genuine love can grow, is very often also the cause of denunciation of everything else.

Vivekananda's thoughts on popular religions' "fanatical crew" echo my own observations on the process of belief, which creates both believers and non-believers. Discussion of this fundamental, human inclination seems to me especially urgent with the recent rise of powerful, "strong men," populist-nationalist leaders invoking religion, especially in influential democratic countries like the United States, India, and Turkey.

The media has been seemingly reluctant to probe into the religious aspect of populism-nationalism, probably justifiably fearful of irrational, explosive reactions. Political leaders and the media seem ignorant or in active denial of the possibility of different levels of human consciousness, implied in Vivekananda's term "lower planes of bhakti." Indeed, many hold the view that all statements have equal value, which is yet another manifestation of quantity taking precedence over quality within society at large. Everything being regarded as having fifty-fifty value has encouraged lies and extremism, which go unpunished. Levels of consciousness will be discussed later in this chapter.

Jnana yoga is a more direct but far less traveled path than bhakti because it requires a relatively unusual combination of rationality and spiritual self-discipline. It is called the yoga of knowledge, but this refers not to conventional knowledge and thinking, but self-inquiry, self-knowledge, and self-realization. Swami Vivekananda asserted that all the founders or prophets of the world's main religions went into a state of mind beyond waking and sleeping states, which he called "supersenuous," to discover knowledge of the Absolute. He pointed out that although the Buddha did not talk about God or soul, he gained enlightenment and knowledge of the "eternal moral law" in a supersenuous state while sitting under the bodhi tree.

Ramana Maharshi, who was highly regarded by Carl Jung ("in India he is the whitest spot in a white space") among many others, agreed with Vivekananda about the relationship between jnana and bhakti:

> The eternal, unbroken, natural state of abiding in the Self is Jnana. To abide in the Self, you must love the Self. Since God is verily the Self, the love of the Self is the love of God; and that is Bhakti. Jnana and Bhakti are thus one and the same.

Karma Yoga

Karma yoga is often described as the way to God through work or action. It recognizes that all human beings are constantly engaged in activity and work, which can be expressions of spirituality as much as the more obvious retirement to a cave or monastery. Karma yoga can thus be guided by either bhakti or jnana, since the main focus of yoga (and deep spirituality generally) is union with the Absolute, a process of embodiment, not just worship from afar. Since most people, including Hindus, follow a devotional path, the ideal of karma yoga is popularly seen as selfless service in the name of God. Mother Teresa, later canonized as Saint Teresa of Calcutta, is a shining example of a modern bhakti karma yogi, even though she was actually a Roman Catholic nun. She stated:

> By blood I am Albanian. By citizenship, an Indian. By faith, I am a Catholic nun. As to my calling, I belong to

the world. As to my heart, I belong entirely to the Heart of Jesus.

A jnana karma yogi, like a true bhakti karma yogi, does not expect recognition or reward for service to others. However, for the former, service is not done in the name of an outer God but flows from the deeper self within, rather than the conventional, grasping, becoming "I" or self. Non-attachment to actions, as in Buddhism, is advised. Ramana Maharshi explained:

> Work performed with attachment is a shackle, whereas work performed with detachment does not affect the doer. He is, even while working, in solitude… Whether you continue in the household or renounce it and go to the forest, your mind haunts you. The ego is the source of thought. It creates the body and the world… The feeling "I work" is the hindrance. Ask yourself, "Who works?"

Vivekananda also described a spiritual way of work or action without wanting or motive, performed with inner silence and emptiness:

> The ideal man is he who in the midst of the greatest silence and solitude finds the intensest activity, and in the midst of the intensest activity, the silence of the desert…
>
> He works best who works without any motive — neither for money, nor for fame, nor for anything else. And when a man can do that, he will be a Buddha and out of him will come the power to work in such a manner as will transform the world. This man represents the very highest ideal of Karma Yoga.

Vivekananda reminds us that each person has unique skills and abilities to offer. What we call activism is the most high-profile form of service, but we can also transform the world by working with individuals through healing, teaching, and more.

Although the parallels between Hinduism and Buddhism are obvious from the quotes above, there are also parallels with Chinese philosophy and spirituality, especially Daoism. The opening paragraph of the *Daodejing* states:

> From eternal non-existence, therefore, we serenely observe the mysterious beginning of the Universe. From eternal existence, we clearly see the apparent distinctions. These two are the same in source and become different when manifested.

The "apparent distinctions" are more commonly known as yin and yang, as depicted in the famous yin-yang diagram, known in Chinese as the *taijitu*. Underlying interactive *taiji* is *wuji*, depicted by an empty circle and representing underlying emptiness and non-action. For decades I have reminded my *taijiquan* students that out of the initial, still, *wuji* standing posture comes the increasingly complex, interconnected, flowing movements that represent *taiji*. However, *wuji* is not replaced by *taiji*; *taiji* takes place within *wuji*. Thus, despite the common confusion and difficulties of a *taijiquan* beginner, it is possible in time and with skill to experience "movement within stillness" — effortless, aware, natural, balanced, connected, flowing mind-body movement. My *taijiquan* teacher, Miss Rose Li, used to say, "In the beginning, you do *taiji*, but later *taiji*

Wuji

Taiji

does you." It is possible to have inner stillness and quiet even amidst what Vivekananda calls "the intensest activity."

Raja Yoga

Raja yoga has been called royal, the king, the best because it describes not only the goal of yoga — union — but the detailed methods to attain it. It appeals to people of a scientific inclination in the sense that it invites experimentation and testing on one's internal states and dynamics, rather than relying on what others have proclaimed or described.

Vivekananda pointed out that most religions are based on faith and belief, usually glorifying the teachings of a certain person or persons. However, these teachings are based on the teacher's personal experiences, which may have appeared to be extraordinary or even unique. But Vivekananda asserts:

> If there has been one experience in this world, in any particular branch of knowledge, it absolutely follows that experience has been possible millions of times before and will be repeated… Without proper analysis any science will be hopeless, mere theorizing… The science of Raja Yoga proposes to give us a means of observing internal states. The instrument is the mind itself. The power of attention, when properly guided and directed towards the internal world, will analyze the mind and illumine facts for us.

Raja yoga practice consists of the eight limbs of yoga (ashtanga yoga), which the sage Patanjali described about two thousand years ago:

1. *Yamas* or the moral imperatives of non-violence, truthfulness, not stealing, sexual restraint, and non-avarice.
2. *Niyamas* or virtuous observances including purity of body, speech and mind, acceptance of others, perseverance or self-discipline, and self-study and reflection.

3. *Asana* or posture, especially a stable seated posture.
4. *Pranayama* literally means breath control. *Prana* can also mean subtle energy or "psychic *prana*."
5. *Pratyahara.* Drawing one's awareness inward away from external objects.
6. *Dharana.* Concentration or one-pointedness.
7. *Dhyana.* Contemplation, reflection.
8. *Samadhi.* Meditative absorption.

Yamas and *niyamas* are moral imperatives and training, similar to those advocated in other religions and spiritual paths, like the Ten Commandments or the ethical part of the Buddha's Noble Eightfold Path. *Asana* and *pranayama* would be covered by the practices known in the West as hatha yoga and the more esoteric kundalini yoga. The latter has in the past been kept secret since it involves the rousing and manipulation of the subtle energy (*prana*). Kundalini, which means "coiled" or, more commonly, "coiled snake," refers to the divine feminine energy called Shakti, which normally resides in the base chakra or energy center called the *muladhara*. Kundalini seeks to awaken the Shakti energy and systematically lead it through the chakras until it unites with the pure consciousness of Shiva, which is regarded as male and resides at the *sahasrara*, or crown chakra, at the top of the head. There are six chakras within the body, not counting the crown chakra. The bottom two chakras are linked with physical survival and procreation; the middle two concern relationships with the external world; and the upper two involve mind and higher mind. Many kundalini practitioners regard it as a complete system leading to full union and enlightenment.

The last four "limbs" of raja yoga — *pratyahara, dharana, dhyana,* and *samadhi* — represent mental training and meditation culminating in the attainment of *samadhi*, when, according to Vivekananda, "all sorrows will cease, all miseries vanish. The seeds of action will be burnt, and the Soul will be free forever." Raja yoga is regarded by many Hindus as a comprehensive "internal science," which, if properly followed, will result in the attainment of *samadhi*.

Qigong

I am not qualified to comment on the finer points of kundalini practice, but descriptions of its *prana* energy and bodily manifestations and movements strike me as similar to my own qi energy experiences in Vipassana meditation (spontaneous) and qigong (formal training and practice).

In kundalini, Shakti energy can be awakened at the base of the spine and directed upwards through the spine and chakras, uniting with the crown chakra. In Chinese qigong, qi can be cultivated and directed for various purposes throughout the human body-energy-mind system, including up the spine. In China, qigong has been used in the martial arts, for self-healing and healing others, and for spiritual cultivation. It is a branch of traditional Chinese medicine (TCM) akin to acupuncture and herbalism, which is gaining ever more formal recognition in the West. The concepts of *prana* in India and qi in China are somewhat similar, but although these concepts are both probably at least three thousand years old, known historical connections and interactions between China and India only date from the opening of the Silk Road, which was about two thousand years ago. Giovanni Maciocia, whom I first met as a fellow student at Miss Li's *taijiquan* classes in London, writes in his celebrated book *The Foundations of Chinese Medicine*:

> Qi is at the basis of all phenomena in the universe and provides a continuity between coarse, material forms and tenuous, rarefied, non-material energies. It therefore completely sidesteps the dilemma that pervaded Western philosophy from the time of Plato down to the present day, i.e., the duality and contrast between materialism and idealism.

In practical terms, qi always interacts and interconnects with body, emotions, and mind. These do not exist in separate, independent compartments as is commonly presumed.

For me, qi is not mysterious, magical, or a product of my imagination or belief system. It is something I feel and consciously interact with and am sure exists in every other living being. Recognizing it and its potential obviously enhances our knowledge of how our mind-body system works. Learning about it can be a powerful tool akin to the knowledge of anatomy or psychology. Qi flows through the body as blood does but is more subtle and interactive as TCM has been describing for millennia. Indeed, the blood circulation system, which is so central to Western medicine, was only discovered by William Harvey as recently as 1628.

My first conscious and undoubted experience of subtle energy or qi occurred during my initial long Vipassana retreat with Dhiravamsa in 1974. In the beginning, I felt just subtle tingling, vibration, and temperature changes. As the retreat progressed, these got stronger and started moving around the body, sometimes feeling uncomfortable and strangely achy. At one point, energy started moving from my genitals in a pulsing, specific way, which I imagined as a line of mercury making its way across my body. It slowly moved across to my right thigh, up my torso and down my right arm to my hand, which was slightly touching the arm of the woman meditator next to me. We had become friendly, and I was conscious of feeling some sexual attraction to her, although I was aware that pursuing that attraction would not be compatible with the purpose of the meditation retreat. Nevertheless, it was clear that my subtle energy was communicating with me in a specific and clear manner — sexual attraction was present.

Towards the latter part of the retreat, I felt a repetitive, generalized "pumping" in my lower body, below my navel, sucking in and out. This pumping sensation then also occurred in the center of my chest, linking with my back, between the shoulder blades. In one particular meditation session, these two pumping energy centers were linked by a sudden burst of energy, like internal lightning. Again, the energy message was clear to me — my sexuality and my heart for the first time were aligned and balanced. I could feel sexual attraction and friendship without acting out the sexual part. Many years later, I discovered that qigong recognized three energy centers, or *dan tians*, which roughly corresponded with the six chakras in yoga. The areas that I had felt connecting were the lower and middle *dan tians*, respectively associated with physicality and with emotions and relationships.

Although I was intrigued and excited by the energy manifestations that I had experienced, I deliberately avoided inquiring or reading about qi, because I was aware that the mind has the power to produce what it wants. Subtle energy had spontaneously manifested through the process of simply paying attention to the breathing process in the present moment. I was determined to follow Dhiravamsa's instruction to let go of thoughts and return to attention in the now. I treated any qi manifestation as I would a thought or an emotion — acknowledge (any meaning or sign), let go, and start over again.

Over time, I felt qi manifesting in my body, especially during *taijiquan* and Vipassana. During meditation, it was often a generalized feeling of energy rising up in bursts through my center core. Sometimes it appeared to be focused on a particular part of the body, releasing and healing, especially if there was stress or injury. I also felt it during my *taijiquan* practice, mostly within my torso, but also emanating through my hands and fingers. *Taijiquan* coordinates movement with breathing and intent. In qigong and the Chinese "internal" martial arts, which includes *taijiquan*, there is a saying, "The *yi* leads to qi, which in turn leads the *li*." *Yi* is intention; qi is subtle energy; and *li* is physical force or strength. In a slightly different context, this reminds me of the Buddha's saying, "You are the result of what you have thought." As in raja yoga, precisely correct posture and breathing in qigong and *taijiquan* are important.

When my daughters were young, I tried to see if they could feel qi without telling them beforehand about qi or what I was doing. One experiment I tried was simply holding each one by both wrists and asking what she felt. They all reported feeling energy moving from one wrist up the arm across the body and down to the other wrist, in the correct direction that I was intending and visualizing. Another experiment that I tried was directing energy by pointing my finger at a certain part of the face, like the earlobe. I did this from a distance while they were otherwise engaged or distracted. Several times, they scratched or touched the precise area I was targeting.

Over time, they accepted qi as something natural and would ask me to give them healing energy when they were sick or injured. They were aware that most of their friends would find the concept "weird," especially at that time around the late-1980s and early-1990s. When my daughter Shuwei was about ten, she recounted an incident at her ballet class. One of her classmates was lazing around while their (very strict) teacher was out of the room and the rest of the class was working strenuously. When the teacher was about to return, her friend became afraid she would be scolded for taking a break, so Shuwei made her hot and sweaty. She said her amazed friend asked her how she did that, but Shuwei shrugged and said nothing, explaining her friend would not understand qi. I had never instructed her in energy projection, but it was just something she intuitively did.

As adults with children of their own, my daughters still occasionally ask me to do qigong healing on them, especially when time is of the essence or conventional remedies are not working.

When I met Dr. Jerry Alan Johnson in 1991 and started learning medical and martial qigong from him in a more formal and comprehensive way, my qi experiences and abilities dramatically increased. I felt that my sixteen years of learning *taijiquan* and the internal martial arts from Miss Li and my subsequent diligent practice were like building a sound and beautiful house. However, not all the electrical wires were connected. Dr. Johnson showed me how to connect them, and my house then functioned fully. I did not have to build a new house.

I qualified as a medical qigong therapist (MQT) from Dr. Johnson's International Institute of Medical Qigong, mainly out of personal interest. The training offered TCM theory for diagnosis plus techniques for energetic cleansing, circulation, building (accumulation) protection, projection, and more. Qigong therapists work in a similar way to acupuncturists, except they utilize direct qi manipulation and projection rather than inserting needles in the qi meridians and channels to treat the organs with which they are connected. Needles cannot be inserted directly into organs. An MQT also prescribes specific qigong self-regulation exercises for the patient. The qi projection is usually done at a short distance from the patient's body, but "distance healing" is also possible since distance is just a matter of degree.

I offered qigong therapy for over ten years, treating a wide variety of conditions. However, I was also asked to treat cases of advanced cancer, presumably as a last-ditch attempt to pull off a miracle. Such circumstances were not ideal, since a desperate patient might conclude that if a miracle was not forthcoming, the qigong therapist was just waving arms about and charging a fee for doing so. Trust was also important in getting patients to do their prescribed qigong self-regulation exercises.

My most successful case was in treating a man with a hard, golf ball–like tumor on the side of his neck. It seemed daunting, but I decided to give it my best shot. After about three weeks of once a week one-hour qigong treatments, I checked the tumor and was surprised to find that it had softened considerably and seemed smaller. After six weeks, it was no longer there! Of all my patients, this man was the most diligent in doing his prescribed qigong exercises, between two and three hours a day. Most patients just did ten to twenty minutes a day. In qigong therapy and healing, it is of the utmost importance that patients take part in their own healing. When I visited a qigong hospital in Beijing as part of Dr. Johnson's group, the patients were enthusiastically lining up to be led through their qigong self-regulation exercises. Their attitude and demeanor were in marked contrast to typical patients in a western hospital.

I undertook my first long distance qigong healing at the request of one of my Toronto *taijiquan* students. Her mother lived in the Vancouver area and was suffering from advanced lung cancer, which constantly filled her lungs with fluid and made breathing difficult. I was not specifically taught by Dr. Johnson how to do distance qigong healing, so I just imagined that the patient was lying on a table in front of me (in Toronto), having beforehand coordinated with her about the starting time of the intended half-hour treatment. After the treatment, she reported that she was breathing much easier and felt less discomfort in her lungs. However, she noted that "something changed" about five minutes before the end of the scheduled half hour. I was astounded because that is precisely when I actually ended the treatment because my concentration was waning. Subsequent qigong treatments eased her discomfort and lengthened the time between the necessary draining of her lungs.

It was another long-distance qigong treatment that persuaded me to cut down and eventually stop offering qigong therapy. I was again asked by one of my students to treat a relative suffering from a severe case of lung cancer. I drove three hours for the first (in-person) treatment of the patient, who was very pleased with the results of the qigong. However, she was disappointed when I said any further treatments would be distance treatments, since I did not have time to undertake all that traveling. I thought her attitude was somewhat presumptuous and needy, but I put it down to her sense of personal crisis. On a subsequent distance qigong treatment, I was on holiday, traveling through Canada's East Coast, several hundred kilometers away from her. I was shocked when I started coughing up blood during the treatment. I always did a special protective meditation before a treatment and my boundaries had always been clear and strong; I had never coughed up blood before. I immediately ended my treatments with her. It was obvious to me there was something amiss in our relationship and that even over distance, I could be affected by that patient. Qi is subtle and is not confined by the physical body.

It has been over a decade since my last formal qigong therapy session, although I have treated family members. I try to practice qigong daily to maintain and optimize my own health and am blessed to have a clean and healthy environment at our rural Harmony Dawn retreat in which to do so. I am aware when something is not in balance in my mind-body system and can usually do specific qigong exercises or perhaps take some herbal medicine to correct the imbalance before it becomes an ailment or illness. I also use self-massage and limited self-acupuncture. In TCM, normal meals are regarded as part of herbal medicine, and so Nicola and I pay careful attention to what we eat, as will be explained later.

Within my own personal Vipassana meditations, spontaneous qi manifestations have become more consistent and powerful over time.

There are many different manifestations, but perhaps the most consistent happens when the mind quiets and is focused on the physical sensations of the breathing process, which, for me, is usually in the lower *dan tian* area below the navel. The physical sensation of the breath morphs into an energy sensation that begins to rise through the solar plexus, heart, throat, and brain to the top of the head, although this rising does not necessarily occur in a linear, predictable way. The breath becomes a whole-body sensation wherein all parts are linked. All is energy. Sometimes energy accumulates on top of the head like a tingling, vibrating cap, and sometimes it explodes upwards through the top of the head, seemingly connecting with the "heavens." At other times, when the mind quiets, everything dissolves into an emptiness in which nothing is lacking; an emptiness that is total and complete.

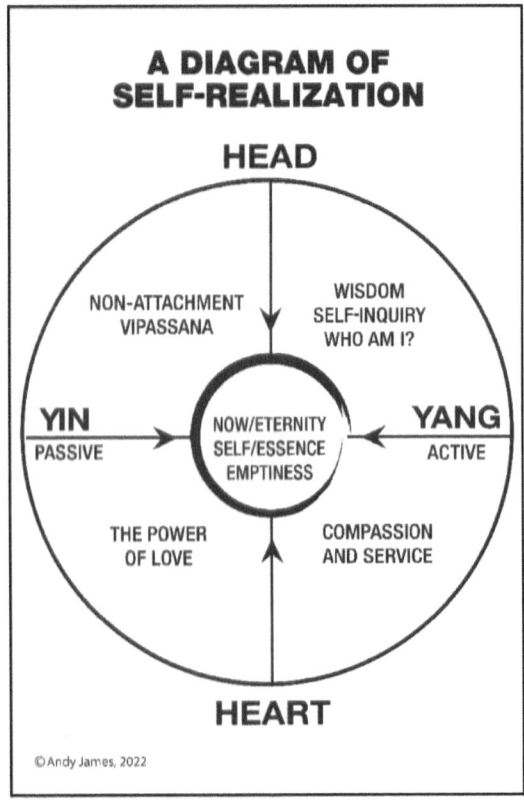

A Self-Realization Diagram

About twenty-five years ago, I started toying with the idea of creating a diagram or other simple visual aid to help explain to my Vipassana students the practice's potentialities and dynamics and how it might fit in with the main global spiritual paths.

In my 2004 book, *The Spiritual Legacy of Shaolin Temple: Buddhism, Daoism, and the Energetic Arts*, I included a diagram that I intuitively felt summarized the primary approaches to self-realization, self-transcendence, union with the Absolute, or enlightenment. It consisted of intersecting perpendicular lines; one horizontal and one vertical. The extremities of the vertical line represented the main paths of head and heart; the extremities of the horizontal line represented yin practices (not doing) and yang (doing, concentration). The center and point of intersection represented realization. I wrote:

> When we take an overall look at the elements necessary for self-transcendence or enlightenment, we can approach through the head or the heart, and the dynamics of our approach can be doing or non-doing (see diagram). It seems that as we approach realization, all elements begin to merge into one.

The main head and heart axis was obvious for me, since the Buddha plainly stated that wisdom and compassion were the necessary ingredients for enlightenment, and they were also the main paths in the comprehensive Indian yoga system, jnana and bhakti. More importantly, from my own decades-long Vipassana practice, it was clear that head and heart always need to be in balance and are so interconnected that they seem to be part of a oneness, even though they are popularly seen as conflicting or in opposition in an either/or way.

After opening Harmony Dawn in 2003, it was obviously much easier to lead meditation retreats as I lived in a retreat center! My self-realization diagram seemed a helpful tool in placing different forms of spirituality in a global context, regardless of my students' specific religious upbringing or background. It also helped me explain the complex in simple visual terms. I intuitively felt that the diagram could be elaborated upon. Over time, I added a circle to enclose the vertical and horizontal axes, and I tried to name or explain what each of the four quadrants of the diagram might represent.

Moving to the Center: A Journey in Consciousness

I saw the outer, enclosing circle as the totality of humanity in its present, conventional state. It reminds me of the circle in the yin-yang diagram and in the Enneagram Personality diagram. Different personalities, races, religions, educational backgrounds, cultures, nationalities, and more, which the Buddha describes as conditioning factors, place us on different parts of the circle and, therefore, give us different perspectives on life. They are all valid in the sense that each person has a view of the whole circle, but that view is only one perspective and is dependent on its particular position. Most people remain in their original position on the outer circle, accepting their conditioning as a given, an inheritance, a right, or even a gift. "I am proud to be me; I am proud of my race, religion, and culture." There is nothing wrong with pride in itself, but pride often brings with it superiority, rigidity, and division.

Relatively few see the wisdom of moving outside the comfort zone of their particular point on the outer circle. The ability to move around the circle would be akin to being able to see from someone else's point of view and to respond to challenges in a manner outside the range of our habitual comfort zone.

Moving towards the inner center of the circle is a journey into the depths of oneself, since it represents the eternal now, true self, essence, and oneness. This journey is usually neither easy nor straightforward. I see my self-realization diagram as akin to looking at the famous spiritual mountain image from above rather than ground level. As climbers reach ever higher/deeper, they move towards the common central point and oneness, and, thus, they also move closer to each other. Wisdom and compassion allow us to transcend our differences as we clearly see and experience the reality of our common ground and nature.

Whenever someone blithely asserts that all religions are the same, I often feel obliged to offer the caveat that this only applies to those who have neared or reached the summit of the spiritual mountain. The foothills may be spread far and wide and some paths that may initially seem promising may end up being dead ends. Even on a well-trodden path that eventually leads to the summit, the climber must be skillful, always aware, and determined. Reaching the summit is not a given.

I see journeying to the mountain peak or descending to the inner center as one of integrating, balancing, and furthering different levels of consciousness. Modern society seems to lack a sense, and perhaps even denies, that human beings are made up of different levels of consciousness, which I think explains many of the major confusions and contradictions that we experience individually and collectively. Indeed, many insist that all perspectives have equal validity, which, to me, seems absurd and illogical.

The nearest that conventional society comes to acknowledging levels of consciousness is in developmental psychology, which focuses on the stages of cognitive and emotional development from infancy to adulthood. Attention is usually only paid to behavior that is outside the parameters of "normality." There seems to be a general, perhaps simplistic, presumption that all "normal" adults are functioning on an equal, rational level of consciousness, and once we reach adulthood, our inner developmental work is done.

Although most people see themselves as logical and reasonable, it is obvious that emotions or gut instincts very often override the thinking mind, a fact that advertisers and political strategists continually and deliberately exploit with great success and profit. At present in many Western democracies, fact-free, emotionally charged demagoguery often sways more voters than logical, balanced, social and economic policies. This is a far-reaching and damning commentary on both leaders and those being led.

The concepts in yoga of the six chakras and in qigong of the three *dan tians* may be seen as an explanation of the evolution of human consciousness, which is paralleled in developmental psychology. The chakras and *dan tians* are regarded both as subtle energy centers and as representing or reflecting levels of consciousness. The lower two chakras and the lower *dan tian* are concerned with physical survival and functioning, which in adulthood also includes sexuality and procreation. The middle chakras and *dan tian* govern relationships with the "outer" world. The upper chakras and *dan tian* represent the thinking mind.

Although these energy centers all function in adulthood, they may not be fully functioning and, furthermore, they may not be in balance with each other. Kundalini seems to allude to this in the system of leading the Shakti energy from the base chakra progressively through the higher chakras, energizing and opening them up in turn, until Shakti finally merges with the energy of the crown chakra. This takes time and is not an automatic process, since certain chakras may be blocked or stagnant.

Qigong features the three regulations of body, qi, and mind, which are approximately represented by the three *dan tians* — lower, middle, and upper. "Regulation" usually includes the cleansing of impurities and blockages, connection and flow within the whole mind-body system, and the infusion of clean, healing qi, which may be absorbed from the external environment and especially Mother Earth. Body, qi, and mind are always interrelated and interacting and never actually operate in the separate conceptual boxes we commonly use.

Even within TCM, it is not easy to ensure balance within these three areas. For example, a TCM doctor or practitioner may detect an energetic imbalance in an organ, say the liver or lungs, and may correctly diagnose the root cause to be emotional, which would be anger or grief, respectively. The TCM practitioner may administer acupuncture, qigong, or herbs to temporarily correct the imbalance, but they usually leave the emotional, root-cause work to the patient, who may or may not seek professional help, perhaps from a psychologist or psychotherapist.

Within my own mind-body system of teaching, the emotional component of a qi imbalance would be covered by skillful Vipassana meditation practice. Many qigong teachers only use active visualization as regulation of the mind, but I hold that a passive, open, wisdom meditation practice, as in Vipassana, is vital since it is capable of awareness of everything within our body-energy-mind system. The thinking and doing mind tends to look for theories and solutions rather than be quiet and aware as we have seen. The mind also tends to dominate the other aspects of our being, including emotions and instincts, which have great wisdom to offer within their own spheres, if we are able to create the space to listen to them. Consider what a mess the thinking mind often makes of food, sex, and relationships by not being in touch with the body, instincts, or heart.

It is important to ensure that all levels of consciousness are healthy and functioning in a balanced manner. The highest level of available consciousness should not suppress and dominate the lower ones, each of which has a specialized function. Displaying ignorance of emotional intelligence and spiritual potentiality, most people seem to admire those who display a special talent or genius in one specific area, say entertainment, and are shocked when that person is found morally wanting or even abusive in other areas of their lives. "Talent" and spiritual maturity and balance are not the same. Because we excel in one area of our lives does not mean we excel in all areas.

If we manage to bring healthy bodies, emotions, and minds into balance with each other, we will function as healthy, global citizens, which would be a huge and much needed accomplishment. We would not need so much remedial care and damage repair, and we would make more creative and compassionate decisions moving forward. There would be less conflict and more cooperation.

Our spiritual potential does not end at the top end of conventional consciousness — the upper chakra or *dan tian*. The ageless wisdom spiritual traditions describe levels of consciousness above the conventional and beyond the limitations of our physical bodies, or, in other words, transpersonal or transcendental consciousness. Ken Wilber, the renowned contemporary philosopher who focuses on transpersonal psychology, identifies four levels of ascending transcendental consciousness, which he calls the psychic, subtle, causal, and ultimate or non-dual.

We are already beginning to see the leading edges of psychic consciousness emerging as it moves beyond conventional, rational, scientific "reality." Out-of-body experiences, shamanic trances, hands-on healing, and, of course, qigong and kundalini are no longer dismissed as lunacy, even if they are not yet widely embraced. The paranormal experiences that may result from the psychic level are fascinating or even intoxicating to some. However, I point out to my students that the psychic is not the ultimate level of consciousness, but just the first level of transpersonal consciousness. To achieve enlightenment and union with all, it takes urgent action now. Thinking you are making spiritual progress and are superior to others because of psychic ability is often self-deception and a form of procrastination from the continuing work of climbing the spiritual mountain.

At the subtle level of consciousness, the mind may start communicating or identifying with archetypal forms like angels, Platonic forms, "heavenly" light and sound, Buddhism's four jnanas with form, and more. Wilber writes of this level:

> Brings a profound insight into the fundamental or Archetypal forms of being and existence itself. It is not Formless, however, or radically transcendent, but rather expresses insight into the subtlest forms of mind, being, deity and manifestation.

Dhiravamsa writes of the archetypes:

> All the archetypes and mythologies are mere symbols of various stages of consciousness or energy patterns manifesting both within us and the external world. As symbols, they are man-made things.

At the causal level of consciousness, transcendence becomes complete and stabilized so that there is no need for forms. There is no self, no god, no sense of separation or duality. This state of consciousness is formless and boundless.

In the ultimate or non-dual stage of consciousness, there is no need to go away from the world in order to experience self-realization or enlightenment. As the Buddhist heart sutra states, "Form is not other than Emptiness and Emptiness is not other than Form." There is no (dualistic) difference between subject and object, manifest and unmanifest.

My favorite depiction of the exploration of consciousness is the delightful series of ten ox- or cow-herding brush paintings created by a twelfth-century Chan Buddhist monk called Shiyuan, or Kakuan in Japanese. The first is "Looking for the Cow." We have lost a sense of who we really are, and the search is confusing; we do not know where to look. We have lost meaning and purpose. This is followed by pictures entitled "Seeing the Traces of the Cow," "Seeing the Cow," and then making progress by "Catching the Cow" and "Herding the Cow." The following commentaries are from D.T. Suzuki's *Essays in Zen Buddhism*, beginning with "Herding the Cow":

> Things oppress us not because of an objective world, but because of a self-deceiving mind. Do not get the nose ring loose; hold it tight and allow yourself no indulgence.

Pictures six to ten describe the more advanced levels of spiritual attainment and then eventual enlightenment, which happens, according to Suzuki, "When one sees into the inmost nature of one's own being, one instantly becomes a Buddha." The sixth picture is "Coming Home on the Cow's Back." Suzuki says, "The struggle is over; he is no more concerned with gain and loss." Number seven is "The Cow Forgotten, Leaving the Man Alone":

> Things are one and the cow is symbolic. When you know that what you need is not the snare or net, but the hare or fish, it is like gold separated from dross.

Number eight is "The Cow and the Man Both Gone Out of Sight." It is represented by a simple circle, which is the same symbol known in Daoism, *taijiquan* and qigong as *wuji*, or emptiness. *Wuji* precedes the interaction of yin and yang but is not a vacuum, since it gives rise to all manifestation. Suzuki writes of this picture:

> All confusion is set aside and serenity alone prevails; even the idea of holiness does not obtain. He does not linger about where the Buddha is, and as to where there is no Buddha he speedily passes on. When there exists no form of dualism, even a thousand-eyed one fails to detect a loophole… All is empty, the whip, the rope, the man and the cow.

The ninth picture is entitled, "Returning to the Origin; Back to the Source":

> From the very beginning, pure and immaculate, he has never been affected by defilement. He calmly watches the growth and decay of things with form, while himself abiding in the immovable serenity of non-assertion.

The tenth and final cow-herding picture is "Entering the City with Bliss-Bestowing Hands":

> His humble cottage door is closed, and the wisest know him not. No glimpses of his inner life are to be caught, for he goes on his way without following the steps of the ancient sages. Carrying a gourd, he goes out into the market, leaning against a stick he comes home. He is found in company with wine-bibbers and butchers; he and they are all converted into Buddhas.

Having attained full enlightenment, the man/sage returns to everyday life without the need to demonstrate his attainment to anyone or show himself as special. It should be noted that not all spiritual-religious traditions feature the four transcendental levels of consciousness discussed above, especially the non-dual, which is about enlightenment in one's present lifetime, not the next or subsequent ones. The extraordinary and ordinary are finally reconciled and embodied.

I see the center of the circle in the self-realization diagram as representing not only enlightenment, union with the Absolute, totality, and emptiness, but also the eternal now. We never actually live in the past or the future, although our minds constantly dwell on those concepts, causing us to ignore or not pay enough attention to the present. The future is but a projection of the past on which we all tend to dwell, individually and collectively. Certain sectors of society are fond of imagining a mythical golden age when everything was perfect and glorious. It never existed. All is now. We cannot do our spiritual transformation work if we do not carefully pay attention to what is arising in the present moment. The *Daodejing* advised:

> A thousand miles' journey begins from the spot under one's feet. Therefore the Sage never attempts great things, and thus he can achieve what is great.

When one no longer experiences duality, there is no separation between inner and outer, manifest and unmanifest. The past and future recede from our consciousness, leaving us in the now. Thus, the center of the circle is both nowness and oneness.

Upper-Left Quadrant: Non-Attachment and Vipassana

I have named the quadrants from the perspective of Buddhist Vipassana practice as I have experienced and taught it, but I sense they probably have wider significance and relevance. I started by placing Vipassana and non-attachment in the upper-left quadrant since it is primarily a head-wisdom practice, and it is passive in the sense of having no specific goals. To clarify the last sentence, we may have a general, long-term interest in trying to follow the Buddha's teachings to end our suffering and reach enlightenment, but within formal sitting meditation, we are just paying attention to what is arising in each moment without control or interference and without wanting to achieve or become anything. Wanting and expectation are obstacles to the practice as they are just forms of thinking. In Daoist terms, our long-term goal may be the thousand-miles journey, but in order to get there, we must mindfully attend to each step, one by one, in each moment.

As I have described before, my initial and ongoing instruction to Vipassana students is to pay attention to the physical sensations resulting from inhaling and exhaling. Since the breathing process is automatic, this does not require conscious effort or doing.

Most meditators are unable to pay bare attention to the breathing process for more than a few minutes or even seconds, since the mind tends to become distracted and veers off in various directions. When the meditator becomes aware that the mind is no longer on the breath, my instruction is to acknowledge that distraction, let go, and start over. Acknowledge is brief and does not require thought or analysis.

Even for a beginner, learning to let go rather than forcing the attention back (which most people do) is a step towards learning what the Buddha's all-important concept of "non-attachment" means. It is refraining from grasping (thoughts, images, emotions, and more) or if one has already grasped, then letting go and beginning anew. In the context of a meditation session, it may not seem important, but it is a step on the way to a radically new way of being. Much is contained in a moment if we pay attention, which reminds me of William Blake: "To see a World in a grain of sand and Heaven in a wild flower, Hold Infinity in the palm of your hand and Eternity in an hour."

Vipassana means "insight" meditation, which will arise if one is able to look at what is arising without getting attached to it. If one simply blocks out thoughts and forcefully returns to the breath, there will not be the space for insight to arise. In my experience, whatever needs to be recognized (and if necessary, released) will eventually arise for attention. This process could involve factors from different levels of consciousness, from lower to higher. In terms of the self-realization diagram, "moving to the center" is not only a deepening of consciousness, but also a process of integration and harmonization — experiencing other segments of the diagram, even those which are unfamiliar or uncomfortable.

Most forms of "meditation" have some form of object on which to focus, whether an image, an idea, a quality, a sound, a prayer, or other. It is a form of one-pointedness or concentration. Other "distracting" objects or impressions are removed or ignored. In Vipassana, we retain our everyday consciousness, but we do not get swept away by objects arising in our consciousness as is common. Consciousness just is. It witnesses without being compelled to react.

Chögyam Trungpa, an acclaimed modern Tibetan Buddhist master, describes Vipassana in his *Meditation in Action*:

> In this kind of meditation, nowness plays a very important part... Whatever one does is not aimed at achieving a higher state or following some theory or ideal, but simply, without any object or ambition, trying to see what is here and now... If one cultivates this intelligent intuitive insight, then gradually, the real intuitive feeling develops and the imaginary or hallucinatory element is gradually clarified... Reality gradually expands so that we do not have a technique at all ... the more one expands, the closer one gets to the realization of centerless existence.

Upper-Right Quadrant: Wisdom and Self-Inquiry

The upper-right quadrant of the self-realization diagram represents wisdom practice in a more active mode than the upper-left. It is perhaps what is called "contemplation" in other forms of spirituality or maybe "concentration" within Buddhism. I do not intend to debate word meanings but describe how Vipassana practice may spontaneously become a more active or directed search for wisdom and understanding.

Within normal Vipassana meditation practice of following the breath without attachment, spontaneous, clear insight and understanding may arise. "Vipassana" means "clear," "special," "penetrating," "thorough" seeing or perception and, thus, is known as insight meditation. In my experience, if such clear insight arises, then direct, choiceless action naturally follows. There is no doubt or second guessing; it is not a matter of weighing options and probabilities.

However, such insight does not usually arise immediately or automatically because of various self-imposed impediments, some of which were described in the earlier section on meditators' questions.

In my experience, two of the most common and subtle impediments are the inability to recognize or be aware of personal behavioral patterns and the operation and activities of the personal self or "I" — both because we are so identified with our "I" or self and the thoughts associated with it. Sometimes, I find it necessary to slightly alter my standard meditation instructions to help individual meditators break through these particular impediments.

Many Vipassana-Mindfulness meditators are attracted by the honest simplicity of the practice, but, ironically, this very simplicity may become a stumbling block. General instruction in Vipassana-Mindfulness meditation found in books or online is usually along these lines:

1. Feel/follow the breath.
2. Notice when the mind wanders or becomes distracted.
3. Gently come back to the breath.

Many meditators I encounter are self-taught or taught by instructors or teachers with little personal experience, so the above instruction tends to be the totality of their meditation practice.

There can be many different interpretations of each of the above three steps and, therefore, many missteps. For example, what does "notice" really mean? What does "come back" really mean? Many mindfulness meditators get so caught up in the process of rigidly and one-pointedly following the breath that their practice becomes a *samatha (samadhi)*, or concentration, practice rather than a Vipassana or wisdom one, which requires an open, aware, non-grasping mind. *Samatha* can give you focus and a sense of peace, but not necessarily the insight-wisdom necessary for enlightenment.

Many meditators "notice" that their mind is no longer on the breath but not on where or how it has wandered away. Sometimes the distraction is trivial, like thinking about the next meal or what chores await, but at other times, it might be a fleeting image or emotion emerging from what is normally subconscious and calling for attention and release. For this reason, I advise my meditation students to "acknowledge" not only that the mind has wandered, but where it has been, in case there is a message coming from within. "Acknowledge" is more active than "notice," but it is brief and not an invitation to analysis or internal discussion.

If (through acknowledging) a meditator recognizes that certain meaningful images, thoughts, or emotions are recurring, it might be necessary to change the object of mindfulness from the physical sensations of the breath to whatever is presenting itself for deeper attention. There are four foundations of mindfulness: body, feelings, state of mind, and mental contents. The sensations of the breath rising and falling are but one aspect of body mindfulness and does not constitute the totality of Vipassana practice. I caution my students to treat all objects of mindfulness in the same way as the breath — acknowledge, let go, start over — without analysis, judgment, or manipulation. In this way, with skillful practice, all can eventually be revealed and released, whether personal trauma, relationship conflict, addictive behavior, or other.

In addition, several of my students have linked troublesome behavioral patterns and relationships with deeper, underlying Enneagram personality patterns, not only their own, but those of others around them. I see personality as a very deep form of conditioning. We cannot get rid of or change our personality, but we can free ourselves from the compulsion of its negative or destructive aspects through letting go in the moment. Personality will be discussed in the next chapter.

As part of my basic instruction in practicing Vipassana meditation, I specifically point out that "I" thoughts should be objects of awareness, just like any other thoughts or impressions. In spite of my reminders and cautions, most people find it extremely difficult not to identify with their "I" thoughts, even during meditation retreats. The "I" thoughts commonly assume the role of meditator, controlling and judging the practice. In such cases, I recommend the practice of occasionally posing the question to the meditator, "Who am I?" This has helped me in my personal meditation practice over the years, especially when the "I" voices and thoughts in my head would not stop.

Who is meditating? Who is making a to-do list? Who am I apart from the names and roles I play, including husband, father, son, teacher, friend, man, Chinese, Canadian, and more? Am I my body, my names, my relationships, my memories? The mind has answers for all these questions, but the answers beg more questions, which is an example of the *dukkha* and conditionality the Buddha pointed out. I see "who" — like "acknowledgement" — as a slightly more active or directed form of awareness, but not reaching the level of "doing." "Who am I?" is self-inquiry, not in order to achieve something or become something, but to delve ever deeper beyond any "answers" in words or thought.

Although I came to "Who am I?" as a natural part of my Vipassana meditation practice, I was aware that some sort of self-inquiry or questioning plays a part in other spiritual traditions. Chan (Zen) used the paradoxical *kung-an* (koan) system of riddles designed to bypass the logical mind. "What is the sound of one hand clapping?" is a famous example of a koan. In more recent times, the renowned Indian sage Ramana Maharshi taught the inquiry, "Who am I?" as the principal means to self-realization. He says:

> After negating all of the above-mentioned as "not this," "not this," that Awareness which alone remains, that I am. The nature of Awareness is existence-consciousness-bliss...
>
> The thought, "Who am I?" will destroy all other thoughts and, like the stick used for stirring the burning pyre, it will itself in the end get destroyed. Then there will arise Self-realization.

The personification of transcendent wisdom (*prajna*) in Mahayana Buddhism is the bodhisattva, Manjushri, which means "gentle glory." He is depicted with a flaming sword in his right hand and a book of the *Prajnaparamita* (great wisdom) sutra supported by a lotus in his left hand. The flaming sword represents transcendent wisdom, which cuts through ignorance and duality, ending afflictions and bringing about enlightenment. Manjushri is known for a straightforward and direct teaching style, jumping directly to the essential and supreme truth, which leads to enlightenment.

In the Greek and Christian traditions, Sophia is the feminine personification of divine wisdom, the word of God or the Holy Spirit. The famous Hagia Sophia cathedral (later a mosque) in Istanbul is generally translated in English as "Holy Wisdom."

Lower-Right Quadrant: Compassion and Service

Vipassana practitioners may come to compassion and service in several ways. Although characterized as a head-wisdom path, it requires a degree of surrender and vulnerability from the very beginning of the meditation practice through the instruction to "let go" of distracting thoughts, emotions, and impressions. Letting go is the surrender of control by the mind, closely intertwined with the notion of "self"; it is an opening of the heart in a very simple and humble way. It is one important and present step on the path.

During a retreat or after some sustained period of personal meditation practice, it is common for emotions to surface, since these are generally suppressed in everyday life. Releasing negative pent-up emotions and patterns requires letting go and opening the heart. This process may be accompanied by a physical-energetic sensation in the center of the chest — opening and pulsating, sending out waves of energy. Opening of the heart is often accompanied by a feeling of expansiveness and widening embrace of others.

In order to facilitate or actively bring attention to the opening process, I sometimes use two brief guided meditations at the beginning of a meditation session: releasing past pain and the more famous loving kindness (*Metta*) meditation. The latter is an active form of meditation based on the Buddha's *Metta* sutra, sending thoughts of love, kindness, and compassion to all beings. Some teachers, including Dhiravamsa, advise sending love and compassion to yourself first and then in widening circles of compassion to include good or intimate friends or family, casual acquaintances, those with whom you have difficulties, and finally all sentient beings.

Some meditators find it difficult to feel love for themselves or others, so I suggest forgiveness. This is not the same as justification of past hurt, but more akin to letting go of any past hurt you carry within yourself relating to certain issues or people. If you let go of your burdens, you are freer to live in the present, taking the next step and meeting the next life challenge. It should be remembered that guided meditations and affirmations are not part of the Vipassana meditation process or dynamic itself but function more as a deliberate, positive reminder.

One can come to love, compassion, and service through wisdom itself. Through my Vipassana practice, I clearly saw how we commonly and unnecessarily create duality, division, and conflict; why our attempts to build a sense of solidity and permanence are doomed to failure; why our sense of "I" is always fragile, even beneath outward bravado; and how our pain and suffering arises from ignorance rather than sin. I saw as a fact that all humans share a deep oneness, even those who want to separate and fight; that all living beings and the planet itself are factually interconnected and interdependent; and that we are all capable of true love, compassion, and contentment if we allow it. The means are available to us all.

A Vipassana practitioner can be of service as a teacher of Buddhism and can bring penetrating and harmonizing wisdom to any particular job, task, or relationship. As the Buddha advised, we can best help and protect others by first protecting ourselves through seeing and living according to the truth.

Lower-Left Quadrant: The Power of Love

Of the four quadrants, I found this one the most difficult to name. What is the passive aspect of devotion? Most devotional paths seem to advocate active practices like praying, chanting, visualizing, ritual, and more.

The Buddha, in talking about the *Satipatthana* (mindfulness) practice, advised:

> Protecting oneself, one protects others; Protecting others, one protects oneself. And how does one in protecting oneself, protect others? By the repeated and

frequent practice of meditation. And how does one in protecting others, protect oneself? By patience and forbearance, by a non-violent and harmless life, by loving kindness and compassion.

Without going out of our way to do good or express love, we can help others by our own behavior and example. We can help others by seeing our interdependence and oneness as a matter of fact, not as ideals or theory. We consequently act in the best interests of all, which is what Buddhists call right action. To me, this is love without being conscious of wanting to love or do good. According to the Buddha, the two necessary ingredients for enlightenment are compassion and wisdom. To me, they are not really separate but different superficial manifestations of a oneness.

This concept reminds me of Hinduism's raja yoga ideal, who acts in the spirit of jnana yoga — right action and work without attachment. Vivekananda points out that although there are four main yoga paths, they tend to overlap and blend into each other. He saw the Buddha as the supreme and perfect example of karma yoga:

> All the prophets of the world, except Buddha, had external motives to move them to unselfish action ... holding that they are Incarnations of God come down to earth or Messengers from God... But Buddha is the only one who said, "I do not care to know your various theories about God... Do good and be good and this will take you to freedom and truth..." He is the ideal karma-yogi, acting entirely without motive ... the greatest combination of heart and brain that ever existed, the greatest soul-power ever manifested.

Emptiness or *Sunyata*

Before I settled on "The Power of Love" as the name for the lower-left quadrant above, it used to be "Emptiness," which I feel deserves a prominent place in discussions of the spiritual path. I have now placed emptiness at the center of the circle, since it is always within us and available to us.

There are many different descriptions of and theories about emptiness, or *sunyata*, as it is generally known in Buddhism and also in Hinduism. For simplicity, I will start with my own experience of it, which is also how I explain it to my students. There are times during my Vipassana meditation practice (and also during my normal everyday life) when the mind is suddenly still, and consciousness just is. This could be described as emptiness, but it is not a nihilistic void or vacuum, since it is full, alive, and complete at the same time. There is nothing to do or to be added. Sometimes there is consciousness of the body and sometimes not. Emptiness can also happen outside of sitting meditation, during *taijiquan* practice or even just walking, standing, or sitting. Often as I gaze out at our meadow, the mind stills and thoughts cease, even though the clouds are moving, the tall grasses are swaying, and birds are flying by. Everything is perfect; it takes a conscious effort to come out of this state of deep peace and completeness, what the Buddhists call "suchness." This stillness can happen even if I am sitting in our house and my gaze lands on something, whether a piece of furniture, an object, or a picture. In these moments, there is no doer, and the heart is fully open and flowing, connected with all. There is no separation.

Emptiness underlies all our activity and, therefore, is always available if we are conscious of it and allow it. There can be space or emptiness between breaths and between thoughts, which is very useful in refraining from reactively saying or doing unwise things in the heat of the moment. Clear, direct action arises out of the neutrality and connectedness of emptiness. It is not programmed and conditioned. This even, or especially, applies in a situation of extreme threat or danger.

Rather than exploring emptiness, most people feel uncomfortable or even fearful of it, and seek to cover it over with activity and "space fillers," which now commonly include a screen of some sort. The constant need to check one's smartphone is akin to addiction, and the young are especially vulnerable. The most absurd incident can now become "viral" and be the subject of fifteen minutes of fame ... until the next fifteen. It is fashionable to have a planet-wide "bucket list" of things to be done in one's life. The more we avoid the state of quiet non-doing, the more afraid we are of it and, thus, the longer we miss the benefits of its profundity and potential. The *Daodejing* observes:

> Thirty spokes unite in one nave and because of the part where nothing exists, we have the use of a carriage wheel. Clay is molded into vessels and because of the space where nothing exists, we are able to use them as vessels. Doors and windows are cut out in the walls of a house and because of the empty spaces we are able to use them. Therefore, on one hand we have the benefit of existence and on the other, we make use of non-existence.
>
> Dao when put in use for its hollowness is not likely to be filled. In its profundity it seems to be the origin of all things. In its depth it seems ever to remain.

Sunyata has always played an important role in Buddhism. In Theravada Buddhism, *sunyata* is implicit in the impermanence and insubstantiality of *dukkha*, the five aggregates, and the doctrine of no-self (anatta). *Sunyata* is also prominent in all branches of Mahayana Buddhism. The famous twelfth-century Chan master Dahui Zhonggao, who promoted the use of the *kung-an* (koan), wrote to one of his disciples:

> If we are free from thoughts, there is no need of teaching any kind of doctrine. In truth, doctrines have no substantiality in them, nor have thoughts any fixed foundations from which they rise. Both doctrines and thoughts are empty in nature. To be thus empty is the character of reality... I pray you to hold all things empty which are thought real; never take them for realities that are by nature empty. If you gain a penetrating insight into this truth, you do away with all the evil karma and

ignorance since the eternal past, and all the doubts you have entertained will melt away like a piece of ice. All the teachings of the Buddha preserved in the Tripitaka are no more than this truth.

In summary, my diagram of self-realization is an attempt to explain my understanding and experience of the Buddha's teaching and, in particular, the practice of Vipassana (insight) meditation. Coming to the center represents a deepening and integration of various aspects of consciousness. However, this journey is not linear, and glimpses of enlightenment, the self, oneness, emptiness, and transcendent wisdom may be experienced along the path and may manifest in any of the quadrants, whether head or heart, active or passive.

I have included quotations not only from various streams of Buddhism, but also Hinduism and Daoism. I see aspects of the self-realization diagram in the Abrahamic religions but do not feel qualified to share my observations.

CONDITIONING AND PERSONALITY

What Is Conditioning?

I have previously mentioned the process of conditioning in different contexts. Here I want to elaborate on it, as it is such a powerful factor in our daily decision-making and our very identity, both individually and collectively. And yet it is little understood or even known.

Twenty-five hundred years ago, the Buddha made the astonishingly profound and prescient observation that all life is constantly changing, interconnected, and insubstantial and, therefore, impossible to grasp or hold. As we have seen, he elaborated on the process of conditionality in his explanation of conditioned genesis, citing twelve factors that keep the wheel of life turning, causing cycles of rebirth and death. These factors, which may initially seem theoretical and remote, are volitional or karma forming actions, consciousness, mental and physical phenomena, the five sense organs plus mind, contact, sensation, desire, clinging, becoming, birth, death, and decay.

Expressing the above in modern terms, it includes the many variables involved in both nature and nurture. There is still an ongoing debate about whether human actions are determined by nature, our biological and genetic traits, or nurture, our external environments, whether natural or human-made, including politics, government, economics, business, finance, race, religion, nationality, technology, and more. There is growing evidence that we are also born with inherited behavioral traits, whether biological, genetic, or other. Esoteric systems like astrology and probably the Enneagram personalities (which will be described below) suggest that we are born with complex behavioral traits already in place.

We are influenced by both nature and nurture (not either/or), since internal and external are interconnected. Our many, ever-changing conditioning factors determine what we think of as our "selves" and "reality." However, although we acknowledge the process of conditioning in certain areas, like early childhood, adolescent trauma, or in how others behave — their race, culture, religion, political party, and more — we generally do not think it applies to ourselves or question our own conditioning. We somehow see ourselves as reasonable, solid, normal, and all right. We do not know how to change, and many do not want to change.

As a Vipassana meditation teacher, I have long used the metaphor of a computer to describe the workings of our thinking mind, since the former was developed to mimic the latter and indeed may soon surpass it. There are four major functions of a computer: input, processing, storage, and output. As a society, we accept the accuracy of people's "output," which is their understanding of and views on life, even despite widely diverse and conflicting perspectives. "Input" and "processing" are rarely scrutinized except in cases of insanity or crime, where someone does something beyond the norms of social acceptability.

Our human "input" varies a lot from person to person, since it is basically our conditioning, whether conscious or not. Parents attempt to pass on to their children their own life lessons and values, which often include their beliefs, culture, religion, and ideology. They also pass on unspoken and unintended lessons, such as underlying emotions that are at odds with their overt words and actions. The unintended lesson may be "do as I say, not as I do" or "don't show your emotions"; intended lessons may be to "be a man," "be a lady," and the like. As a child grows, there is conditioning from different sources, like schools, universities, workplaces, culture, politics, and now the internet, from increasingly early ages. Much content on the internet is designed to persuade rather than to be objective, neutral, or educational in a positive manner.

Our input experiences/conditioning are different but so is the way we process them, our software. It is an obvious fact that all our conscious words and actions arise from within ourselves, but only a very small percentage of us are brought up or even encouraged to inquire about how our beliefs, self-image, likes, dislikes, notions of right and wrong, and ambitions come into being. As we have seen in the earlier chapters on Buddhism and Vipassana, our logical thinking process is often overwhelmed by emotion and instinct (a fact routinely exploited by political spinners and marketers), and its objectivity compromised by our identification with our conditioning, especially beliefs. A very deep form of conditioning is our personality.

As a result of the above, we stumble through life without really understanding ourselves, why we do what we do, and if our efforts will bring us happiness or contentment. We implicitly trust our "output" without any persistent or skilled examination of our internal dynamics and often react in a knee-jerk way without thinking. At present, there seems to be a growing reaction against self-reflection and self-inquiry in favor of simply blaming and demonizing others for our own discontent and anger. It is always someone else's fault, never our own.

These processes, of course, also operate within those who impact society as leaders in politics, business, technology, science, religion, culture, law, and more. Although they may excel in one or some aspects of life, that does not necessarily reflect deep self-knowledge or knowledge of human nature generally. This personal blind spot or lack of deep self-knowledge is extremely dangerous in those who make decisions that impact humanity, like the leaders of the more powerful countries and in technology, especially social media and artificial intelligence. Astonishingly, in the approach to the 2024 U.S. presidential elections, Elon Musk joined Donald Trump in continuing the false, conspiracy-driven narrative that the previous election (in 2020) was stolen from Trump. Trump is a powerful political figure and wealthy in his own right. Musk is perhaps the world's second richest person, the owner of global social media platform Twitter/X (which he freely used to promote falsehoods), and in the forefront of AI development, which will shape the future of humanity. He also spent about $130 million of his own money promoting Trump's election campaign. So much concentration of power in two such volatile individuals does not seem healthy for democracy. It should be a huge red flag.

We know that disturbed individuals may suddenly and unexpectedly run amok in knife or gun rampages. Yet our low level of emotional intelligence, amply evidenced over time, allows us to vote into power obviously narcissistic, corrupt, volatile, and bullying leaders who are in charge of weapons and policies that could destroy the world.

We live in times of rapid change driven primarily by technology, but most people resist change as it challenges their beliefs, expectations, and patterns — the conditioning with which they identify. They feel unstable, vulnerable, confused, and helpless. Consequently, many want to turn the clock back to a mythical time where life was happier, easier, and "great" — a golden age that exists only in wishful thinking.

Not surprisingly, mental health is worsening worldwide and definitely in the United States. A 2017 *Scientific American* article on mental health in the United States reported:

> The mental health of the nation may have even declined in the past 20 years… Suicide rates per 100,000 people have increased to a 30-year high. Substance abuse, particularly of opiates, has become epidemic. Disability awards for mental disorders have dramatically increased since 1980.

The Buddha counseled, "You are the result of what you think" and "Be a refuge unto yourself." Our distorted and mistaken views of reality, including of ourselves, take place within us and operate from moment to moment. Thus, if we want to dissipate our confusion and suffering, we have to learn to pay attention in each moment and let go or be non-attached to our destructive compulsions and reactivity. If we understand ourselves at a deep level, we will also understand others at a deep level. The Chinese classic *Daodejing* states:

> Without going out of the door, One can know the whole world; without peeping out of the window One can see the Dao of heaven. The further one travels, the less one knows. Therefore the Sage knows everything without traveling; He names everything without seeing it.

The Enneagram of Personality

In my personal experience, probably the most comprehensive explanation of a very deep form of pervasive, perhaps universal, conditioning is the Enneagram Personality Types. I have related that my teacher Dhiravamsa shared his knowledge of the Enneagram of Personality to help my wife and me understand why we were having difficulties with our daughter, Shuwen, who was two years old at the time. It enabled us to see life from her personality perspective and speak her "language," resulting in a dramatic and positive change in our relationship. Over the decades, it has proven to be an invaluable relationship tool that I have shared with family, students, and close friends, who have in turn benefitted from it.

I see personality as a deep form of conditioning very likely in place at birth. It is a form of nature conditioning akin to our physical bodies. It is our "relationship body" since it overwhelmingly determines how we perceive and react to others. It very often determines the types of jobs, partners, spouses, and ideologies we choose. We are born with both "bodies" and cannot exchange them for different ones, but we can learn to understand, take care of, and use them optimally.

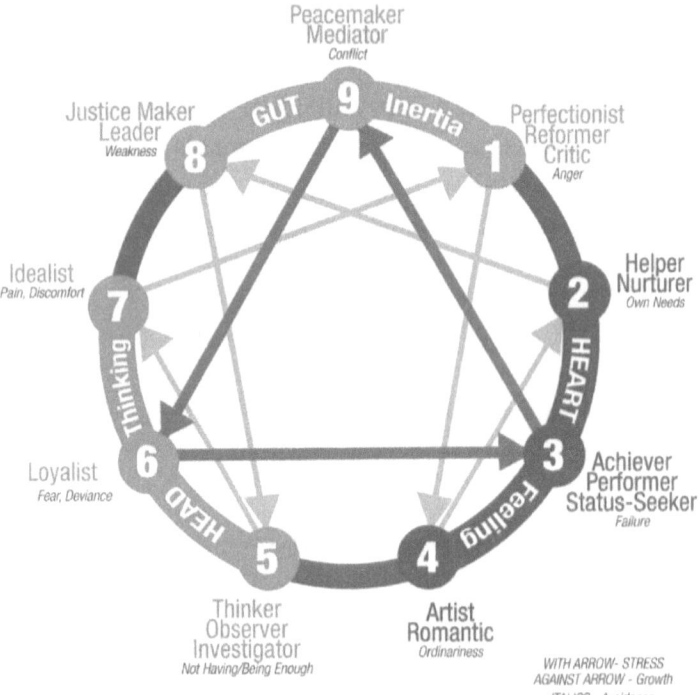

The Enneagram of Personality is not part of the Buddhist tradition. Dhiravamsa became aware of it before published books because the recognized founder of the modern Enneagram of Personality system, Claudio Naranjo, was a Vipassana student of his when he lived in Berkeley, California. It is an esoteric system from the Middle East associated with the Sufis who used it to help their students understand their conditioning patterns and habits.

The Enneagram is a nine-pointed symbol first introduced to the West in 1916 by the Armenian philosopher, George Gurdjieff. The symbol consists of a circle containing an equilateral triangle, the points of which are numbered three, six, and nine. Superimposed on the triangle is another series of lines connecting points on the circle numbered one, four, two, eight, five, and seven. The former represents the three major universal forces — creative, destructive, and sustaining or inertia — and the personalities grouped around those points operate from the heart, head, and gut (instinct), respectively. The latter sequence is called the Law of Seven because if one is divided by seven, the result is 0.142857 recurring. The Law of Seven is supposed to demonstrate the non-linear progression of events, of which the musical scale is supposed to be an example.

All the lines connecting personalities/points on the circle have directional arrows. Moving in the direction of the arrow means that a personality is under stress and disintegrating. It will begin to display some negative characteristics of the personality it is approaching. Moving against the arrow suggests that the personality is healthy and integrating. It will display positive characteristics of the personality it is approaching.

The above helps to explain the seeming complexity of the Enneagram diagram and is helpful in finding one's personality type and subsequently using that knowledge. The most important step, however, is identifying your particular personality type, which may require some help from someone familiar with the Enneagram system.

I regard the Enneagram of Personality as an invaluable tool for understanding the main drivers of one's own personality and seeing its specific dynamics in operation from day to day. Even for people who are aware of the Enneagram Personality Types, it is easy to become embroiled in everyday relationships and forget that one's reactions are falling into patterns predictable according to personality type.

The compulsion of the personality types is very strong, and to change, we must be aware of what needs changing as well as the ability to let go, which is why Vipassana practice is always necessary. As the Buddha advised, if we take care of ourselves, it is also the best way of taking care of others. My version of this advice to my daughters is comparing relationships to a pipe or conduit. The best you can do is to keep your own end of the pipe free from obstruction. Ultimately, we cannot really change others, but only ourselves. Krishnamurti observed, "Life is a movement of relationship."

The Enneagram of Personality is also very helpful in understanding someone else's personality patterns in relationship conflicts or where the other person is exhibiting unusual or antisocial behavioral patterns. It is useful to see from someone else's perspective, even if you do not agree or if you have a very different perspective.

In my personal experience, I was already aware of my main personality patterns from my practice of Vipassana, but knowledge of the Enneagram Personality Types filled in more detailed behavioral dynamics. I see each personality as viewing life from a particular perspective point on the Enneagram circle. That perspective is valid but not universal or total, as many feel their perspectives to be. As previously mentioned, personality may be regarded as our "relationship body" comparable to our physical body in that it may not be perfect and may contain both positive and negative features, but it is what we have, and we must try to use it the best way we can. If we realize that certain personality patterns are negative or destructive, it would be helpful to let go of those compulsions, which is where Vipassana comes in — the ability to be aware in each moment and to let go if necessary. If we can let go, then we are not confined in our responses to just one place on the circle but can move around the circle to appropriately respond as the challenge of the moment demands. There is no one-size-fits-all way to appropriately respond to life.

Certain personality types gravitate to certain roles, jobs, and activities and, thus, influence the perspectives of those particular communities. For example, many leadership positions in business and politics are filled by the Type 8 personality (the Boss or Leader) and by the Type 3 personality (the Achiever or Performer). The former exudes and wields power while the latter is focused on success and is persuasive, sometimes to the point of "bending" the truth or outright fabrications. Type 6 personalities gravitate to the police and military, Type 1s to teaching, Type 2s to the caring professions, and Type 4s to the arts.

Awareness of basic personality traits would help enormously in our collective decision-making, since some leaders act so predictably and compulsively according to their personality patterns. It could easily be taught in schools and universities as it is just knowledge. The process of actual change is more difficult since it requires letting go and non-attachment, which is a deeper process, as we have seen. I see the purpose of the Enneagram as enabling us to understand our deep conditioning patterns for the purpose of release and freedom from our compulsions. It should not be used to manipulate, exploit, or make excuses for bad behavior; it should not be used to pigeonhole people for the sake of convenience or manipulation.

Below are very brief sketches of each personality type, which may help readers recognize patterns in themselves or others. If such patterns exist, that means those forms of conditioning are determining behavior, probably at an unconscious level, regardless of what one thinks about the origins or validity of the Enneagram system. Many books have now been written about the Enneagram of Personality containing analyses and descriptions much more detailed than what I include here. I learned the system before books, in the original oral tradition.

The Type 1 personality is the Perfectionist, who is part of the inertia triad along with Type 8 and Type 9. They operate from gut instincts and share the feeling that life should be maintained in a certain way, which in the case of the Type 1s is "perfection." Growing up, they are the model "good boys and girls," trying to behave properly. They often have a picture in their heads of how things should be and strive for that, being critical of those who fall short of that notion of perfection, including themselves. Their attempts at perfection and self-improvement make them hardworking, detail-oriented, and self-reliant. They often see themselves as clearing up chaos and making things tidy and orderly. They have a respect for authority and tradition, often seeing some period in the past as a perfect "golden age."

Type 1s tend to be rigid in their views and often even in their bodies, being subject to muscular armoring. Their personal images of perfection are so powerful they find it difficult to comprehend that others do not share them. This can lead to blame, frustration, and anger, which they cannot permit themselves to show since that would not match up to the image of perfection. They can benefit from directly seeing that perfection is only an idea they carry, albeit a fundamental and compulsive one, which in the Enneagram system sometimes is called the "fixation."

For each personality, the fixation is the source of both positive and negative traits as it is their fundamental perspective on life, often what they see as the most important thing in life. In a sense, each personality is trying to justify its fixation and build ego-defenses around it, but this inevitably fails because that particular life perspective is not the totality, or whole, and also life changes so nothing can be grasped. When Type 1s disintegrate, they go towards the negative aspects of Type 4 (the Romantic/Artist), retreating within themselves. Healthy Type 1s are more sociable and relaxed, demonstrating some of the more positive traits of the Type 7 (the Idealist). In Enneagram terminology, "disintegration" refers to the personality coming under stress and going towards its negative tendencies. "Integration" is the personality being in a balanced and healthy state, able to resist its negative tendencies.

In society, many Type 1s are to be found in the teaching professions and among political conservatives. The English Protestant Puritans were examples of the Type 1 personality, being independent, hardworking, with a sense of righteousness, "pulling themselves up by their own bootstraps." Pleasure is postponed until after all the work they feel needs to be done is done. For some Type 1s, there is never any time for leisure or idling. As regards countries, China displays strong Type 1 personality traits. The Chinese have a respect for their ancestors and China's long and glorious history; they work hard and are self-sufficient. China is and will continue to be a global power, so it would be wise for other countries to understand their national characteristics and history, which includes exploitation by the Western industrialized powers over much of the last two centuries.

The Type 2 personality is called the Helper, Giver, or Independent. Type 2s, along with Type 3s (the Performer/Status-Seeker) and Type 4s, are in a different triad from Type 1s. They operate from the heart and are concerned about relationships and how they are seen or, in other words, their image. Type 2s in relationships need approval and want to be liked. They achieve this by trying to be empathetic and helpful, often adapting themselves to fit in with those around them. They often appear bubbly and entertaining and are generally very sociable and people-oriented; they are likeable and attractive people. They take quiet pride in others' reliance on them but tend to deny their own needs or make them of secondary importance; they also take pride in being associated with important people. Type 2s gravitate to the helping professions, often becoming nurses, social workers, or therapists; they may also be private secretaries to powerful people.

Despite their pride and their sense of being independent, Type 2s need positive feedback and approval. If they do not receive it, they may become deflated, resentful, and angry. Because they go out of their way to do things for others, they may sometimes feel that the recipients of their generosity take them for granted and expect too much from them. In relationships, Type 2s will often cater to their partner's needs and likes early on, but as the relationship continues, they may resent their dependence on their partners and rebel against them, wanting "freedom and independence." The pride of the Type 2s makes it very difficult for them to listen to even well-meaning advice, much less criticism. They often think along the lines of "I help others, and they need me; I don't need help." Their pride is often their stumbling block.

Just as the Type 1s need to acknowledge that they are not perfect and never will be, the Type 2s need to swallow their pride and acknowledge that much of what they do is to win the approval and affection of others and, in that sense, they are dependent; they need others. Type 2s can come to balance by acknowledging their own needs and setting boundaries for themselves; they can be helpful but need not be overly so. Healthy Type 2s are capable of spending more time by themselves, doing what pleases them, not others. In this way, they can be personable, fun, and helpful without any underlying motives or hidden needs. When Type 2s are disintegrating, they begin to show their anger and frustration.

The Type 3 personality, situated on the equilateral triangle, is at the center of the heart or image triad and is called the Performer, Achiever, or Status-Seeker. Image and status are of the utmost importance to the Type 3 and, therefore, "success" or peer group acclaim is continually sought. A one-time success is not enough, even if it brings financial security. Type 3s feel that they must always be busy, trying to achieve ever more to continue their success and peer admiration, whether measured by money, celebrity, power, or other. The Type 3 personality is often called the Performer, and as children they were probably praised for their achievements. For this personality, the greatest fear and avoidance is being seen as a failure, or "loser" in the current vernacular, as this would tarnish or damage the all-important image.

In addition, because the Type 3s are so good at manipulating the superficial trappings, images, and aspirations of everyday life, often "bending" the truth or even offering up "alternative truth," they can lose track of what is actually true or false, sometimes even questioning whether it even matters as long as they personally succeed. They can not only lose track of what is true but who they are, if anything, underneath their performance roles. The renowned English actor, Sir Laurence Olivier remarked:

> I am far from sure when I am acting and when I am not, or should I more frankly put it, when I am lying and when I am not. For what is acting but lying and what is good acting but convincing lying.

He also said that he knew how to play any role except how to play himself. Of all the Enneagram Personality Types, I have found the Type 3 to be the least attracted to Vipassana meditation, probably because it consists of quiet "not doing" and of delving ever deeper into what lies beneath the surface, which is often frightening for a Type 3. Vipassana also offers no chance of "success" and acclaim, since all attention is turned within as we take refuge in ourselves and right action for its own sake, not expecting reward or acclaim.

Type 3s are attracted to business, acting, media, marketing, sales, and, of course, politics, all of which largely depend on the art of persuasion. The United States is an obvious Type 3 country — successful, powerful, and admired, especially because of the image-making magic of its entertainment industry. The major Hollywood studios have been active since 1910, and their mood and decision manipulation skills pervade American culture and politics. The American dream is nothing if not the ultimate success story and it is influential not only in the United States but throughout much of the world, especially in the spheres of entertainment and popular culture.

An apposite, instructive, and somewhat concerning example of an extreme Type 3 personality leader and Type 3 country coming together is Donald Trump's entry into American politics and subsequent presidency. Early on, Trump openly boasted that he could do and say whatever he liked and would be able to persuade others to support him. On the 2016 campaign trail, he actually said, "I could stand in the middle of Fifth Avenue and shoot somebody, and I wouldn't lose any voters." Although it sounded outrageous at the time, Trump's core supporters, almost half of Americans, have stood by him through repeated outrageous and unprecedented personal presidential acts that would have long destroyed most politicians. These, of course, included an attempt to overturn the election of his successor, President Joe Biden, calling for an attack on Congress and attempting to overturn voting counts and procedures. He has also openly admired the power of authoritarian "strong men" and vowed to punish his political opponents.

If one pays attention, Trump's personality and manipulation playbook quickly become transparent: create an image and storyline, even if not based on fact; double down on it; never admit you are wrong; blame others, especially for what you yourself are doing, as it "muddies the waters" for many people; tell each particular audience what they want to hear, even if in doing so you contradict yourself; make simplistic appeals to people's basest, knee-jerk instincts, including race, gender, and religious prejudice; and divide and conquer. The only constant in this strategy is that Trump always focuses the attention on himself and puts his own interests first. This strategy works on those (very many) who do not pay consistent attention and/or want to believe him anyway so avoid any questioning, not unlike many believers in popular religion, which has already been discussed.

In a way Trump personifies a familiar, love-hate, American archetype — the snake oil salesman, carnival barker, the reality TV star; one who appears to be living the American dream and flaunting its excesses. At some level, many know what is being said is too good to be true or probably an outright lie, but they buy into it anyway. Trump and his core followers seem to represent America's ever-present shadow side, which goes back to the founding of the country. Trump is nothing without his audience, a feeling that Sir Laurence Olivier would no doubt have understood. He openly and repeatedly boasts about his crowd sizes and poll numbers.

According to the Enneagram system, Type 3 and Type 6 (the fear-based Loyalist) are related via the arrows of compulsion. Disintegrated Type 6s move to Type 3s, bringing their fears and reactivity with them, which makes for a volatile and unstable mix, especially as many Type 6s are in the army and police. Healthy Type 3s move towards the positive side of Type 6, displaying more loyalty to and caring for family and the greater community. Disintegrated Type 3s move to the negative side of Type 9, often collapsing into inertia, with some even unable to get out of bed.

The Type 4 personality is called the Tragic Romantic or the Artist and is the third and final personality in the feeling-image triad, acting from the heart and concerned with image and relationships. Most Type 4s feel a sense of loss, abandonment, or regret concerning the past; they might feel targeted by life for a tragic existence. They spend a lot of time imagining how life would be different if something had not happened to them or if they had acted differently in certain situations in the past. They tend to constantly ponder the many ways in which life might be different in the future and write scripts in their heads, which some Type 4s turn into their actual profession, becoming scriptwriters or authors.

This preoccupation with the past can spiral into moodiness, melancholy, and depression. Type 4s highly value feelings and emotions, and their introspection makes them feel different from other people — more sensitive and refined. However, this aloofness and withdrawal from the world can become a double-edged sword, making them different from and envious of others who seem to be leading relatively carefree and happy lives.

Because of their rich and active interior lives, Type 4s gravitate to the arts, especially writing, acting, painting, design, and high fashion. They often credit their suffering for inspiring their creativity, in some cases holding on to their mental and emotional pain even if it is damaging their health. Type 4s often find Vipassana meditation difficult since they are always thinking and find it difficult to let go of it or to distinguish thinking that they are meditating from actually meditating, which, of course, does not require thought.

Many Type 4s yearn for a future, passionate, real, authentic, romantic relationship. Under stress, Type 4s move towards the dependency of Type 2s, hoping for a "white knight" to ride in to rescue them. Balanced and integrated Type 4s move towards the hard work and practicality of the Type 1s. It is good for them to work more with the body rather than just the mind, to embrace the ordinariness of getting things done in the everyday world. Much of the Type 4s' ruminations focus on finding "authenticity," which is to be found not in the merry-go-round of their minds but in participation in the real world around them.

The Type 5 Enneagram personality is the Observer and is probably the most private and reclusive of the nine personality types. The Type 5 likes to observe life from a safe distance, free from emotional involvements, relationships, competition, and obligations. Social situations and interpersonal contact are uncomfortable for many Type 5s and are often avoided for the comfort and safety of home. The Type 5 is part of the head-fear (thinking) triad and uses observation of the world to try to understand and predict it in an attempt to exercise some control over it. Type 5s often read and research a wide variety of topics, collecting and storing bits and pieces of useful information, which often makes them excellent intellectuals and scholars. They know a little bit of everything and are good at integrating information. They tend to limit material possessions and comforts in order to simplify their lives and their dependence on others.

Type 5s' constant detached observation of life may eventually make them feel isolated and trapped. Their treasured privacy may turn into loneliness and isolation. They often do not know how or are afraid to reach out to others; they may be cut off from their own emotions after spending so much time in their heads. Type 5s may have great ideas and insights but feel afraid to test them in the nitty-gritty of everyday life, lest they be proven wrong or incorrect in their thinking.

When Type 5s disintegrate under stress, they go to Type 7 (the Idealist), getting lost and trapped in their own world of ideas, ideals, and fantasies. Healthy Type 5s begin to demonstrate the assertiveness and power of Type 8s (the Boss/Leader), daring to test their knowledge in the competition of the real world, opening themselves to social interaction, engagement, competition, and possible rejection. Instead of just observing life, healthy Type 5s also more fully partake in life. They walk their talk.

Type 6 is called the Adventurer, the Loyalist, or the Devil's Advocate. As the Type 6 is at the heart of the fear-thinking triad, fear plays a major role in the personality, which is probably the most reactive and seemingly contradictory in the Enneagram system. Type 6s are distrustful of any form of authority (apart from their own adopted ones) and instinctively react against it, hence the description of them as the devil's advocate. The authority may be the government, political party, or religion, but it could also be just something in casual conversation that sparks the defensive reaction and counterattack.

When I first started offering Vipassana meditation classes to the general public, there would often be at least one person in the group questioning and challenging why it was necessary to sit on a cushion or cross-legged, even though this was just my suggestion, not a compulsory requirement. They were invariably Type 6s and I was seen as an authority figure, which they did not fully trust even though they had enrolled for classes of their own volition. Their constant scrutiny and judgment were palpable.

Type 6s may be either phobic and openly fearful or counter-phobic, trying to conquer their fears and demonstrate it to the world. The latter often engage in mind-over-matter activities like marathons, triathlons, mountain climbing, and martial arts.

The Type 6s are also called the Loyalist because even though they react against authority generally, they are seeking an authority of their own that they can trust (to the best of their ability). Once they find that authority, they will be loyal to it and try to protect it. Many counter-phobic Type 6s gravitate to the police, firefighting, and the armed forces because it allows them to fight their fears through dangerous physical activities while fighting for a just cause or authority. Loyalty and obeying orders are expected in those organizations, which also suit the Type 6 personality as they do not have to continually question it.

The Type 6 personality is also called the Adventurer because it is restless, always wanting to try something new. This is caused by their constant anxiety, self-doubt, and need for stimulation to occupy their minds. They continually scan their environment for potential threats, but their attention is selective, and often they may spot something that they blow out of proportion as a potential threat, resulting in a form of paranoia. They are given to projection, blaming others for what they themselves feel. Even if a Type 6 personality is in a reasonably settled life situation, there is always the temptation to move on to try to find something that is even better, safer, and more stimulating.

As mentioned earlier, degenerated, under-stress Type 6s move towards the negative aspects of Type 3 (the Performer), getting lost in fear and lies, and possibly lashing out. Balanced and integrated Type 6s display the positive aspects of the Type 9 personality, which is the Peace Maker and Mediator. They begin to realize that their fears cannot be conquered if not acknowledged and faced, which is a difficult first step for them. Acceptance of the fact of their own fears makes accepting others easier; calm and the feeling of being more settled and stable may gradually replace their constant struggle and reaction.

The Type 7 personality is called the Idealist or Epicure and is the third and final personality in the fear-thinking triad. They fight their fears by being compulsive optimists and idealists and by having a good time. Pleasure is highly valued and indulged. They are sociable, lighthearted, charming, smiling, eloquent, and good storytellers. They feel themselves to be special, some perhaps even enlightened, and tend to spend their time making idealistic and visionary plans for the future. As spiritual teachers, their ideals and charismatic delivery make them very appealing, especially since they tend to avoid mentioning anything negative. They ignore the dark side of reality and shy away from hard work, difficulties, and pain. Type 7s often seek groups of the like-minded to keep up their positive outlook and spirits and to have fun together.

The hippie and counter-culture movement of the 1960s and 1970s very much reflected the Type 7 perspectives and worldview. The flower child was a symbol of peace and love. "Make love not war" was a major rallying call, and many dropped out of the conventional rat race and joined the like-minded in idealistic hippie communes. Drugs and especially psychedelics offered not only pleasurable "highs" but a promise of expansion of spiritual consciousness.

Type 7s are now commonly found in New Age communities and in globalist, charitable, and ecological organizations. A few years ago, my wife, Nicola, and I hosted members of a well-known environmental group at Harmony Dawn. We were surprised that few of them had meditated or were even interested in self-inquiry. We were more than surprised when they partied late past midnight, not only keeping us awake but rummaging through our private cupboards for wine glasses and music CDs. They were surprised when we reprimanded them because they were caught up just having fun. Several environmental groups we hosted were interested in improving the external natural environment but did not pay much attention to their own inner environment, the source of all their perspectives and choices.

Because of their fear of commitment and the routine, hard work needed to get things done, the grand, idealistic plans of Type 7s often fail to materialize. They may then display the anger and frustration of the Type 1 (the Perfectionist) or may become more narcissistic, focusing on their own well-being and pleasure. The more balanced and integrated Type 7s go to the positive side of Type 5 (the Observer), turning inward and allowing themselves to stay in the present, accepting and examining what they normally avoid, such as fear, boredom, and hard work. In other words, it is beneficial for them to adopt a practice like Vipassana meditation, which they normally find difficult and boring.

The Type 8 personality is the Boss, Leader, or Justice Maker and is in the gut-inertia triad together with the Type 1 (the Perfectionist) and Type 9 (the Peace Maker). Type 8s admire and seek power and strength, avoiding what they see as any weakness in themselves. They see themselves as using their power to protect and guarantee justice for those in their community or group. They do not shy away from conflict or from expressing their anger and will deliberately push people to see how they will react. Their view is survival of the fittest and strongest, and they like to be in control. They tend to see situations in simplistic terms of black or white, right or wrong. They are often physically powerful and imposing. Many bosses and leaders are Type 8s, since people are commonly drawn to their display of strength and power. Many lawyers and gang members, like the Hells Angels, are Type 8s.

The negative aspect of the Type 8 personality is that they suppress any tenderness, softness, sensitivity, or compassion in themselves as signs of weakness. This affects their ability to love and be loved, causing them to withdraw and perhaps compensate with sensual excess in food, drink, sex, and drugs. Also, their idea of right and wrong is subjective and instinctive, not much tested by the heart or head, and in imposing it on others, they may become bullying and abusive.

Type 8s come to balance by realizing that their idea of justice is not shared by everyone else and that listening, empathizing, and reasoning is not weakness. Indeed, this will make them better informed and more empathetic bosses and leaders. It will also open them up to real relationships rather than controlling ones. When Type 8s deteriorate, they withdraw within and isolate themselves.

The final Enneagram Personality Type is Type 9, who is the Mediator or Peace Maker and is at the heart of the gut-inertia triad. They want everything and everybody to be settled and peaceful. They like routine, detailed, impersonal work and shy away from unpredictable interactions with others and from decision-making, which they find stressful. Even when there is work to be done, they may get distracted by trivia, perhaps gravitating to "couch potato" TV mode, games, and crossword or jigsaw puzzles. Many accountants, dentists, judges, and bureaucrats are Type 9s.

Type 9s often have a sense of having been overlooked and not heard, so they are reluctant to assert their own opinions. This makes them good at listening to and understanding the opinions of others. Seeing all sides of a situation also makes it easier for them to not have a personal perspective or priority. They are not good self-starters but will allow themselves to be led into new activities and ventures if others take the initiative and encourage them along.

Type 9s under stress will demonstrate the negative aspects of the Type 6 (Loyalist/Devil's Advocate) personality, becoming anxious and indecisive and, therefore, looking for some structure, group, or belief system in which to shelter. They may react with increasing passive aggression. Integrated and healthy Type 9s begin to realize that true peace is not just the lack of superficial turbulence but results from full inquiry into the elements of any conflict, even if this process is initially uncomfortable. They become more confident in undertaking new projects and ventures, going to the positive side of the Type 3 (the Achiever) personality.

The main perspective or fixation of each personality has some validity but cannot be made to work for all situations, since it is just one point on the circle of life. In order to move around the circle and obtain other perspectives and strategies, each personality must learn to let go of those personality compulsions that lock them into unhealthy negativity. This means that they must first acknowledge that quality or aspect of themselves they usually avoid or deny. Knowledge of the Enneagram Personality Types can help us quickly identify healthy and unhealthy patterns in ourselves and others, which is most useful in navigating meaningful and impactful relationships, whether intimate, family, personal, professional, or political.

However, it must be remembered that actual change can only come through letting go of old patterns and compulsions. We can only change ourselves. While we cannot change others, we can much better understand them if we are able to stand in their shoes and speak their particular personality language, which may be very different from our own.

REALIZING A DREAM

I have recounted that I met my present wife, Nicola, in 1998, five years after Yolind and I separated. In the first few months of our relationship, we agreed on so many issues that I began to be suspicious. Was she just feeding my own opinions and preferences back to me? It seemed uncanny. Over time, I began to realize that maybe we were indeed kindred spirits or even "soul mates," and that she was a gem that I had stumbled upon. She was not only very attractive, but also obviously intelligent, intuitive, creative, hardworking, sociable, and loving. Astonishingly, we never argued. She had an absurd British sense of humor that I shared. She enthusiastically attended most of the classes I taught, especially *taijiquan*, qigong, and Vipassana meditation, and we practiced in our private time together. She wholeheartedly embraced my daughters as well as my Chinese and Guyanese backgrounds, especially the cuisines, as she was a foodie. What more could I want? Time has answered that question — not much, if anything.

Very early in our relationship, I shared with Nicola my vision or dream of someday building an off-grid, sustainable-energy house in the country, which could initially serve as a retreat center and later a retirement home for us and a country refuge for our children and any future grandchildren. I had been attracted by the notion of sustainable living as early as the 1970s while living in London, but the technology then was rudimentary and impractical. About a year before I met Nicola, my daughters and I had visited an off-grid house in our Toronto neighborhood that had just won a national, Canadian "Healthy House" design competition. I was very surprised and inspired by the advancements in sustainable technology, which was now more practical and affordable, even if still more expensive than building a conventional house.

I had no intention of acting on my vision at that time, since I was only forty-nine years old and quite happy living in Toronto and teaching at the nearby Tai Chi and Meditation Centre that I had founded. Nicola, however, was really excited about my dream of an off-grid house in the country and suggested that we should at least start looking at properties to see what was available and at what price range. I saw no harm in looking, especially as it gave us a reason to get out of the city and enjoy country road trips.

In determining our search area, we drew a semi-circle around Toronto, since its southern border was Lake Ontario. We figured that any property functioning as a retreat center should be within a reasonable driving distance from Toronto, taking into account the many weekend cottagers who pour out of Toronto in all directions. Any property should also be affordable, of course, and meet certain feng shui requirements that we had determined, like being near a lake or river, having a pleasing mix of forests and meadows, and preferably having some undulation. I knew something about feng shui from the yin-yang principles inherent in *taijiquan*, qigong, and traditional Chinese medicine. Nicola had recently taken a feng shui course and had a certification in it.

We spent a few months looking at properties, mostly farmhouses, throughout our search zone and eventually gravitated to Northumberland County, about an hour-and-a-half drive north-east of Toronto. Properties were generally cheaper there and it featured rolling hills, rivers, and lakes, reminiscent of Northumberland in north-east England. This seemed somewhat synchronous since Yolind's mother, Anne, was from that area and Miss Li also lived and started teaching *taijiquan* there.

Eventually, in 1999, we found a fifty-acre property without any buildings that ticked most of our boxes and seemed perfect — accessibility from Toronto, a central hill surrounded by meadows and mature woodlands, and within walking distance of Rice Lake, a popular fishing destination. Years later, the vendor, and by then our neighbor and friend, revealed that our estate agent had told her what we were looking for and she severed her hundred-acre property to fit our requirements. She also sold us three acres on the lake itself. The land was comparatively cheap at that time, since it was regarded as agricultural and not very good for that purpose. Our intention for the property was quite different. We put in a basic dirt road on the main property and contemplated building a small cabin on the lakeside property when we had some extra money.

Another Wake-Up Call

September 11, 2001, was a shock to the system for many people, including Nicola and me. For me, the shock was not only seeing planes crashing into the Twin Towers in New York City, but also how quickly and profoundly the American psyche was shaken. Yes, the attacks were unprecedented — three thousand people died and the economy took a dive — but it was not a national attack, invasion, or war. I was afraid that the United States would overreact, and they did, which is not a good sign for a superpower possessing a nuclear arsenal and the mightiest military in the world. Polls show that after the terrorist attacks, seventy-seven percent of Americans wanted some kind of military retaliation, and President George W. Bush duly obliged them with an invasion of Iraq, which was not involved with the 9/11 attacks. By the end of the Iraq invasion and war, seven thousand Americans and over 200,000 Iraqis were dead; the United States spent well over $100 billion on the war and reconstruction.

What disturbed me besides the terrorist attack itself was the obvious (to me) growing propensity for U.S. government officials and politicians at the highest levels to consciously mislead their citizens for dubious personal or partisan motives. I have already mentioned the Bush administration's largely successful and destructive attempts to debunk climate science and, therefore, the fact of climate change itself. The oil industry was an early and major force in promoting global warming denial, and both presidents George H. W. and George W. Bush had deep ties to and financial interests in the Texas oil industry. Frank Luntz's infamous memo advising George W. Bush how to discredit the solid scientific evidence concerning global warming occurred in 2002, about the same time the Bush-Cheney administration started spreading disinformation about Iraq.

The decision to invade Iraq was logically groundless and the deliberate deception of the public was blatant. Unable to prove any links with the 9/11 attacks, the administration alleged that Iraq had weapons of mass destruction (WMDs), which could possibly be nuclear, chemical, or biological. It was clear to me, even looking on from Canada, that there was no proof of WMDs and that the Bush administration was "cherry picking" intelligence information to justify a war with Iraq that they clearly intended to initiate. Indeed, the director general of the BBC at the time, Greg Dyke, went uncharacteristically public by declaring that America has "no news operation strong enough or brave enough to stand up against the White House and Pentagon" and that American news networks "wrapped themselves in the American flag and swapped impartiality for patriotism." I wrote about the folly of invading Iraq in my 2003 book, *Ageless Wisdom Spirituality: Investing in Human Evolution*, years before most "experts" openly acknowledged that fact.

It did not help dispel appearances of doubtful propriety and suspicions of ulterior motives that Vice President Dick Cheney seemed to be exercising undue influence in decision-making. Haliburton, a company from which Cheney resigned as CEO to become Vice President, received a $7-billion contract to service troops in Iraq while no other companies were allowed to bid. Cheney was defense secretary under H. W. Bush (George W.'s father) and played a big role in sending U.S. troops to Iraq in 1991 after it attacked Kuwait. The Iraqi army suffered a swift and major defeat, and second-guessers subsequently questioned why the United States did not remove Saddam Hussein then, especially when, in 1993, Hussein was blamed by U.S. intelligence for an assassination plot against H. W. Bush. Some suggest that George W. Bush and Cheney both had personal reasons to avenge H. W. Bush by removing and eventually killing Saddam Hussein.

I already knew that most societies, despite general public complacency, rested on fragile foundations. However, 9/11 and its aftermath surprised me by the scope and speed of the volatility it engendered, especially in the world's most powerful and ostensibly stable country. U.S. politics and decision-making also seemed to be getting steadily more polarized and volatile, which would, of course, impact other countries, especially its neighbor and major trading partner, Canada. In hindsight, it seems that the Republican party decided back then to continue its policies of disinformation and division because they appeared to be effective in consolidating its dwindling base. These policies exploded into the open during the Trump era.

Nicola and I sensed major winds of change approaching and decided that our dream sustainable, off-grid, rural retreat needed to be built sooner rather than later! We liquidated and mortgaged most of our assets and again took a plunge into the unknown, initiating the design and subsequent building process, hoping we would somehow have enough funds to complete our project. It reminded me in some ways of another plunge I took when I decided to leave the business world to try and become a *taijiquan* and meditation teacher eighteen years earlier.

Building with Green and Subtle Energy

Nicola and I wanted to use yin-yang principles not only in the selection of our land but also in the placement of our building and in the design of the building itself. We wanted a unique building that would incorporate both the latest sustainable, green energy technology and age-old, subtle energy (qi) principles, not only for our own private benefit and enjoyment, but also as an example of what is possible for any future retreat guests who might want to build their own sustainable houses. We felt that if people felt truly safe, comfortable, and well nourished (food was an important part of what we offered), it would make them curious about the intentions and strategies that went into creating our unique retreat center. Hopefully, without being told or lectured, they would naturally experience the power of its underlying yin-yang principles, which had also been the foundation of my decades-long teaching of *taijiquan*, qigong, and, in a sense, Vipassana meditation. Vipassana is, of course, normally associated with

Theravada Buddhism rather than Daoism, but from my experience, Buddhism and Daoism undoubtedly overlap.

Having initially consulted with several leaders in the green design field, we were fortunate to eventually meet a newly qualified green architect, Carolyn Moss, who was open to and enthusiastic about meshing as many sustainability principles as possible with our ideas on feng shui, functionality, and aesthetics. It was a wonderfully creative process.

Based on my retreat experience, I originally envisioned three separate buildings linked by walkway greenhouses. They would function respectively as a studio or meditation hall, a central sleeping and living area, and a kitchen-dining area. However, local regulations stipulated we could only have one building and Carolyn determined that there was not enough southern exposure for the "greenhouses" to successfully function as such.

We finally created one building with three separate areas as planned, each set back a bit from the other to increase air and qi flow, since qi moves like air and water. The central part, which contained the living room, washrooms, and bedrooms, was a three-storied, cedar-shingled, wood-framed building with a sloping metal roof that was not dissimilar in appearance to some others in the locality. We did not want this internally unconventional house to look obviously weird from the outside.

The central section of the building was conventionally built, but very well insulated with blown insulation, a strategy Carolyn called "tight and light." The ground flooring consisted of large, dark slate tiles to capture solar heat; the upper floors were bamboo, which is hard-wearing but grows much faster than traditional hardwood. A central staircase wound around the stack of a wood-burning masonry fireplace, the heat from which rose upwards through a gap around the stack to supply heat to the upper floors. Above the stack was an openable skylight to vent the summer heat upwards through the roof, a strategy long used in many hot countries. All of this was low tech but highly effective. It utilized thoughtful design rather than expensive materials and active technology.

The central, conventional-looking building was flanked on either side by modules with flat, water-collecting roofs, cinder-block outer walls covered by rigid insulation and stucco, and south-facing, floor-to-ceiling windows, which Carolyn described as the "mass and glass" building approach. They featured concrete floors heated by built-in hot-water tubes. The inner-facing sides of the cinder blocks were not covered over so that they and the concrete floors could function as "heat sinks," absorbing direct sunlight and later radiating the captured solar heat back into the building.

All three modules of the building faced true south to maximize the capture of solar energy, not only for active energy through our solar panels, but also for passive energy to heat the concrete floors and the interior of the cinder-block walls. All the windows minimized outward heat loss. We tried to give all south-facing windows some form of permanent awning to minimize the sun hitting the floors in the summer. In the winter, the sun is lower in the sky and penetrates deeper into the building, providing more passive solar heat.

We protected the cold northern side of the building by having smaller windows and by partially "berming" the ground floor and basement with earth pushed up against the building. This passively used the constant, deep ground temperature to provide heat in the winter and cooling in the summer. Carolyn explained that at a depth of at least 3 meters, or about 10 feet, the temperature of the earth is a constant 13 degrees Celsius, or 55 degrees Fahrenheit. As I write in 2024, with global and local heat records being regularly broken, that 55-degrees number recently came to my attention. An article pointed out that in the Australian town of Coober Pedy, which operated as an opal mine, most of the 2,500 inhabitants live underground in old mine shafts and tunnels using that 55 degrees Fahrenheit. The outside summer temperatures there reach 126 degrees Fahrenheit. The article also mentioned the underground cities in Cappadocia in central Turkey, which date from the eighth century. These were built not only to utilize the constant earth temperature, but also to protect inhabitants from invaders.

Amazingly, we were able to combine the green technology elements described above with the feng shui principles in a most pleasing win-win manner. In situating the building, we used the five-element theory — fire to the south, water to the north, metal to the west, wood to the east, and earth at the center, where you stand. What more fire is there than the sun's energy absorbed from the south? Directly north of our building is the ample water energy of nearby Rice Lake and the building's north-side "berming" provided a protective "turtle shell," the animal associated with water energy and the ancestors. The western side of the building is dug into the top of the hill, providing metal energy. To the east is woodland and a seasonal stream to provide movement and flow. The view southwards from the building is very peaceful and pleasing, featuring an open, flat grassy meadow with wildflowers surrounded by undulating woodland that slopes downwards to a small ravine. The feeling is open and spacious but not exposed, being protected on all sides by trees.

The interior of the building was designed to facilitate both horizontal and vertical air flow for feng shui purposes as well as for preventing stagnant and toxic air. We stayed away from carpeting and the use of chemical cleaning products to limit any noxious gas emissions. The light from the large south windows compensated for the smaller ones to the north. We tried to limit the size of the building's footprint but compensated with ceilings at least eight feet high, even in our extensive basement. The earthiness of the slate tiles, cinder-block walls, and concrete floors was balanced by the woodiness of light pine doors, stairs, and wood trim. Walls within the central module were painted white, all of which gave the building a simple and natural Scandinavian-Japanese feel.

The building, just by its design, moderates heat and cold evenly throughout the changing seasons so that comparatively little active energy input is needed, even though we sometimes hosted groups of up to twenty-two. In the beginning, our renewable energy sources were a small wind turbine and some solar panels. We later sold the former because it broke down and the manufacturers were by then only building much bigger ones not suitable for our property. Instead, we increased our solar array when we had the necessary funds, and they worked very well. Over time, the cost of solar panels fell thanks largely to growing Chinese output.

Our non-renewable energy sources consist of propane and diesel. The propane provides hot water for the showers, for the kitchen, and for heating the floors and washrooms. The diesel fuels our backup generator when there is not enough sun, usually during the months of December and January. The generator is normally not used at all for six months of the year. The system works very well and is dependable, which is important, as we offer accommodation to groups averaging between fourteen and twenty guests. Our masonry fireplace uses only wood from fallen trees on our property and is not very much needed as we burn just over half a cord of wood per season, which is unheard of in our locality. A cord is a pile of wood that is eight feet by four feet by four feet.

In August 2003, just before our building was completed, fifty million people in the eastern parts of the United States and Canada lost power because a branch fell on some power lines and the software alarm system failed. Our building workers at that time were unaware of a blackout until they returned home. It was a timely reminder of changing times. Since then, extreme weather conditions have several times caused power outages in our area, but usually we are not aware of them unless someone tells us.

Harmony Dawn

Two thousand and three was a momentous year in our lives, not only because we completed the construction of our retreat center building, but also because of something that, in hindsight, assumed much greater significance — the outbreak of SARS (severe acute respiratory syndrome). SARS was a warning about just how rapidly infectious diseases could spread around the world because of air travel. The Covid-19 pandemic, which started in 2020 and killed over seven million people worldwide, was a type of SARS. On a personal level, SARS permanently decimated the student numbers of our Tai Chi and Meditation Centre in Toronto, because the general public, spooked by news coming mainly from the United States, associated SARS with anything Chinese related, even in Canada. The Chinese students in our organization could be counted on the fingers of one hand.

The grand opening of our retreat center was held in early October 2003 and was greeted not only by enthusiastic guests but also by a complete double rainbow, which recurred on that same weekend in October for several years afterwards. We called our retreat "Harmony Dawn" because my three daughters shared a common Chinese name, "Shu," which means "dawn." Their names are Shuwen, Shuwei, and Shuhan, respectively meaning "tinted clouds of dawn," "dawn glow," and "dawn blossom." Dawn is when light begins to manifest and grow. The "Harmony" part was a reference to my yin-yang background and teaching. The name expressed a hope that our retreat — activities, buildings, land, and guests — would help encourage or accelerate the growth of a wiser and more compassionate human consciousness and way of being.

Our dream manifested slowly as there were less than ten retreats (including two of my own) booked at Harmony Dawn in the first year and there was still some final finishing work to be done to the building. Despite trying to cut financial corners by buying a used battery bank and generator, our funds were exhausted, and we were forced to sell our house in Toronto.

Nicola and I moved from Toronto to Harmony Dawn in the spring of 2005 with little idea of what to expect of our retreat center and no experience of country living, since both of us had always lived in big cities. It was another step into the unknown. Moving from a big, bright, and noisy city to the dark and silent countryside was unsettling at first. Moreover, we were away from family and friends and had only a few retreats booked. We had moved into our dream house, but now what were we supposed to do with ourselves? Neither of us were ready or had the funds for retirement.

A few weeks after moving to Harmony Dawn, Nicola had an enlightening experience. Standing in our kitchen, her personal power spot, she said she suddenly felt a "bolt of lightning" shoot through her head and body and had a sense of some sort of "seismic shift" as if her personal universe was realigning itself. She then clearly felt that, somehow, she was now in the right and proper place and time in her life. A few days later, telephone inquiries started pouring in, even though we had not done any additional advertising or reaching out. We both intuitively felt that by moving to Harmony Dawn permanently, we had made a true commitment, which then caused a major shift in our lives. That was not the first time that commitment had made a pivotal difference to my own life path. I likened it to getting married, committing to Buddhism and *taijiquan*, starting to teach, and then having to recommit when my seafood business collapsed in the early days of teaching and I began to doubt myself.

Our retreat groups rapidly increased to the point that most weekends were booked. This was a great relief because it seemed that our vision was indeed resonating with people, and on a more practical level, it was a source of income to pay our bills and hopefully save something for our retirement since neither Nicola nor I had pension plans. We also loved our life at Harmony Dawn. A win-win-win situation!

We closed for December and January because of the holiday festivities and the inclement winter weather, which made our half-kilometer, hilly driveway difficult for city drivers, especially since many had no snow tires. Most of our groups were yoga, but we also hosted meditation, environmental, and inter-religious groups. I did a few meditation and tai chi-qigong workshops every year, and the demand for them increased over time.

Nicola and I, by popular demand, offered hands-on Harmony Dawn cooking workshops since groups loved our cuisine, and several individual guests had told us that they returned to Harmony Dawn mainly for the food. Guests wanted to learn how we cooked. One guest, who regularly traveled to resorts around the world, said that Harmony Dawn cuisine was the best food she had ever experienced. Nicola wrote two Harmony Dawn cookbooks, which were and still are very popular — *The Dao of Harmony Dawn Cooking* and *Eco Harmony Dawn Cooking: Balancing Your Internal and External Environments*. I wrote the first chapter of the latter book.

Although we loved the fact that our guests loved our food, there was method in our proverbial cuisine madness. Food was and is a big part of Harmony Dawn because we both knew from personal experience over decades just how important it is to one's health, along with mind-body exercises. Indeed, everyday eating has long been regarded as herbal medicine in traditional Chinese medicine, a perspective that is slowly gaining traction among Western medical communities. Our cooking workshops always featured two introductory Vipassana sessions as well as one on qigong. We encouraged our participants to improve their nutrition knowledge, their kitchen skills, and rediscover the joy of cooking and eating in the company of others, which has long been the tradition in so many countries. We also suggested that families make a conscious effort to take time to regularly cook and eat together.

As in the building itself, we used yin-yang principles of balance without being obvious or trying to advertise it, applying them not only in East Asian cuisine, but also in foods from around the world. In my mid-twenties, I became a vegetarian for a couple of years before gravitating to a diet based on yin-yang principles of balance. I felt that, as a vegetarian, I was not getting enough protein to fuel me for all my martial arts training. I started eating fish and seafood but no meat and chicken. I also drastically reduced my intake of dairy and sugar and tried to eat brown rather than white (processed) flour and rice. The composition of my diet for decades has approximated recently recommended portions of grains, proteins, fruit, and vegetables. It has served me very well (together with my mind-body practices) as my health to this point has been excellent. I have never spent a single night in a hospital bed.

When Nicola and I met, she embraced my diet and added her own food experience and expertise, having cooked from a young age and worked in the restaurant business. She is an excellent baker and has always had an eye for beautiful food presentation, especially in the use of different colors. We now know that nutrition experts recommend eating foods of a variety of colors, as that represents different plant-produced nutrients, or more technically, phytonutrients or antioxidants. This is another form of food balance that can be easily understood and implemented.

There is now broad agreement among nutrition and medical experts on how to eat healthily, taking into account worldwide cuisines. The problem is getting people to accept and embrace change, as we have already discussed in several different contexts in this book. Experts say that healthy eating is more of a lifestyle rather than trying to stick to specific diets or superfoods. From personal experience, I would wholeheartedly agree, since in my youth I loved meat, processed foods like bacon and pepperoni, soft drinks (pop), and salty and sugary foods, all of which I devoured in large quantities. I have not missed or craved any of that once I clearly decided to change my eating habits. I try to listen to my body rather than my mind, which like everyone else's is continually assaulted by marketing. I have found that what is right and appropriate for me has subtly changed as I have aged. It is not a matter of "one size fits all" forever.

The most recommended diet is the Mediterranean diet, which many deem to also include a balanced Chinese- and Japanese-style diet. In terms of proportions, about half your food intake should be fruits and vegetables (of many colors), one quarter a variety of healthy grains (preferably not white or processed), and one quarter a mixture of healthy proteins, including lean meat, but also chicken, seafood, nuts, seeds, beans, and pulses.

The standard American diet is regarded as generally unhealthy as it contains too much fat, salt and sodium, sugar, red meat, and processed and refined foods, which in themselves already contain salt, sugar, and additives. Poor diet in the United States causes over $50 billion annually in health-care costs, much of that to treat heart disease, stroke, diabetes, and obesity. It is estimated that about 75 percent of Americans are either overweight or obese. Poor diet can cause a variety of diseases, including cancers, and even affect mental health. As a recent example, a study presented at the 2024 Alzheimer's Association International Conference found that risk of dementia increased by 14 percent when people ate one ounce of processed red meat per day, equivalent to two three-ounce servings a week, compared to people who ate three servings a month. If the one ounce of daily consumed processed red meat was replaced by nuts and legumes, the risk of dementia fell by 20 percent. Red meat has been strongly linked with colon and other cancers, diabetes, heart disease, and stroke, while nuts and legumes are anti-inflammatory foods.

Americans generally eat more protein than they actually need, and much of that is in the form of meat, which negatively impacts personal health and the production of which adds to greenhouse gas emissions, especially carbon dioxide and methane. Everything is interconnected, as we have seen. If we do the little, fundamental things right, then we do not get big problems later, to paraphrase the *Daodejing*. Nothing is more fundamental than eating, except perhaps breathing.

Many of our return guest groups are now like family and, indeed, many of them say that coming to Harmony Dawn each time is like "coming home." They have learned theories about sustainable living and live it at Harmony Dawn. They economize on water usage, turn off lights when not in use, and try not to use too much power at night and early in the morning to conserve our battery bank until the sun comes up. They are happy to share bedrooms and washrooms, a practice we predict will be a necessity in the future. The food they enjoy is not only delicious, but also balanced and nourishing in the best ways. A win-win situation all around.

Our guests give Nicola and me much in return. They punctuate the peace and silence of our normal lives with stimulating interaction, sharing, and often genuine, deep affection. We also learn from them. Several early guests taught us about the geology and history of our property and its surroundings. We discovered that the many oval, undulating hills of our local Northumberland County are called drumlins, deposits left behind by glacial ice flow. Our building actually sits on a drumlin, and apparently the trees on one side of the drumlin are slightly different from those on the other side. Rice Lake, which our building overlooks, was part of a popular travel and trading route for Indigenous peoples, and the lake itself teemed with wild rice and fish. One of the last major inter-tribal battles in North America was fought in the immediate vicinity of our property. At present, the Hiawatha First Nation is just north of us across Rice Lake and the Alderville First Nation is to the south. Both are Michisaagig

Anishnaabeg (Mississauga Nations of the Ojibway). A guest who was an archeologist found ancient stone tools on our property and guessed that the reason we built where we did, on a hill overlooking a bountiful lake, would have also motivated people to settle here over past millennia.

A few years after our opening of Harmony Dawn, we noticed that one of our group's guests, who happened to be a renowned Quebec shaman, was lying and convulsing under the ancient oak tree behind our building. Nicola and I considered calling the emergency services, but the shaman got up not long afterwards. During the lunch break, she approached us and said that, in her trance, the ancestors, animals, and even rocks wanted her to tell us that they all blessed our efforts in creating and offering Harmony Dawn as a retreat and healing place. She said that according to her wisdom tradition, we had placed our building (albeit using Chinese feng shui principles) in the best place possible, being in the middle of a giant medicine wheel, the center of which was just in front of our studio, where all our groups did their practices. In 2009, Nicola and I got married in the center of the medicine wheel and our guests danced there.

Even though we did not display any religious or esoteric symbols apart from some depictions of the Buddha, which are now part of popular culture, some guests on first entering our building have remarked that they immediately felt a sense of awe or something radically different. Some said it was like entering a temple. A Shaolin master who was a guest teacher at a retreat, immediately sensed that "feng shui masters" had created the building and wanted to meet them. Nicola and I humbly owned up to our feng shui input into the building design.

Perhaps one of the most surprising and unexpected of such interactions occurred when one of the guests excitedly came up to our kitchen window, waving a copy of my *Ageless Wisdom Spirituality*, which she said covered many topics she and her husband had been discussing. They were Canadian but living in Houston, Texas. When we asked why they decided to live there, she said her husband was an astronaut (Jeremy Hansen), who would be part of the Artemis II moon orbit scheduled for 2024 (but now delayed). The fact of Jeremy being an astronaut had enhanced their global views and sense of interconnectedness of the planet. He wanted to be able to speak meaningfully about this in any upcoming media opportunities. Our guest was Dr. Catherine Hansen, who has now given up her OB-GYN medical practice to help her patients in a broader and more meaningful way than just treating their physical symptoms.

A New Life Stage

Moving to the country and operating an off-grid retreat center would represent a big change for anyone, but in my case, it also represented a deepening of my spiritual life and connection to nature. In hindsight, I reflected that Chinese astrology considers that one has lived a "full life" at the age of sixty, having experienced the twelve animals of the Chinese zodiac going through the stages of the five elements. After that, one begins a new life. Nicola and I moved to the country when I was fifty-six and we got married in 2009, when I was exactly sixty years old. Our wedding was not planned to accord with astrology but came about because we felt the time was right.

Although I had meditated almost every day of my life since 1974, mostly in cities, the pervasive silence and harmonious mixture of trees and meadows at Harmony Dawn automatically deepened my meditations and everyday awareness. We are influenced by our environments, both natural and human-created, so the external silence and spaciousness facilitated our internal silence and spaciousness. The nearest house is almost half a kilometer away, and there are no streetlights, so the sky is dark and the stars are bright. There is much physical work to be done in maintaining our property, but it does not require much thinking, just awareness, and can be done in mindful silence. Nicola and I try to meditate and do our *taijiquan* together daily. We are together at Harmony Dawn all day and every day (apart from occasional trips to the city), but we have our separate jobs as well as the jobs we share, like cooking, cleaning, and property maintenance. Nicola loves gardening. We still do not have any arguments.

My personal spiritual practice also benefited from leading more meditation retreats at Harmony Dawn. They not only increased the intensity and duration of my own meditation sessions, but also challenged me to find new ways to explain a complex and profound process in simple terms to participants of varying ages, religions, cultures, experience, and personalities.

Most retreats are on weekends, but we also run ten-day retreats if there is a demand. My retreat participation began increasing consistently starting from around 2017–2018 and this continued after the Covid-19 pandemic restrictions. This was encouraging for me since, for over thirty years, silent meditation retreats had been a hard sell. What also encouraged me was the participation of a few young, China-born retreatants who were open to and enthusiastic about my teaching, despite the fact that my Chinese language skills were almost non-existent and Vipassana was in many ways not "typically Chinese," being open-ended and questioning, even of tradition. Something seemed to be subtly shifting at a deeper level.

The Indigenous ancestors, land, animals, and birds also provided us with opportunities for subtle connection and deepening. In early 2003, before our official opening, about half a dozen of my senior students and I participated in the very first group meditation at Harmony Dawn. Even though we entered without any preconceptions or expectations (as is our practice), every participant subsequently recounted some experience connected with the land or Indigenous peoples. I myself felt that the ground was rising up to meet me, which was a weird and unprecedented feeling since I was sitting on a cushion.

Walking in the forest behind our house, close to Rice Lake, Nicola once heard people running through the forest close to her, but there was actually no one she could see. One morning, walking our dog, I noticed a pervasive smell of sweet tobacco throughout the forest, but again there was no one around. I then realized that the previous night was the summer solstice, which is very important in Indigenous traditions. Over the years, guests have occasionally reported having vivid dreams about the land and ancestors; a few have reported having dreams in which our house itself was communicating with them.

We've learned to recognize many kinds of visiting and resident birds, from the smallest to the largest, and eventually to have a relationship with some of them. We recognize individual birds returning from their annual migration, like a raven who hopped because one leg was damaged; some birds recognize us as individuals as well, landing near us but not our guests. If the bird feeder is empty, they fly up to one of the dining room windows to let us know. One year, a family of barred owls nested in the forest behind our house and allowed us to approach, but if we got too close, the mother owl would let us know by flying to a branch just in front of us and staring us down. Quite often during a full moon around midnight, the barred owls come to the oak tree just behind our building and start calling out. A few days before our Quebec shaman guest visited, two golden eagles, rare for this area, arrived and stayed for a day in sight of our house.

Several times I have revived small birds, including woodpeckers, who fly into our windows, and sometimes, even after recovering alertness, they would prefer to sit on my hand for quite a while rather than be put into a tree or bush. At the beginning of one particularly intense meditation session, a bald eagle appeared in a tree quite close to our studio, which was unprecedented. When I looked at it, it appeared to be looking directly at me. At the end of the session, I checked to see if it was still there, and it was, but then it immediately flew away after our eye contact. Having a "bird brain" may be a misguided insult.

The deer often sleep in the tall meadow grass or under the evergreens close to our building, presumably because we are the only substantial, non-hunting property in the locality. They know we mean them no harm. They occasionally appear during the day and normally run away when they see us, but sometimes they make eye contact with us and decide to linger in our vicinity, sometimes up to ten minutes at a time.

In June 2008, I heard an unusual, prolonged crying or wailing, which normally means that something is being killed by a predator. In the dark of our forest, I found a young fawn pinned by a fisher cat that was gnawing at its neck. My appearance startled them, and the fisher let the fawn go, but scurried up a nearby tree, staring us down, still intent on having the fawn. I called the fawn to me and was surprised when it hesitantly walked over and leaned against my leg; I could see the wet gnaw marks on its neck. I told it to follow me, which it did, and I was able to escort it to the safety of our open meadow, where it ran away to freedom. Later that afternoon, I heard that at the very same time this fawn incident was happening, my mother was being admitted into hospital for what would be the last day of her life. Her main trait was gentleness, which is associated with the deer in Native American animal medicine. A month earlier, she'd had an operation on her leg and had complained, "My leg feels like it's biting me!" I felt that, like the fawn running away to freedom across the meadow, she was freeing herself from her bodily pain.

We have visits from coyotes, foxes, and occasionally black bears. A few years ago, four fox cubs visited us around the house for about a week. My neighbor said that their den was probably close by and that their mother had probably kicked them out to be on their own and explore the world. They were very curious and even came to us a couple of times when we were sitting under our oak tree, and I called out, "Foxes, come!"

As enriching as these bird and animal encounters were, they could not compare to the company of our big dogs as they frolicked in their personal paradise. Nicola and I did not have dogs in the city because of our lifestyles. However, Nicola has always loved dogs and jumped at the opportunity to take care of Bear, our daughters' dog, as they grew older and eventually left for university. He loved coming to Harmony Dawn with us and ran to the door of his home when he heard any of my daughters mention the word "retreat." He spent the last blissful year of his life with us, often content to sit under the oak tree and gaze out over the property. He was very big but intelligent, gentle, and loving. He was an unusual Shepherd-Rottweiler mix. Years later, a guest at Harmony Dawn saw his picture in our dining room and said, "He looks just like my dog!" I said that was strange since I only ever saw one other dog who looked like him, back in our Toronto neighborhood. It was missing one of its back legs. She said, "That was my dog!"

When Bear died in 2005, it took us five years before we could contemplate getting another dog. We eventually got Rosie, a female

Rottweiler because we liked the breed's qualities of strength, intelligence, and being family-oriented and protective, especially as we lived in the countryside by ourselves. Trespassers or those with more negative intent can suddenly appear unannounced, while little dogs are in danger of being carried off by coyotes and wolves. In the early days before moving in, we had an eight-hundred-pound generator stolen and the house burgled.

After Rosie died in 2020, during the Covid-19 pandemic, we got Reggie and then Bella, again Rottweilers. For me it has been a fascinating study in consciousness to see how they interact with each other, with Nicola and me individually and separately, with guests, and with the wild animals they encounter. They still have strong hunting and primal instincts, but also human qualities and even language, acquired no doubt from the estimated thirty thousand years dogs have lived with humans. They know our routines, by ourselves and with guests, and they adapt accordingly. I have no doubt that they can often sense our intentions and emotions even without visual or auditory clues. They love and are loved; they are good at letting go and moving on, unlike most humans.

Although I stopped going into Toronto to teach classes at the Tai Chi and Meditation Centre in 2018, my mind-body practices have continued to be part of my life not only in formal practice sessions, but also in the physical work of maintaining our property — lifting, pushing, bending, squatting, climbing, and even jumping. This was especially helpful in my late sixties and beyond. Sometimes even my martial skills have been called on. One early spring, I went into our ravine to cut up a large tree trunk that had fallen between the main branches of another tree. As I cut off the bottom of the tree trunk, it jumped up into the air like a released spring, spinning, and then started falling right where I was standing. I instinctively knew I could not jump out of the way fast enough as I was wearing heavy boots in over one foot of wet snow and holding a fifteen-pound chain saw in my right hand. My *taijiquan* training and instincts kicked in and, without moving my feet, I shifted my weight to the left and, turning my torso, used my free left forearm to swipe at the thick, eight-foot-long tree trunk, knocking it about ten feet away ... to my great surprise and relief! It was a literal, possibly life and death, demonstration of a famous *taijiquan* saying: "Four ounces can deflect one thousand pounds." This saying sounds fanciful, but it is true, as I have experienced several times in my life.

Of course, nothing more obviously defines later life than being a grandparent. In 2012, Shuwei became the first of my daughters to get married and it brought me together with Dhiravamsa for the first time in about twenty-five years. I had thought that perhaps I would never see him again in person, although we occasionally communicated by email. Shuwei, who was born during our year on San Juan Island, had always felt some kind of connection with Dhiravamsa and had traveled from Singapore to Spain to attend one of his retreats. Subsequently, she and her husband, Leon, invited Dhira to officiate at their wedding in Istanbul, which they chose because it was the historic meeting point between East and West, and it reflected their family, friends, and lifestyle.

In 2017, Dhira invited Nicola and me to stay with him in his small Las Palmas (Canary Islands) apartment, which was surprising since he is a very private person who enjoys his own company. I tried to think of questions on Buddhism and spirituality I could put to Dhira when we had private time in Las Palmas, but when I did, he surprisingly told me that I already knew everything I need to know and that we should just enjoy each other's company while we were together. A few days later, we were having coffee with Dhira and a few of his students when one of them inquired how long I had been studying with Dhira and was shocked to hear that it was forty years. Dhira interjected that I was a "complete master," not only in Vipassana, but also in tai chi and qigong. Later that day, Nicola was taking a picture of us outside the cathedral made famous by Christopher Columbus, when Dhira jokingly commented to her, "Just two enlightened guys hanging out."

I was shocked to hear Dhiravamsa speaking about me in such complimentary terms, since he had never before commented on my spiritual development or attainment except to tell me, towards the end of my San Juan Island training with him, that I was ready to be a

Vipassana teacher. He always spoke from the heart and with deliberation, so I was pleased to hear his comments. However, it did not make a difference to me, because by that time I had come to a place where I was satisfied just to "be," without wanting to become or achieve anything. Indeed, often in our recent times together, Dhira and I rarely talked about anything deep since we agreed on everything of consequence. It was almost like being with myself.

I was blessed to have Dhiravamsa not only as a great teacher, but also as a very close personal friend. Ann Bancroft, in her *Modern Mystics and Sages*, began her introduction to Dhiravamsa:

> The two Buddhists in this book, Trungpa and Dhiravamsa, both seem to emanate characteristics of serene cheerfulness and calm good sense. This latter quality belongs in particular to Dhiravamsa. Although not physically large or imposing, as soon as Dhiravamsa stands up to speak, his personality quietens and brings together a waiting audience. When he addresses groups of people in his clear careful style, even the most irrational or persistent questioner is transported to an area of practical common sense.

I have witnessed the above dynamic many times over the years. Once on San Juan Island, Dhira and I were walking towards the meditation building and casually chatting. As he entered the building and made his way to his dais, he seemed to somehow get larger, more elevated, and deeper at the same time. He was shifting his consciousness to get ready for the group meditation session and it was palpable to me.

Over the years, Dhira's "serene cheerfulness" expanded into a soft, loving playfulness and laughter, without ever losing his penetrating insight and wisdom. He showed me his human side, which was as instructive and precious for me as his enlightened side. There was no duality.

At present all my daughters have children, giving us four grandsons and two granddaughters: Bodhi, aged ten; Grey, seven; Emmie, four; Indie, three; Nolan, three; and Riley, one. I have no expectations of them and just make myself available for whatever they want to do or not. They all love coming to Harmony Dawn to frolic in the clean, open fields and forests and discover frogs, garter snakes, exotic insects, and occasionally deer and foxes. My tractor and ATV are big draws, and Leon, my son-in-law, bought the two older boys their own smaller ATVs, which they race through our meadows. We have an insulated cabin about 300 feet from our main house and it is like a big doll's house to them, especially as it has an inbuilt ladder to an upper sleeping area between the sloping roofs. They call it "the little house" and it is a favorite destination.

They love exploring all the nooks and crannies of our unusual three-story main building, especially the basement where Nicola and I live. That is where we store all of our private possessions and mementos, and where the power systems are located. The kids look through our photo albums and retrieve from our storage area whatever they find fascinating, like my *taiji* sword, fighting sticks, and staff, and even an old solar-powered transistor radio, which has become their prized possession. When they saw a TV program on tornadoes, they asked if our basement would function like a bunker — which it would. Grey, who is now seven, told us that when we die, he will come and live at Harmony Dawn to take care of it for the extended family. They want to learn how the building works and why we built it the way it is; they are eager to help with property maintenance chores like weeding, digging, and road repair and with food preparation and cooking.

It is interesting to see their personalities emerging and the developing dynamics with their parents' personalities. Occasionally they ask about meditation and martial arts. The world that they will have to navigate, and perhaps lead, in about twenty years will likely be much more challenging and volatile than ours. My hope is that they will begin to rediscover our ageless but often forgotten wisdom and be lights for their own generation.

Harmony Dawn retreat under construction 2002.

Harmony Dawn retreat 2024.

Andy leading intensive 10-day Vipassana meditation retreat.

Andy's Taijiquan and qi gong retreat 2023.

Taijiquan under Harmony Dawn oak tree 2023.

Guest Yoga group.

Andy's and Nicola's wedding at Harmony Dawn 2009.

With Nicola's parents Derek and Margaret and Andy's daughters, Hana, Shuwei, Shuwen (left to right).

With Andy's brothers Brian, Ray and Michael.

Dhiravamsa at Shuwei's and Leon's wedding, Istanbul 2012.

Dhiravamsa and Andy at Shuwei's Wedding.

Visiting with Dhiravamsa in Grand Canaria, 2015.

Andy teaching Taijiquan workshop for Miss Li's students in Newcastle UK, circa 2012.

Newcastle Taijiquan group 2012.

Sister Georgene Wilson visits Harmony Dawn 2018.

Woodpecker revival at Harmony Dawn.

Dining room at Harmony Dawn.

Andy and Nicola leading a cooking workshop.

Nicola demonstrating veggie sushi rolls at cooking workshop.

Tai Chi & Meditation Centre Instructors 2024.

Instructors' Christmas party 2024.

Harmony Dawn fun with grandsons Bodhi and Grey.

Favorite Harmony Dawn (non) activity.

CONCLUSION

Considering the amount of power and knowledge we humans have at our disposal, it is probably an understatement to say we do not seem to be using them wisely. To begin with our most urgent self-created challenge, there is a real possibility we could suddenly and overwhelmingly destroy most of our present civilization through nuclear war, deliberately or erroneously triggered. The main reason that we have not so far is the theory of mutually assured destruction, which, as crazy as it is, seems to be reassuring since nuclear war is apparently not a major concern for most. Experts, however, warn that the risk of nuclear war is real and is now at its highest levels in decades, as Putin of Russia and Kim of North Korea routinely threaten it. Words have power and are power.

To date the United States is the only country that has used such weapons, namely the two bombs dropped on Hiroshima and Nagasaki in 1945, which killed between 150,000 to 250,000 people, mostly civilians. Modern nuclear bombs are about eighty times more destructive than those dropped on Japan, and just one could easily wipe out any major city, killing millions of people. A nuclear explosion will create a fireball within ten seconds, and its intense blast, heat, and radiation will race out in all directions at a speed of hundreds of miles an hour, causing firestorms. A war between enemies using nuclear weapons will create hundreds of such firestorms, causing soot and smoke to blot out the sun and likely trigger a "nuclear winter," which is severe and prolonged global cooling, causing crop failure and famine. Apart from the immediate destruction of a direct hit, there will be lingering, cancer-causing radiation in the atmosphere. I think it is appropriate to repeat a quote from Albert Einstein used earlier in this book:

> We must never relax our efforts to arouse in the people of the world, and especially their governments, an awareness of the unprecedented disaster which they are absolutely certain to bring on themselves unless there is a fundamental change in their attitudes towards one another as well as in their concept of the future. The unleashed power of the atom has changed everything except our modes of thinking.

I see Einstein's warning as echoing the Buddha's teachings on the difference between the two main streams of Buddhist meditation. There is *samatha* (one-pointedness, focus, concentration), which can be seen as leading to power, as in a laser or a fire hose, or as being "single minded." The other stream is Vipassana or jnana, which is the penetrating wisdom necessary to wisely use power and, more importantly, to end suffering and gain enlightenment. Power by itself never has and never will end suffering. It can be used for constructive or destructive purposes. I personally would re-phrase Einstein's call to change "our modes of thinking" to "our level of consciousness," which, as we have seen, is possible but is neither straightforward nor widely discussed. Now is an apt time to start such a conversation.

Although technology and spirituality are commonly cast as antithetical, the rapid advancement of science and technology is ironically raising fundamental questions that the Axial sages and mystics have long raised: Who am I? What is a human being? What is the true purpose of life? These are no longer remote and arcane questions for a scant few, but necessary for crucial societal decision-making in times of great crisis and ominous tipping points. Science and technology are also validating the Buddha's insights into life as constantly changing, insubstantial, interconnected, and conditioned. Nothing is fixed and solid, including ourselves.

Another example (apart from nuclear war) of great power lacking the guidance of wisdom is artificial intelligence (AI), which has been under development for some time. I wrote about it in my 2003 book *Ageless Wisdom Spirituality*, but it has only recently come to popular attention. Preeminent AI leaders, including those representing competing giants Microsoft and Google, issued a blunt and stark public warning in May 2023:

> Mitigating the risk of extinction from AI should be a global priority alongside societal-scale risks such as pandemics and nuclear war.

After this warning, nothing substantial has been done to address the risks, and in fact, AI development has raced ahead as companies compete with companies and nations with nations. Speed is of the essence in competition. The present U.S. governmental and economic system encourages competition and discourages regulation and cooperation, so it is difficult to see how we can "mitigate the risk of extinction" under our present system. The rest of the developed world generally follows the U.S. lead.

AI is only one of the twenty-first-century technologies that carry both great promise and great risk. In 2000, Bill Joy, co-founder of Sun Microsystems, wrote a much discussed and still relevant article for *Wired* magazine called "Why the Future Doesn't Need Us." An excerpt:

> Accustomed to living with almost routine scientific breakthroughs, we have yet to come to terms with the fact that the most compelling 21st century technologies — robotics, genetic engineering and nanotechnology — pose a different threat than the technologies that have come before. Specifically, robots, engineered organisms, and nanobots share a dangerous amplifying factor: they can self-replicate. A bomb is blown up only once, but one bot can become many and quickly get out of control.

Joy pointed out that all the above technologies can be used for military purposes and also be incorporated into human beings.

Knowledge is power, different from nuclear weapons, but also capable of displacing most humans by making them obsolete in the capitalist market or by perhaps creating a hybrid, sci-fi-like "super race." It must be clearly noted that knowledge and intelligence (intellectual capacity) in the conventional sense is not the same as wisdom as understood in the ageless wisdom traditions. Knowledge is conditioned, dependent on beliefs, theories, and assumptions. I think of wisdom as alive, responsive, and capable of resolving apparent conflict and contradiction by integrating not only different (horizontal) issues, but also different levels of (vertical) consciousness.

The devastation of the planet and the related effects of global warming and climate change are powerfully and rapidly manifesting now, yet leaders and citizens alike, especially in the United States, demonstrate an astonishing lack of real concern and effective remedial action. As we have discussed, much of this seems to be the result of the powerful fossil fuel lobby and the Republican party under George W. Bush successfully casting doubt on solid scientific evidence and making global warming/climate change a political issue. Republican mouthpieces routinely describe those concerned about the environment and climate change as "radical leftists" or "Marxists." Sebastian Gorka, a former adviser to President Trump, addressing the Conservative Political Action Conference (CPAC) in 2019, described the Green New Deal as a watermelon:

> Green on the outside, deep communist red on the inside ... they want to take your pickup truck, they want to rebuild your home, they want to take away your hamburgers. This is what Stalin dreamt about but never achieved.

The theater of the absurd would be redundant on this subject since many find such statements reasonable and true.

As we have seen, the planetary devastation we are witnessing is the result of 250 years of material "progress," measured in consumption, much of which is "conspicuous" to show social status. This has been driven by the coming together of unprecedented technological advances and free-market capitalism. We have been taught that endless, conspicuous consumption will bring us happiness. Most know that it does not, and statistics show that the constant struggle and competition it entails cause us debilitating stress. We are not happy and content, even the more fortunate; an increasing number of people feel they are struggling to stay afloat or even sinking in debt. Yet we persist in pursuing various iterations of the American dream and, in the process, devour and despoil our planet and its creatures, triggering what many scientists believe is the onset of the planet's sixth extinction of species. The fifth extinction occurred 65 million years ago and was responsible for wiping out the dinosaurs, among the countless other species. Species are again disappearing at a highly accelerated rate.

Societal change, especially economic, is difficult because most do not understand its complexities and because our leaders offer no real alternative, just variations of the old circular patterns. U.S. voters almost always prioritize the "economy," validating the Democratic strategist James Carville's adage, "It's the economy, stupid!" Most people feel they never have enough, and the only exercise of power being offered to them is to vote for someone other than the incumbent, which they almost automatically do. To me, this constant alternation of political parties clearly signals that voters do not logically evaluate an administration's actual economic performance. They are also not aware of or deliberately ignore the fact that boom-and-bust cycles and inequality are inherent parts of the free-market capitalist system. The much-touted free-market "rising tide" lifts the boats of the rich much higher and faster than those of the poor or middle class.

No U.S. political parties mention the fact of growing inequality or the approaching scarcity of vital resources (including water and food) because they presently have no solution to these problems. U.S. voters consistently feel that Republicans are better at managing the economy even though recent history shows that, in fact, the Democrats do a better job. As with climate change, facts do not necessarily prevail against fact-free "spin," which is now turbo charged by social media, AI-enhanced misinformation.

Adding to economic volatility, the stock market, an influential measure of financial health, is often clearly emotional and irrational in its reactions and overreactions. It is also swayed by the interests of the rich, especially corporations, and includes a bias against taxation. The top ten percent of U.S. households own about 90 percent of stock market wealth. The bottom fifty percent own 1 percent of wealth. It should not be surprising that "insiders" tend to make the biggest fortunes in the stock market.

So how can Einstein's call for "fundamental change in their attitudes towards one another as well as in their concept of the future" come about, and who are the "we" to arouse the peoples of the world and their governments?

Our power has grown enormously, but our consciousness and behavior seem largely unchanged over centuries and millennia. The stories and lessons of Greek and Roman literature are still familiar and relevant today. Nearer our time, we see reflections of ourselves in the works of Shakespeare from 400 years ago and the lesser-known Niccolo Machiavelli from 500 years ago. The latter has a regularly used word named after him, "Machiavellian: cunning, scheming, unscrupulous, especially in politics." Although "Machiavellian" has often been used in a derogatory sense, his advice on "political realism" has been and still is very influential and apparent:

> Power is the pivot on which everything hinges. He who has the power is always right; the weaker is always wrong.
>
> Politics have no relation to morals.
>
> The ends justify the means.
>
> Whoever wishes to foresee the future must consult the past … this arises from the fact that they are produced by men who have ever been, and ever shall be, animated by the same passions and thus they necessarily have the same results.

I agree with the above quotes as observations of how politics is often (but not always) conducted, but I disagree with Machiavelli's conclusion or supposition that people "ever shall be" animated by the same passions with the same results. I know what is required for radical change, and I know that radical change is possible. I am far from alone in this regard as deeper forms of global spirituality, including mysticism, have existed for millennia and their aim is union with the divine, absolute truth, enlightenment, and such ... in other words, liberation from the passions of which Machiavelli speaks.

I also know that different paths up the spiritual mountain converge the higher the ascent. Perhaps my most striking personal reminder of this fact is my very good friend, Georgene Wilson, a Wheaton Franciscan nun, whom I met when we were both members of the Forge Guild, an international organization of spiritual teachers and leaders. Despite our disparate religious and cultural backgrounds, we have arrived at the same place in heart and mind, content in ourselves, and valuing solitude, oneness, and compassion for all. We are one.

Modern society has been ruled by a dualistic perspective of life. It is thought to be composed of distinct, separate, contrasting, often opposing pairs of forces, qualities, or entities. This view has its ancient roots in the widely revered Abrahamic Bible starting with Genesis, which introduces God, the creator, and man, the creation; man and woman; and good and evil. In current society, we have innumerable examples of duality including mind and body, individual and collective (society), East and West, political Left and Right, progressive and conservative, past and future, science and religion, church and state, rich and poor, black and white.

In terms of opposing groups of people, they generally become polarized as believers and non-believers, whether religious, political, or ideological. The stronger one's belief is, the more rigidity is generated and, therefore, the greater likelihood of conflict. Belief is not truth, regardless of the number of believers. Belief and polarization seem to be on the rise at present, creating greater volatility and conflict and thereby hindering any efforts at cooperation in our shared challenges. As has been pointed out, as soon as we celebrate "I" or "we," we create a separate and opposing dualistic "other." This dynamic should be glaringly obvious by now, but apparently it is not. Even liberal and progressive intellectuals cannot resist the temptation to emphasize some distinguishing identity, whether national, religious, racial, gender, or other.

The *Daodejing* millennia ago pointed out:

> From eternal existence we clearly see the apparent distinctions. These two are the same in source and become different when manifested. This sameness is called Profundity. Infinite profundity is the gate whence comes the beginning of all parts of the Universe.
>
> When all in the world understand beauty to be beautiful, then ugliness exists. When all understand goodness to be good, then evil exists.

The mental process that perceives life as consisting of pairs of opposites is endless ("infinite profundity") and, therefore, creates the increasing complexity we all experience. Complexity creates ever more issues and problems to solve, which then become overwhelming. As Krishnamurti pointed out, we cannot solve complexity by more complexity, but only by simplicity, which must be personally discovered. Simple in this sense is not the same as simplistic.

It is difficult for experts in different fields, for example technology, science, finance, or politics, to grasp or want to promote an inclusive, interconnected, and total perspective, since they are so invested in their particular field or proverbial piece of the overall pie. They are rewarded in various ways, whether with fame, money, or power, because of their specialization ... because of their ability to analyze and deconstruct life into ever smaller parts.

The *Daodejing* and yin-yang theory acknowledge the existence of the apparent or seeming opposites but point out that the two are always in relationship, contain elements of each other, and, in fact, their extremities give rise to each other. Taking Machiavelli's quote on the use of power as an example, a dictator may indeed use power to bend subjects to his or her will, but if this continues too long or too brutally, the weak will eventually band together, becoming strong enough to overthrow their oppressor.

As a practitioner of *taijiquan*, which ideally is a mind-body embodiment of yin-yang principles, I can attest to many occasions when I (and other practitioners) have turned superior physical force into weakness. A simple example is when an attacker tries to be too aggressive or uses too much force, but the opponent moves and so there is no target to hit. At that point the attacker is unbalanced, maybe stumbling, and therefore vulnerable to counterattack. In a sense this is what happened to the U.S. military in Vietnam. They had vastly more powerful military might, but the enemy would repeatedly attack and then retreat and disappear, wearing them down over time. The *taijiquan* classics have long described how "four ounces deflects one thousand pounds" and how to lead incoming force to "fall into emptiness." This is not fanciful lore but a description of what is possible and what actually happens. Yet we seek to seize and exercise ever more raw power, erroneously believing it to be the solution to all our problems and that the presently weak and manipulated will remain forever so.

The *Daodejing* states that the seeming opposites are interconnected and that they arise from the same source, which, before existence, was non-existence or emptiness. The fact that all life on this planet is interconnected and interdependent is being increasingly proven by studies in a wide variety of areas, including ecosystems, food webs, genetics, climate change, politics, economics, communications, and information systems.

Despite our obvious interconnection and interdependence, too many of us behave as if we are isolated, independent islands bounded by our skins ... until, of course, things go wrong and then we expect help from the greater community. A recurring example of this dynamic is the U.S. southern, Republican red states, where the majority deny the fact of climate change and rail against Big Government despite the fact they are being hit by an increasing number of climate change–related hurricanes, floods, and droughts. When these occur, citizens invariably expect immediate help from

FEMA (Federal Emergency Management Agency), a national Big Government body funded by tax dollars.

Jiddu Krishnamurti, in a 1984 talk at the United Nations, pointed to the individual as the only vehicle and source of real change within society:

> Why is it after all these millions of years human beings don't live in peace?... Every form of violence, terrorism, wars, we are responsible for it... Unless we realize the one major factor in our life, that psychologically we are one, we are going to be eternally in conflict. And no organization in the world is going to change that fact. So what is a human being to do if he is seriously concerned with the world?... Become aware of his condition and radically change.

I enclose a few quotes from Mahatma Gandhi, which suggest some ways Einstein's (and Krishnamurti's) call for behavioral and attitudinal change can come to realization:

> The future depends on what we do in the present.

> Our greatest ability as humans is not to change the world but to change ourselves.

> The world has enough for everyone's need but not for everyone's greed.

> Even if the paradise of material satisfaction were realized on earth, it would not bring mankind either contentment or peace.

> It's easy to stand in the crowd but it takes courage to stand alone.

Happiness and peace cannot come from external means because they are states of mind that originate from within us. Even the wealthiest of the wealthy are often discontented and still seeking more. In addition, the planet's resources are not infinite. There is enough for a comfortable life for all, as Gandhi noted, but we have to share and monitor our resources, especially since the world's two most populous countries, China and India, are rapidly raising their standards of living. A family has a budget, as does a town, a country, and also our planet. We do not live in isolation; we are always in relationship. We all deserve basic human rights, but we also have responsibilities to other humans and to the Earth, our home.

Einstein says "we" have to arouse awareness in the peoples of the world and their governments of the need to change their attitudes to each other and to the future. It stands to reason that "we" cannot do so if we share and promote present conventional thinking, attitudes, and norms. We first must change ourselves (which Gandhi sees as our greatest ability) before we change the world. We have to act now to safeguard the future for ourselves, our children, and our grandchildren.

Although our personal transformation benefits the world, it primarily benefits us. The personal transformation process is a huge win-win in this sense. Health statistics show a dramatic increase in stress-related illnesses, and many are already at the final exhaustion or collapse stage of the stress syndrome theory popularized by Dr. Hans Selye. We are not good at dealing with change, which is particularly consequential in an era of accelerated, perhaps unprecedented, change. Our personal transformation process may not be easy, and we will also need the courage to "stand alone" or walk the "path less traveled."

Gandhi's advice echoes the Buddha's insights and teachings that he shared with the world so long ago. The Buddha counseled to "be a refuge unto yourself" since "even Buddhas can only point the way." He taught that all life is impermanent (ever-changing), insubstantial, and conditioned, with all manifestation being interconnected and interdependent. Conditionality as a fact of life is being increasingly recognized by advances in science and technology.

The Buddha pointed out that we suffer because we try to hold on to the positive and push away the negative, but this is impossible. Life is fluid and changeable. We must learn to flow with life rather than trying in vain to resist and control it. We cannot flow if we hold on, consciously or subconsciously. In modern terminology, any compulsive behavior — whether habit, addiction, belief, or ideology — is a sign of attachment and rigidity. If these operate on us, we are not really free but acting according to the compulsion of our knee-jerk conditioning.

As already explained, perhaps the most important single practice in the Buddha's Noble Eightfold Path is the cultivation of mindfulness, which he described in his early and foundational *Satipatthana Sutta*. It is the basis of all Buddhist meditation. "Mindfulness" meditation has recently become popular, but I prefer to describe the meditation I practice and teach as Vipassana, or insight, meditation, since insightful wisdom is a necessary part of enlightenment, as is compassion. One can be "mindful" enough to reduce stress yet not experience the deep transformation that comes from direct insight wisdom.

We can and must start our journey of transformation now, since all thought and action only ever occur in the present, even though we are commonly preoccupied with the future and the past. The former is a projection of the latter; it is impossible to envision a future without past experiences. All our aspirations, hopes, and beliefs are conditioned by the past, whether experiences, memories, personality patterns, or inherited genetics. Krishnamurti disagreed with Machiavelli's famous proposition, "The ends justify the means," pointing out instead, "The means is the end." What we think and do is what we are. All is ever now. The Buddha advocated urgency in our spiritual practice, "as if your head is on fire."

Krishnamurti's quote echoes the opening lines of the *Dhammapada*, the famous collection of sayings of the Buddha:

> All states have mind as their forerunner, their chief, and are mind-made. If one speaks or acts with a polluted mind, then suffering follows as the wheel follows the hoof of the ox pulling the cart.

> If one speaks or acts with a pure mind, then happiness
> follows one as one's shadow that never departs.

As the Buddha advised, we can only break through this conditioning by letting go of our attachment. No matter how much information we have about our problems and possible solutions, we cannot change by holding on, however subtle our evasive strategies. I see Vipassana meditation as a humble, non-manipulative, open-ended practice since, in essence, what we are doing is setting aside time to pay attention to what is taking place within our consciousness, whether pleasant or painful, without any preconceived opinions, beliefs, or goals.

In Vipassana practice, we try to switch our personal two-way radio to "receive" rather than "broadcast," which is our normal setting. We generally like to trumpet our opinions and identities, seeking the company of like-minded others (easy in these days of social media) to justify ourselves and feel more secure and "right." This, as yin-yang theory points out, automatically creates those who are not like-minded and "wrong," in turn generating tension and eventually conflict. Fanatics seem to find it hard to conceive that someone else may be just as fanatical as they but hold opposing beliefs. It is possible to be secure in one's identity without emphasizing it, which often provokes reaction.

If, even for a few minutes, we can let go of the intrusive compulsion of our own thoughts and feelings, then we create space (or emptiness) that will lessen the compulsion of our reactivity and afford us some insight into our attitudes and behavior. Insightful wisdom will enable us to distinguish inherent quality in something or someone rather than basing our judgment on mere quantity, perhaps measured in dollars, "likes," "friends," possessions, celebrity, and more. We can resolve conflict by seeing things in a both/and rather than an either/or way, by recognizing the existence within ourselves of different levels of consciousness.

If we continue our skillful practice, we will eventually gain insight into who we are underneath even the patterns of our personal individuality and identity. We can experience growing wisdom and compassion, which are the necessary attributes of enlightenment. If it works for you — if you are a kinder person making better decisions — then just trust the process and keep on walking the path on your thousand-mile journey to ever more expanding enlightenment.

The more we understand ourselves, the more we will understand others since we will discover the deeper common ground of our humanity, not as an ideal but as an observable day-to-day reality. The *Daodejing* reminds us that without opening our window or going out of our door, we can nevertheless know the whole world. The Buddha similarly advised that the best way to safeguard and protect others is by first protecting ourselves.

By clearly understanding ourselves and others, we will make wiser and more compassionate decisions in our lives, whether in one-on-one relationships or generally in society. As mentioned, we may be able to manipulate others temporarily, but we cannot really change them; we all can only really change ourselves. The best we can do is perform right action, which takes into account not only ourselves and our desires, but the well-being of our greater environment. Enlightenment is not the power to control and manipulate life but the wisdom to flow with the totality of it, maintaining balance, wherever and however it may take us.

Wisdom in this sense is deep insight into the nature of life, including specific issues and people, even seemingly remote public figures. It is like having a master key that opens all individual doors. Our collective problems do not exist in isolation and, therefore, cannot be solved in isolation, as we presently attempt. Moreover, they are invariably the result of human decisions and behavior, especially greed and conflict. As is obvious from attention and observation, we tend to think mostly about our own self-interests and mostly of the short term, which is not a good recipe for living together and promoting the well-being of our children and their descendants and the health of the planet and its diverse, beautiful species.

There are many scholars, researchers, and activists, like the young environmentalist Greta Thunberg, coming up with creative ideas, inventions, and solutions regarding a wide variety of issues. I have personally witnessed the rise of Singapore, over the last fifty years, from a third-world country with blackened, polluted rivers and open gutters to a glittering, spotless, high-tech modern city-state with the second highest per-capita income in the world at over $100,000. Singapore attracts profitable investments from around the planet while looking after its environment and providing affordable housing, healthcare, education, and transport for the citizens who need it. Some naysayers point out that Singapore is relatively small, with a population of six million. However, the world's population is now concentrated in cities, so countries like Singapore have many lessons to offer, if we are open-minded enough to inquire and learn. As a Canadian, it is apparent to me that Canadians look mostly to the United States for innovative ideas, while Americans rarely look outside their own country.

There are also many suggestions for the long-overdue restructuring of politics and government in democracies. Of utmost importance, the United Nations must become a more representative body with real power to be an effective vehicle for global policies and cooperation. Five permanent members of the Security Council have wielded the considerable power of a unilateral veto on all major decisions, not only military or "security" matters. These five are the "winners" of the Second World War — the United States, the United Kingdom, Russia, France, and China — and have often acted in blatant self-interest.

All of these specific remedial suggestions are, of course, commendable and necessary. However, we need an integrated and holistic approach since our challenges are interconnected, and more importantly and crucially, we need the collective will to change. No matter how powerful the technological innovations we create, whether AI or a miraculous new source of energy, we still have to confront the issue of how to share and cooperate, which is our fundamental human problem. We need the collective will to change, which involves examining, questioning, and probably discarding many of our fundamental beliefs and assumptions. As we have seen, we tend to resist change because we identify with our established beliefs and habits as our self or "I."

A more enlightened consciousness will be capable of both/and thinking and action rather than dualistic either/or. A fundamental source of either/or conflict is our sense of separation, not only from the external world, but also within ourselves, which is felt as internal conflict. We are actually both separate and connected. By resolving internal conflict and separation, we also resolve our feelings of separation from others and the world generally. By healing ourselves, we enjoy mind-body health, which is essential to all our activity, and are able to live lives that are more compassionate, cooperative, sustainable, and harmonious. We can experience deep contentment and peace, which is different from the momentary fun we commonly seek for stimulus and distraction.

We need light in our times of darkening, unprecedented threat. This can only come about by nurturing it in ourselves, whether we are ordinary people or leaders in our communities. Whatever our position or function in society, we can bring light, wisdom, and compassion into our actions, decisions, and relationships. Individual lights growing together in brightness will illuminate the collective way forward for all. The next step on our journey is now, as it always is.

About fifteen years ago, when my daughters were in their early twenties, I wrote a short poem to help them in difficult times. Although I am by no means a poet, they have found and still find it a helpful reminder.

When Everything Goes Wrong

>When everything seems to go wrong, with no end in sight,
>
>When you don't know what thought or action is right,
>
>Take a deep breath and come back to now.
>
>Now is all there ever is,

And includes all —

Ups and downs, wrong and right,

Young and old, dark and light.

The pot of gold is not at the end of the rainbow,

But in each step of the journey there.

We all are blessed and loved,

But lose sight of that now and then.

Open and expand your heart and mind

And you will your self find.

ACKNOWLEDGMENTS

I am very grateful to Patrick Crean for his invaluable editorial input, insight, and experience.

Acknowledgment for permission to use quotes is gratefully given to:

Janine Jutima, Escuela de Meditación Dhiravamsa, for all Dhiravamsa quotes and book excerpts.

Dr. Carrie Bernard for her meditation journal excerpt.

www.ingramcontent.com/pod-product-compliance
Lightning Source LLC
Chambersburg PA
CBHW020228170426
43201CB00007B/355